THE SMART GUIDE TO

Healthy Grilling

BY BARRY FAST

The Smart Guide To Healthy Grilling - Second Edition

Published by

Smart Guide Publications, Inc.
2517 Deer Chase Drive
Norman, OK 73071
www.smartguidepublications.com

For information, address: Smart Guide Publications, Inc. 2517 Deer Creek Drive, Norman, OK 73071

SMART GUIDE and Design are registered trademarks licensed to Smart Guide Publications, Inc.

International Standard Book Number: 978-1-937636-15-9

Library of Congress Catalog Card Number:
11 12 13 14 15 10 9 8 7 6 5 4 3 2 1

Printed in the United States of America

Cover design: Lorna Llewellyn
Copy Editor: Ruth Strother
Back cover design: Joel Friedlander, Eric Gelb, Deon Seifert
Back cover copy: Eric Gelb, Deon Seifert
Illustrations: James Balkovek
Production: Zoë Lonergan
Indexer: Cory Emberson
V.P./Business Manager: Cathy Barker

ACKNOWLEDGEMENTS

This book exists because Sally McMillan, my agent, believed I could research and write it. I treasure her wise counsel and encouragement. She has been my business partner, my "sister," and for over thirty years among my dearest friends.

The grilling community reflects the values that outdoor cooking embodies: generous, sociable, creative, and fun loving. Many expert grillers have shared their recipes, techniques, and advice with me, and they are referenced and thanked throughout this book. I am particularly grateful to Jonathan Martinez of the *Celebrity Grill Show* for his enthusiastic help from day one. Ed Hamlin of Grill Innovations has generously shared recipes and advice during the nearly two years I worked on this project. Their moral support was a constant source of inspiration and motivation.

My wife, Carol, has endured countless grilling failures as I've tested, reworked, or invented recipes. As a fine cook in her own right, a super taster, and professional baker, her critiques and suggestions have been invaluable. She patiently read each chapter, offering much appreciated editing advice. And she never nagged me—at least not about working on this book.

My grandchildren, Connor, Caroline, Jace, and Callie, willingly consumed many grilled meals and gave advice from a kid's standpoint. I can't thank them enough for being my tasters and for never spitting out any of the food. Although he's not yet fully verbal, I know our youngest grandchild, Gavin, loves my grilled veggie pizza because he hides half eaten slices and begs for more. This affirmation from him and his siblings and cousins was all I needed to maintain my enthusiasm for this project.

This book is dedicated to my daughters,

Nancy and Rebecca,

in gratitude for completing our family and staying close.

TABLE OF CONTENTS

PART TWO: *Healthy Grilling and Delicious Eating* 31

3   *Beef Burgers* 33

INTRODUCTION

Grilling is the most sociable and friendly way to cook. It's not just for special occasions or weekend cookouts. It can be the most frequent way you feed your family and entertain friends. Better yet, it can be the healthiest way to cook for yourself and your loved ones. In the pages ahead we'll emphasize the healthy ways to grill everyday food that tastes great.

Grilling vs Barbecuing

Grilling is not barbecuing, although the terms are often used interchangeably. Barbecuing is a specialized form of meat and, to a lesser extent, poultry preparation, where the pork, beef, and chicken are cooked "low and slow" over a smoky indirect heat source, often hickory or other hardwood charcoal. Barbecuing takes many hours and requires special equipment to be done right. The best meats for barbecuing tend to be the cheaper, fattier cuts—absolutely delicious but reserved for special-occasion enjoyment or at barbecue huts run by expert pit masters around the country.

Grilling, in contrast, is a highly diversified cooking technique that employs direct or indirect heat, often from charcoal but much more frequently (and conveniently) produced by propane or natural gas. My kind of grilling is the healthiest way to cook because you can prepare almost anything on the grill and end up with lower-fat, fuller-flavored, less-salty, and naturally sweeter food than just about any other cooking method. The nutrients your foods contain are not washed out in a cooking liquid or swimming in butter or fat from a frying pan. Instead, the vitamins and minerals are concentrated. You get more nutrients in each chew of grilled food.

The lively clean flavors of vegetables and fruit are enhanced by grilling. Meat is leaner but still succulent, and chicken and fish, grilled my way, take on light smoke-accented flavors enhanced by marinades and rubs that don't add fat and calories. Healthy grilling means nutritious meals that kids love. This is food that is not processed and is free of chemicals we can't pronounce—in other words, food that is real.

Instead of that rather daunting contraption out on your deck, the traditional provenance of men in the thrall of flame and smoke, you'll reimagine your grill as a creative cooking appliance that has more flexibility than your kitchen stove and is more fun too. Healthy grilling is easy, enjoyable, and deeply satisfying.

How *The Smart Guide to Healthy Grilling* Is Organized

There are three parts to Healthy Grilling:

> ➤ Part One: The first part discusses why you should include grilling as the cooking technique for regular family meals as well as for festive entertaining and celebrations. What equipment you'll need, what kind of grill you'll want to purchase, and what accessories and fuel you'll find best suited to your lifestyle. We discuss the health issues in detail, including low-fat heart-healthy grilling, reduction or elimination of potentially harmful chemicals that all high-heat cooking can produce in meat, fish, and poultry, and the importance of a well-rounded diet that follows guidelines from the most reliable medical and scientific research. What we eat affects how we feel, how we look and how we age, as well as how we impact the environment. That's what healthy grilling is all about.

> ➤ Part Two: The second part of the book takes you through the food groups that are ideally suited for healthy grilling. We explore steaks, pork, chicken, and fish, of course, but how about an entire chapter dedicated to corn. And other chapters devoted to vegetables, bread, pizza, and fruit. Grilling clams and oysters, the best lobster you ever ate, and how to make a low-fat burger taste as juicy as one with twice the calories. We go over what raw products you should buy, how to prepare various foods for the grill, and offer loads of information on grilling techniques for different foods. There are plenty of surprises ahead for those of you who think grilling is pretty much about hot dogs, bratwurst, and burgers.

> ➤ Part Three: The third and final part of the book is bursting with grilling creativity—real examples, recipe by recipe, showing you how to think differently about family dinners on the grill. We'll take you on a culinary adventure with your grill as the magic carpet. We'll explore complete meals from soup to nuts—OK not nuts, but grilled roasted chickpeas that taste nutty and are so delicious your kids will think they're eating junk food.

The grill is the centerpiece in this section, providing healthy family meals, celebrating the seasons and special-occasion dinners. Over two hundred recipes in all, from flavor-boosting marinades to nutritious pizza, *The Smart Guide to Healthy Grilling* will give you plenty of inspiration and specific grilling ideas for years to come.

Be sure to check out the resources section that will take you beyond this book to some significant online sites, how-to videos, my favorite grilling personalities, accessories, sauces, rubs, books, and more.

Sidebars

Sidebars throughout the book provide information relating to the topic being covered in the text, highlighting or expanding on the subject. Here is a brief description of the sidebars:

> ➤ Fat Fighters: Ways to help you lower the fat and calories in your daily diet

> ➤ Tasty Tips: Tips to help you enhance the flavors in everything you grill

> ➤ Grilling Tech Talk: Advice on how to hone your grilling techniques and food knowledge

> ➤ Grill Speak: Explanations of the specialized vocabulary we grillers use to describe a piece of equipment, a flavoring method, or some other jargon that you may not be familiar with

A Note about Ingredients

Here are some definitions to help you have a better understanding of the vocabulary we use:

> ➤ *Olive oil* means extra-virgin olive oil, unless otherwise noted.

> ➤ *Oil* means a neutral high-heat oil such as canola or corn oil.

> ➤ *Salt* refers to kosher salt unless table salt or sea salt is specified.

> ➤ *Flour* means all-purpose flour unless another kind is named.

> ➤ None of the recipes or grilling techniques will instruct you to heat the grill, or, worse yet, use the nonsensical word *preheat*. As the late, great George Carlin pointed out about ovens, they are either heated or not. I assume you will always turn on your gas grill or get a good charcoal fire going before you start cooking, just like you do with your oven.

Books, E-books, and the Web

Books in print form have stood the test of time—from Gutenberg in the fifteenth century to our time in the 2000s. E-books have certain advantages for learning, researching, and entertainment, which is why many will find the e-book edition of *Healthy Grilling* useful. But I find printed cookbooks especially user friendly—you can lay them flat on the counter for frequent consulting, you can spill sauce or a drink on them without shorting them out, and there is something comforting about a page smudged with an ingredient that was on your finger two years ago when you last touched that recipe. However, a paper book is not dynamic—it's immutable till the next edition. That's where the trusty old Internet comes in. Go to my website, www.healthygrillingtoday.com for the latest updates, additions, insights, links, and, dare I say it, maybe even corrections, as you and I continue to experiment, create, learn, and refine our grilling skills.

PART ONE

Healthy Grilling: Getting Started

CHAPTER 1

Grilling and Healthy Eating

In This Chapter

➤ Grilled foods as part of a varied and healthy diet

➤ Grilling: the powerful weight-loss program

➤ Reducing or eliminating the cancer risk in grilling

One of my grilling friends likes to say, "We cook because we have to, we grill because we want to." An oversimplification? Not if you use your grill several times a week like we do. Grilling routine meals year-round, especially in our northeastern winters, may seem a little strange. But grilled food tastes so good it's a shame to restrict that cooking method for occasional weekends in the warmer seasons. If your grill is in the right location, close to the house on an easily accessible deck or patio, sheltered and well lit, it's almost as convenient as your kitchen stove, even in winter.

The Benefits of Grilling

Grilling is so easy and versatile that once you nail down a few basic techniques, you'll develop a set of recipes and menus that quickly become family favorites. Boneless, skinless chicken breasts, often disdained as rather dry and tasteless, will instead offer such a wide range of culinary possibilities they'll become a staple in your refrigerator. Burgers with ketchup on a white bread roll? You'll be way past that tired old presentation when you unleash your grilling creativity, inspired by the pages ahead. Did you ever think you'd see your kids looking forward to vegetables on their plate? Wait till you've explored the methods and recipes in this book. Grilling will transform the way you feed your family and entertain your friends. And believe me, you'll never send out for fatty, greasy pizza after you grill one of mine.

This is what you'll learn in the chapters ahead:

➤ Grilling forms the core of a long-term weight-control program, low in fat and calories, high in flavor and versatility.

➤ The cancer risks associated with high-heat cooking can be greatly reduced, or even eliminated, with the use of meat, poultry, and fish marinades, as well as by using a different grilling technique I call grill-roasting.

➤ Grilling can promote a heart-healthy diet for adults and kids, offering tasty alternatives to salty sauces, sugary desserts, and other overprocessed dinner fare.

Fat Fighters

Over 60 percent of us are overweight, many to the point of obesity. There is little debate about the causes—enormous serving sizes, sugar-packed soft drinks, processed foods high in fats and salt, lack of exercise, and general ignorance of how many calories we're consuming every day. To maintain a healthy weight, we adults should consume on average 1,800–2,400 calories a day, depending on how much exercise is included in our daily routine.

Calorie-conscious people consume far more vegetables than those of us who may be less motivated. Grilled veggies are so tasty you'll never feel unsatisfied. A splash of olive oil, a sprinkle of lemon juice, and the grill. Irresistible!

Grilling is easy and fun; it's our most ancient cooking technique—and like most good things, it takes some practice to get it right. It's worth the effort to perfect your grilling skills. The result is great-tasting meals that are good for you and those you love.

Everything Tastes Better When It's Grilled

The dry heat of grilling concentrates and enhances the innate flavors of the food you're cooking, and caramelizes the natural sugars. These attributes, and the effect of rubs, marinades, and spices, result in food that you and your family will love. The grill gives meat a richer taste. Vegetables become more substantial, needing nothing but a little salt and oil, and grilled fruits are sweet enough to satisfy even the most sugar-craving kid. Sandwiches are transformed when served on bread brushed with olive oil, laced with attractive grill marks and the delicate flavor of smoke. Pizza comes off the grill with a delicious twist over the standard oven-baked pie, a rustic bread more in touch with its roots in the ancient wood-fired brick ovens of Rome and Naples.

Grilling Helps Us Eat Better

This diversity of tastes and ingredients is so important because our typical American diet is often missing key nutritional elements. We don't eat enough vegetables and fruit, partly because we prepare them so poorly that our kids quite rightly dislike them. To make vegetables acceptable, we bury them in goop from the supermarket. These buttery, creamy, cheesy sauces turn vegetables into another source of too much fat, too much salt, and too many calories.

We should be making vegetables that taste good on their own. Trying to fool children into eating something is a losing proposition over the long term. The problem is not just getting kids to eat enough fruit and vegetables—it's getting kids to love eating them. As you'll see in Chapters 11, 12, and 13, your grill is the solution.

A Healthy Diet

Nutrition experts tell us that the healthiest way to eat is to make sure your diet is varied and has a heavy emphasis on unprocessed

Grill Speak

Grill heat has two effects on the intrinsic sugar in the food we're cooking. It draws sugar to the surface, and then browns the sugar to a caramel color. Those are the grill lines we find so attractive. They taste as good as they look.

Caramelizing is a process that uses heat to convert sucrose into two simple sugars, fructose and glucose, which taste sweeter and richer. It is accelerated by higher acidity so some fruit caramelize more quickly than vegetables, and acidic marinades help meat, poultry, and fish caramelize in less time over high heat—a good thing as you'll learn here. So when you sense that grilled fruit or vegetables taste sweeter than these foods cooked most other ways, you're right.

Tasty Tips

Out-of-season fruit can be a real turnoff, often under-ripe or just plain tasteless. But wait till you see what your grill can do to change the way hard pears, bland peaches, and lackluster melons taste. Chapter 13 is all about grilled fruit alchemy, literally changing leaden flavored fruit into dessert gold. Your grill is not just about burgers and hot dogs anymore.

Tasty Tips

The variety of vegetables that can be made on a grill, the many ways they can be spiced, herbed, and marinated, their attractive appearance and texture will keep your family happy meal after meal. The grill makes fresh vegetables a welcome part of everyday food. And wait till you learn how leftover veggies can keep the family eating healthy snacks and nutritious pizzas in place of fatty processed convenience foods.

fresh foods, lots of vegetables, fruits, and whole grains. You will notice that I practice what they preach. In Part Two of this book, for instance, there is an entire chapter devoted to corn, just corn. Another chapter describes how vegetables from all over the world can be prepared on your grill. Fruit has its own chapter to do those delightful ingredients justice, and I provide a significant part of the chapter on bread and pizza to the use of whole grains and home-made unprocessed dough. Part Three is loaded with specific recipes and meal plans incorporating these ingredients that form a healthy diet.

Fat Fighters

Healthy grilling does not mean you eliminate brats or give up steak. It does mean that foods like those, as delicious and traditional as they are in grilling, are going to assume their proper role here. That role is a player in the food orchestra, not the conductor, not even first violin but definitely a valued contributor, albeit a little slimmer than we might be used to. We're talking about portion control, not eliminating portions. You'll see what we mean in the Part Two chapters ahead. For weight-loss programs, portion control is the single most effective strategy because you don't have to give up food you enjoy; you just eat less of it. This kind of diet works—it's not denying, it's controlling.

Sticking to a Healthy Diet

In our family, the average daily calorie goal is approximately 2,000–2,200 (a little more if it's a big exercise day). This is a comfortable amount of food for most adults who don't want to get fat. We try to keep our routine weekday dinners at around 800 calories per serving, leaving us with about 1,200 calories for the rest of the day's food. That is a veggie-packed dinner menu with some meat, poultry, or fish on the plate—not a lot, around 4–6 ounces for most portions, which won't make you feel deprived.

We keep our daily fat intake below the RDA limit of 65 grams, of which 20 grams is saturated fat. A 90 percent lean 6-ounce burger, for instance, has about 17 grams of fat, and a third of that is saturated fat. The recommended daily allowance (RDA) for sodium is a little over 2 grams, which translates into a teaspoon of common table salt a day. Eating a lot of processed food, often high in sodium, can easily put you over the salt limit. We kept that in mind as we developed the recipes for this book.

We Love Burgers, But . . .

Burgers are a wonderful American food, perfected right here in our country. Healthy grilling celebrates the burger in all its glory (twenty-three recipes in Part Three) while recommending that you lower the fat, reduce the size just a little, and grill it differently than most "experts" instruct. Serve burgers as part of a grilling medley that includes lots of fresh veggies and fruit.

Reimagine Your Grill

Think of your grill as a food source, not just an appliance. Grilling transforms the raw materials into flavorful foods, packed with vitamins and other valuable nutrients. Everyday dinners, from simple to elaborate, can be fully and completely prepared on a grill. Start with grilled vegetable salads or barbecued shrimp, scallops, or oysters as an appetizer, or perhaps a soup such as charred corn chowder. Move on to a main course of grilled pork, chicken, beef, or fish accompanied by corn on the cob, grilled stuffed cabbage, or a wild mushroom medley—or a family-size pizza or other grilled flat bread topped with arugula, mushrooms, onions, and a little crumbled sausage meat. End with a dessert, lovely slices of grilled pineapples, pears, or peaches.

Grilling Tech Talk

Slicing cantaloupes and other melons can contaminate the fruit with knife-borne listeria or E-coli that is carried from the melon's skin into its interior. These bacteria cause serious, occasionally fatal infections. When you grill melon slices, you kill these germs and eliminate the risk of infection. Grilled fruit is a delicious dessert treat as it concentrates and caramelizes the sugar—and it's a surefire method of getting rid of germs that can harm us.

This kind of eating is so healthy and richly diverse. You and your loved ones are eating mostly fresh unprocessed ingredients. You don't feel deprived; you're not "being good."

Grill Speak

Gas grills have burner plates that cover the gas burners. These long V-shaped plates are also called flavor bars. They protect the burners, keeping them from getting clogged with fat and other food residue that drips and falls through the grates above. Just as important is when these fats hit the plates, they burn, producing a smokiness that helps provide that grilled flavor we all cherish. Use a wire brush to clean off the burner plates when you see them getting layered with old burned grease.

Fat Fighters

Most people fail at weight loss because most diets are based on a form of deprivation. It's just natural for us to crave what we can't have. If your diet makes you unhappy, you'll never stick to it—and sticking to a diet for many months is the key to successful weight loss.

Before you begin a diet, don't think only about what and how much you're allowed to eat. Just as important is to plan how you'll cook your food. Grilling provides more low-fat, low-calorie food choices than any other cooking method.

Eating this way routinely is not a burden—it's easy, as you'll see in Part Three, which is full of menu planning ideas, recipes, and suggested side dishes, salads, and desserts.

How Grilling Aids Weight Loss

Grilled foods combine two powerful weight-loss advantages:

1. Grilling makes food taste better without the extra fat you would use when sautéing, frying, or saucing it. Grilling intensifies the natural flavors of your ingredients by caramelizing the sugars in meat, vegetables, and fruit, and concentrating those flavors by significantly reducing moisture, especially in fruits and vegetables.

2. Grilling reduces much of the intrinsic fat in meat and poultry, as well as removes some of the fat you may be adding in marinades or, in the case of veggies, olive oil or other oils that you've brushed on for added flavor. The fat falls away onto the charcoal or burner plates and adds a light smokiness to whatever you're cooking. For instance, instead of a burger that has cooked in its own rendered fat in the stove-top frying pan, you end up with a juicy grilled burger that has significantly less fat—and fewer calories—than the meat you started with.

High-Heat Cooking and Cancer

Meat, poultry, and fish cooked over high heat from any source (or deep fried) develop chemicals called heterocyclic amines (HCAs). When these same foods are cooked over flames from burning fat that is dripping on coals or on burner plates, they can develop another chemical called polycyclic aromatic hydrocarbons (PAHs). Both HCAs and PAHs are carcinogens that in high doses have caused cancer in laboratory animals. According to the National Cancer Institute, the federal agency coordinating and interpreting much of the cancer research in this country, "whether such exposure causes cancer in humans is unclear." What is clear, however, is that you can reduce the amount of HCAs and PAHs that form in meat, poultry, and fish by as much as 90 percent with a few simple practices, thus greatly reducing any cancer risk.

Grilling Tech Talk

Practice safe grilling by reducing the time you cook meat, poultry, and fish over direct high heat. Do not grill directly on coal embers and do not allow flames to lick your food on the grates. Prevent flare-ups with a water spray for charcoal and by removing visible fat on meat.

Marinate meat, poultry, and fish in a beer- or acid-based marinade—spices are good, too—for at least an hour. Cut meat—especially poultry, which you can't cook rare—into smaller pieces like you would for kabobs. The less time over heat the better. Grill-roast, meaning briefly sear to caramelize natural surface sugars (attractive grill lines), and then finish the longer grilling time over indirect heat—400°F or lower is best.

Eliminating PAHs

According to the National Cancer Institute, you can virtually eliminate PAHs by preventing flare-ups—flames from burning fat that scorch your food. This means when cooking over charcoal, you should monitor the grill and spray water if flames form. Bank the coals on opposite sides, leave a clear space in the middle, and use a disposable aluminum drip pan to catch dripping fat.

After heating the grates of a gas grill, turn off the middle burner(s) to create an indirect, cooler heat zone between the front and rear burners. You may want to reduce the heat under the remaining burners—monitor the grill thermometer to adjust cooking temps. (For two-burner grills, turn off the rear burner for the indirect roasting area).

Make sure your heat is not so high you have fat-fueled open flames curling around the burner plates. Trim fat—the less fat on your meat, the less dripping onto the coals and burner plates that can cause flare-ups. After a quick searing, move the food off direct heat and roast it in a closed cover grill over indirect heat, which means it's cooking at a lower temperature with no flare-ups.

Reducing or Eliminating HCAs through Cooking Methods

There are two ways to reduce HCAs by as much as 90 percent. One is your cooking method and the other is using marinades.

Exposure to direct high heat causes the formation of HCAs. Longer high-heat exposure creates more HCA formation. Roasting meat, fish, and poultry using indirect heat greatly reduces HCAs or keeps them from occurring. Lower and slower cooking is the key here. I call this grill-roasting.

As you'd expect, grill-roasting does take a little longer to achieve desired doneness, resulting in the unintended consequence of a juicier outcome because leaner meat can quickly dry out over intense high heat. Follow the recipes here and practice a few times. You'll get it right.

Grilling Tech Talk

Grill-roasting is easy. Whether using charcoal or gas, make sure the grilling area is divided into a hot direct-heat zone and a cooler indirect-heat zone. For charcoal, you can bank the coals against the sides, leaving the middle for indirect cooking. For gas, after you've got hot grates, you simply reduce or turn off one or two burners and leave the other(s) on high.

First, over direct high heat, sear your meat for two to three minutes per side, then flip again and move the meat to the indirect cooking area. Close the lid and grill-roast till the meat or poultry is done.

This slower cooking enables lower-fat meat, fish, and poultry to retain juiciness while preventing the formation of potentially harmful chemicals.

Reducing or Eliminating HCAs through Marinades

The second technique to reduce the formation of HCAs by as much as 90 percent is by marinating meat, poultry, and fish in an acid-based mixture using vinegar or lemon juice and olive oil or other oil. All marinades with acid inhibit the formation of HCAs. Garlic and rosemary in a marinade also inhibit HCA formation. Rubs containing cumin, turmeric, and rosemary interfere with HCA formation. Marinating in red wine is also effective against HCA formation, but a beer-based marinade has been found to be even more effective in inhibiting HCA formation. Marinate at least an hour to reduce HCA formation by as much as 90 percent.

Grill Speak

We talk a lot about searing our food on the grill, particularly meat and other protein foods. Searing always refers to high-heat grilling, which creates those attractive grill lines. Grilling for the entire cooking time at this high-heat level is probably not a good idea due to the formation of HCA. You need to sear only for a very short period till the food releases from the grates—that's when the grill marks form too. This can be as quick as a minute or two. Acidic marinades speed the searing process so grill marks appear sooner. Experiment with the aim of keeping your searing time as short as you can while still getting the taste results you want.

According to the Tufts University Health and Nutrition Newsletter (a very reliable and informative source for overall health advice), a Portuguese study comparing unmarinated meat to beer-marinated meat showed an 88 percent reduction in HCA in the beer-treated meat. Comparing wine-marinated beef to unmarinated beef showed a 44 percent reduction in HCA in the wine-treated meat. A tasting panel preferred the beer marinating over the wine, which seemed to change the taste and texture of the beef in negative ways. Beer marinating actually improved the flavor for many of the tasters.

In another study at Kansas State University, food scientists found that meat marinated in oil, acid (vinegar), and spices had lower HCA after high-heat cooking, ranging from 57 percent to 88 percent less HCA than meat that had not been marinated.

Tasty Tips

Throughout this book, when olive oil is mentioned, unless otherwise noted, it means extra-virgin olive oil. The taste really matters, especially when added to cooked meat, fish, vegetables, and poultry after grilling. Neutral oils for oiling grates include corn and canola oil. Sunflower oil has a neutral taste and is very nutritious and high in omega-3, as is grape seed oil.

Tasty Tips

Prolonged high-heat grilling can easily dry out leaner cuts of meat and scorch fattier meats, neither of which is desirable. A nice char, the result of searing meat, poultry, or fish for two to three minutes over high heat, is not the same as scorching. Charring caramelizes the natural sugars; scorching burns them to a bitter taste. Color is the key. A golden to tan color is the goal, not black tar.

Grilling Tech Talk

Most barbecue sauces don't have enough acid to protect against HCA formation. The higher sugar content of many sauces can cause that unpleasant burned taste if applied too early in the grilling process. If you like to use barbecue sauce you'll still need to marinate. Brush on your BBQ sauce when you move meat, fish, or poultry to indirect heat for roasting, or just before you're finished grilling.

Grilling Tech Talk

The good news is that you don't have to even think about PAHs and HCAs when you're grilling veggies, fruits, breads, and any nonanimal protein foods. These chemicals do not form in those ingredients. Another good reason to eat your vegetables.

Reduce HCA with a Rub and Grill-Roasting

You can't marinate burgers but you can use a rub with turmeric, cumin, and/or rosemary. You should grill-roast burgers. By doing both, an anti-HCA rub and grill-roasting, you can virtually eliminate the formation of HCAs. No one is saying for sure that these carcinogens accumulate enough in frequent grilling to cause cancer in humans. But there is evidence in the lab and in some population studies to suggest that they may play a role. Reducing PAHs and HCAs to a point where they pose no threat is a healthy grilling practice that is easy to do and sensible. The food tastes as good, or better, than using the old-fashioned high-heat grilling that most experts still recommend.

Grilling to Your Heart's Content

A heart-healthy diet is low in animal and dairy fat and high in water-soluble fiber—the kind found in fruits and vegetables. The so-called Mediterranean diet is rich in these ingredients, and your grill is the ideal place to put this way of eating into practice.

When you grill meat, you provide a place for the rendered fat to drip away, so even if you begin with meat that has more fat than you'd like, you'll end with meat that has significantly less fat when served. And the same is true for marinades that contain fats you've added, like olive, canola, or sesame oil. These are generally heart-healthy oils but can add too many calories if you're dieting. The good news is they too will tend to drip away from the food as it's heated on the gill. Compared to frying, braising, or roasting, grilling removes more intrinsic fat and much of any added fat.

Tasty Snacks

Obesity and heart disease go hand in hand. Childhood obesity is heart disease destiny. Getting children to eat a heart-healthy low-fat diet is a constant struggle. So whether your kids are overweight or not, try these kinds of after-school snacks instead of potato chips, cookies, and other processed high-salt, high-fat foods:

> ➤ Sweet potatoes: Thinly slice sweet potatoes, brush with a little canola oil, and lightly sprinkle with ground cinnamon and a touch of salt. Grill over medium heat, a few minutes on each side till done. You want them softened but still firm, with pleasing grill marks—don't let them burn. Serve warm or at room temperature.

> ➤ Chickpeas: Rinse fully cooked chickpeas or simmer dry chickpeas in water till soft, usually one and a half hours. Cool and let dry. In a bowl, lightly coat them with olive, sesame, or canola oil. Salt to taste (crunchy kosher or sea salt is best). Spread the chickpeas evenly on a perforated grill pan (see Chapter 2 on grilling equipment) and roast over low indirect heat about an hour till they have the texture of nuts with nice background smokiness. Kids love these nutritious low-calorie snacks. (This is easy to do when roasting other foods on the grill and will keep for weeks in the fridge.)

Grill Speak

We talk about grilling temperature, but how can you tell? Here's the simple measurement we grillers use: how long can you keep your hand above the grilling surface before you are in pain? Granted, we all have different pain thresholds, but this will give you a pretty good guide. As you get to know your grill, your fuel, and your grilling results, you won't need to do this.

The number of seconds you can hold your hand about 2 inches above the grates before it hurts is a rough estimate of the temperature of your grill. Here is a guideline:

➤ 1–2 seconds: High heat

➤ 3–4 seconds: Medium-high heat

➤ 5–6 seconds: Low heat

Low heat is indirect heat where your food is basically roasting away from the heat source—in the middle with charcoal banked against the sides, in the middle between two gas burners, or for a two burner grill at the rear with that burner off. Both charcoal and gas with the lid closed because you are roasting the food.

➤ Pita-Veggie pizzas: Chop leftover cooked mushrooms, peas, or corn—or any vegetable—by hand or in a food processor to a spreadable consistency. If desired, mix in yogurt cheese or low-fat cream cheese at this point. Grill one side of whole wheat pita on oiled grates over medium heat. Remove when toasted. With the grilled side up, top pita with the veggie spread and, if desired, a layer of your favorite thinly sliced cheese, and put back on grill. Close cover and grill for a few more minutes, checking carefully, till pita is toasted and veggie cheese spread melted.

These are just three snack ideas that you can create on your grill. And after you've seen how easy it is to grill frequently throughout the week, how delicious and healthy the food is, and how much your family enjoys these meals, your grill will rival your kitchen stove as the principle source of everyday dinners.

Grilling Tech Talk

Gas grills provide cooking convenience, just like turning on your kitchen stove, and good flavor too. It's impractical to wait for a charcoal grill to reach the right temperature when you're making a healthy snack for your kids, or for that matter when you're preparing a weekday family meal after working all day. With the lid closed and a little smoke from the burner plates, your gas grill will come quite close to that earthy appeal of charcoal. Soaked wood chips also add smokiness. Convenience trumps authenticity when you grill frequently like we do. Save the charcoal grill for special occasions or leisurely summer weekends.

As you'll see in the following chapters, healthy grilling is easy. It creates the tastiest food for your friends and family. The best part of grilling is that it's liberating. You're not stuck in the kitchen hearing the distant laughter of your friends and family. Grilling is cooking with those you love all around you.

CHAPTER 2

Selecting and Caring For Your Grill

In this chapter I'll help you decide what kind of grill to buy, what features are worthwhile and what are not, and try to make a seemingly daunting task a lot easier. If you are new to grilling or have no family grilling lore to learn from, here is the place to begin. If you're an experienced griller, this chapter will act as a refresher and help organize your decision-making process. Buying a grill is a fairly big decision since you may be spending several hundreds to thousands of dollars for an appliance that is intended for frequent, long-term use. Yes, a careful analysis is called for, but that doesn't mean it has to be stressful. It's actually simpler than you may think.

Planning Your Grill Buying

The debate over whether to buy a charcoal, pellet, or gas grill is easily solved once you determine your grilling practices and preferences. What model grill, how big, how elaborate—in other words, how much you can or want to spend—is a function of your budget, your family size, and your food preferences. Will you do a lot of entertaining using your grill, just grilling for the family, or plenty of both? Then there are the details—the types of grates, the arrangement of burners, the add-ons and features. Each of these apparent dilemmas is actually quite solvable, even for the least-experienced grill buyer.

Ask yourself these questions before you go grill shopping:

➤ How often do I plan to use my grill, and when? Just every few weeks and mostly on weekends? More often, and on weekdays as well? Seasonally or year-round? Or once in a while when the weather is real nice and friends are invited for a cookout?

➤ How many people will I regularly be feeding?

➤ What kinds of foods do I plan to grill? Good, healthy meals featuring lots of vegetables, lean meats and poultry, fish and fruit? Or more elaborate meals and for special occasions doing roasts and slow-cooked barbecues? Or just the traditional sausages, burgers, and dogs nearly every time I grill?

➤ How much money do I want to spend—or will I have to spend? My budget, in other words.

Let's deal with each of these questions in order to arrive at a set of attributes that will determine the kind of grill you should buy.

Grilling Tech Talk

There are many charcoal lighting gizmos on the market, from old-fashioned, smelly, and occasionally dangerous lighter fluid to elaborate battery-powered heating elements with blowers built in. None hold up when stacked against the chimney starter for ease of use, cost, and simplicity. Charcoal goes in at the top, a wad of newspaper below, and in fifteen minutes you have a fully functioning coal fire. Chimney starters are available at stores wherever grills are sold or online. Follow the directions and enjoy this eco-friendly, low-tech, reliable charcoal lighter.

The Special Occasion Griller

If you are a special occasion griller who plans to barbecue several times a month, mostly in nice weather, grilling steaks, burgers, and dogs, and mostly for entertaining family and friends, you probably should opt for a charcoal grill or a pellet grill for two good reasons:

1. Most people think of a festive cookout taking place on the traditional hardwood or charcoal grill

2. When you are planning a special occasion grilling event, you'll usually have the time to prepare and have the patience to develop the ideal cooking temperature. You'll want those gray ash coals with a solid heat glow, achieving sizzling temps of 600°F or more at the grates. Or you'll want the lower and slower smoky heat of a pellet grill. Or both.

So, from a traditional and perhaps festive point of view, a charcoal and/or pellet grill are your better choices if you are a weekend and special event griller.

Grilling Tech Talk

Thanks to YouTube and the web, you can see pellet grills in action. Nothing beats these online demos for clarity. You'll be able to compare the charcoal and pellet technologies to decide which will work best for your grilled food preferences. You'll be a much better informed consumer if you spend a couple of hours exploring pellet grills, especially on the website for MAK Grills at www.makgrills.com, which in my opinion is the best overall performer on the market.

The Every-Occasion Griller

If you plan on frequent grilling, most weekends for friends and family and for weeknight routine dinners, you should opt for gas. Frequent grilling with a wider variety of food dictates a practical resolution of the charcoal/gas quandary. Gas is practical and convenient. What may be lost in aroma and that traditional charcoal background flavor can be made up by ease of use. Like your kitchen stove, a gas grill is ready in minutes and gives you better control over your heat. The last thing a working mom or dad needs at the end of a long day is fussing with charcoal while the kids do a variation on the "are we there yet" car trip. Gas is practical, and it can deliver great grilled food. With rubs, marinades, and flavored wood, you can even surpass charcoal for the rustic, smoky taste that you thought only charcoal could provide.

Choosing Charcoal

For charcoal grills, I prefer lump charcoal made from pieces of hardwood instead of briquettes. Those uniform briquettes were originally developed by Ford from the leftover sawdust and wood chips it collected in the manufacture of the classy wood trim in its autos and "woody" station wagons. Briquettes are compressed and bonded with added chemicals.

Lump charcoal, on the other hand, is a more rustic product, the result of burning hardwood with so little oxygen that it chars instead of being consumed by flames. Charcoal burns hotter than wood and will not flame-burn food if you monitor the arrangement of coals and food on the grates. Lump charcoal also burns hotter than briquettes. Don't even think of using briquettes impregnated with lighter fluid—the so-called easy lighting product. Smelly! Ugly taste.

Choosing Gas

For gas grills, always have a second full tank of propane gas in reserve. There is nothing worse than running out of fuel halfway through a grilling session. With a patio full of hungry mouths to feed you're rushing to the propane store. Believe me, I've been there—a mistake you only make once.

When propane tanks get near empty the gas pressure drops, resulting in a lower flame under your burner bars. Lower pressure equals cooler gas flames, which can lead to an underdone grilling disaster almost as bad as running out of fuel altogether. So check your tank before starting to cook, either by the gauge on the tank, the weight scale on your grill, or by simply lifting it to get a feel for the weight. You'll get to know when a tank feels so light it's nearly empty. When in doubt, it's better to waste a little propane and hook up a full tank before you start cooking.

Choosing Pellets

Like charcoal briquettes, pellets are made from sawdust, but with a big difference. The sawdust leftover from manufacturing hardwood products and lumber is compressed under tremendous force, and in the process a natural "glue" in wood called lignin is liquefied, binding the sawdust into hardwood pellets with all the attributes of the original wood. No added chemicals, just natural wood in pellet form. So, for instance, if you choose apple wood pellets, you'll get the aromatic apple wood smoke you want for your cooking with none of the inconvenience and plan-ahead soaking. Or you can choose citrus, alder, oak, cherry, mesquite, and more. There are many online sources for pellets, and some grilling supply stores carry a good variety.

Grilling Tech Talk

Nothing beats the convenience of a natural gas line from your kitchen to your outdoor grill. If you can locate your grill on the patio or deck in a place where it's practical to run a gas line, you will never again have to lug propane tanks. You'll need a grill outfitted for natural gas, or a conversion kit for your existing propane grill. This added expense up front is paid for several times over during the life of your grill—and not just in the cost of propane and fuel for your car. One less disruptive errand in your busy life and less strain on your back handling heavy tanks.

Tasty Tips

Some of us will never use a gas grill because we miss that smoky charcoal flavor. But there are ways to compensate. Soak some hardwood or fruit wood—oak, hickory, mesquite, apple, citrus, cherry, etc.—and wrap the wet wood in aluminum foil with a few fork holes in the foil. Place the wood along the outside edge of your burners, not under the food, and in a few minutes they will give off their smoky goodness. Keep a water spray bottle handy to douse any flames that may develop, and after you're done cooking, spray the charred wood so you don't leave it smoldering in your grill. Neighbors get nervous at 3 a.m. when they awaken to the smell of wood smoke during a warm summer night.

Grill Size

When deciding on the size of your grill, consider how many people you usually cook for. When you grill for a crowd on special occasions, do you usually grill all the food at once or in batches and stages? The factors determine how much cooking surface you need. Grill size is expressed in square inches of cooking surface. Make sure the grill manufacturer does not include an upper warming rack in this calculation because you're not cooking there, you're just holding food there to keep warm.

Figure about 100 square inches per person, about 10 inches by 10 inches of grilling surface for each chicken breast, steak, burger, or tuna steak (including an arrangement of grilling vegetables). You don't want the food crowded together on the grill. So for a dinner for six you'll want 600 square inches of cooking surface. In

Grilling Tech Talk

Just as there are arguments among passionate grillers about charcoal versus gas, there are disagreements about the type of gas we should use. Propane or natural gas, meaning those tanks we exchange or fill, or the same gas piped to our homes powering the stove and perhaps clothes dryer. Propane burns hotter than natural gas and is under more pressure, which explains why you need a natural gas conversion kit for the generic gas grill. There are two reasons I prefer natural gas. The obvious one is convenience—never having to lug tanks, never running out of gas. But the other is important too. I don't strive for the hottest heat I can pump out of my grill. Virtually all my grilling is done the healthier way over medium to medium-high heat with grill-roasting for most meat, poultry, and fish.

general, for most family and friends grilling occasions I've found plenty of grilling room in the 600–700 square inch category. If you regularly cook for a crowd and grill the kinds of foods that must all be served at the same time, you will probably want a larger grill—800 square inches or more.

Advice from an Expert

I asked one of the most knowledgeable grilling experts, Bruce Bjorkman, what the ideal size for a grill is. Bruce broadcasts weekly on Oregon's KXL-FM radio station and can be heard on his audio podcast (iTunes and other podcast providers) *Cooking Outdoors with Mr. BBQ*. He has been working in the grill manufacturing industry for over twenty years, so you can count on his insider experience for good advice. He said he's often asked this question and has a very simple answer. Always buy a bigger grill than you think you need. If you're serious about grilling, says Bruce, you will get better at it over time and attract friends and neighbors. If your original grill can't adequately accommodate your newfound popularity, you'll have to purchase a bigger one. So start off with the assumption that the social aspects of grilling—the reason we all love it so much—will prevail over time. This is one of the few times when more is better, more grilling area means more enjoyment for you and your friends.

Tasty Tips

I know serious grillers who swear by gas for convenience and better heat control. For grilling fish, poultry, pork chops, vegetables, and fruit—gas is the preferred fuel because these products are generally more delicate than a big, beefy steak.

But beef may be a different story. Many grillers insist you just can't get that steak sear, that crunchy goodness on the outside and juicy tenderness inside when you use gas. Gotta get your charcoal under that sirloin, many serious grillers say. I say, why not do both? For less than $100, you can buy an excellent charcoal grill reserved for steaks and a few other charcoal-demanding foods, while your day-to-day grilling is conveniently accomplished on your workhorse gas grill.

The Great Grate Debate

Grill grates are not all created equal, and choosing your grates can make a substantial difference in your grilling success. There are three basic categories and each has some advantages.

Stainless Steel

Stainless steel grates are light and easy to remove and clean. They are thicker than wire but in my opinion, not thick enough to give you the attractive grill marks we all like to see on meat and veggies. There are two basic grades of stainless steel, 400 and 300. The lower number is the higher quality in terms of durability and corrosion resistance.

Smaller, lighter portable grills seem to use stainless steel grates more often. Tailgaters and picnickers like them for ease of handling. Boaters, including me, almost always use stainless steel for the over-the–transom grilling anchored off a favorite beach. A marine environment requires stainless steel for corrosion resistance.

My advice is to avoid stainless steel on your home grill and choose one of the two other options. The only exception is pellet grills, where you are doing virtually all your grilling over indirect heat. In this case, stainless steel is fine because searing is not the primary objective and even heat distribution results from the convection oven effect.

Cast Iron

Cast iron grates are heavy and outshine stainless steel for heat transfer and grill marks. Like a cast iron skillet, though, cast iron grates must be seasoned and maintained to keep them rust-free. If you go long periods without using your grill, cast iron grates tend to rust. For frequent grillers cast iron is the number one choice.

Always get preseasoned grates. For charcoal grillers, make sure the grates have a hinge so you can add charcoal while cooking—these are real heavy, so removing hot grates to add more fuel can be a dangerous chore. They are easy to keep clean with a wire brush and will last forever. I like cast iron grates because I grill frequently and they stay rust-free.

Porcelain

Porcelain-coated cast iron grates win my affection too, but they are actually more difficult to care for than advertised. These grates have all the attributes of cast iron without the rust problem. They are relatively care-free for less frequent grillers. If you are a seasonal outdoor cook, porcelain is a good choice. But these grates do have one problem. If you use a wire brush for cleaning, and you do this frequently and with a lot of pressure, you can degrade the porcelain finish and end up with pitting. That makes the grates even harder to keep clean. Don't ever use a scraper on porcelain.

Burners

The arrangement of burners in your gas grill makes a difference. Facing your grill, the burners, and the flavor bars covering them, can run front to back or left to right. I prefer an arrangement of three or four front-to-back burners.

Many recipes instruct you to grill food over indirect heat. Others call for searing your meat over direct heat. But after you sear your food, you will most often be using my healthy grilling method I call grill-roasting. That means you'll be doing most of your grilling time over indirect heat, not directly over the burners. You will move your meat, fish, or poultry to the back of the grill, turn off the back and middle burners, and roast your food under the closed grill cover. The front burner heat will distribute more evenly across your food with this burner arrangement than if you were creating an indirect cooking surface on one side of the grill. The shape of the grill and cover induces convection that is more even front to back than left to right. This makes for better roasting because your heat flow is balanced across the entire grill instead of more heat on one side than the other.

The Cost

What should you spend on a gas grill? Assuming you can afford up to $1,200 (and you can spend twice that for the top of the line, loaded with accessories), in other words, you've budgeted as you would for a kitchen stove, what amount makes sense. I come down pretty much in the middle. Around $500 to $800 should get you just about everything you'll need or want. Add up to $100 additional cost for natural gas, if possible, to avoid the inconvenience of propane. This will buy a really nice Weber Genesis or equivalent. You can spend more for a top-grade Bull Grill—very much worth it, in my opinion—or less for a workable Char-Grill or similar. But keep in mind that a cheap grill is just that. Even if you don't plan on using your grill very often, you should always opt for quality over frugality when it comes to an appliance that will be handling heat, grease, and weather.

Charcoal Grill Costs

If your workhorse grill is gas, which it is for most of us, it is a good idea to have a charcoal grill for veggies, various flatbreads, and every now and then a big juicy steak. You can buy a very good small kettle grill for under $100. Large well-made charcoal grills from Weber can run around $200 and up, well worth it, and other manufacturers will certainly qualify with quality products.

Pellet Grill Costs

My favorite MAK pellet grills start at around $1,300 and top out over $2,000. These grills are built to last, using top-grade stainless steel throughout and a nonclogging augur feed system for the pellets. They have plenty of innovative features and are easy to use and keep clean. Top-of-the-line price and worth every penny.

There are about a dozen other pellet grill manufacturers with prices as low as $400. Do your research before you buy. If most of your grilling will be low and slow, and if you're a big smoke fan, pellet grills are a better choice than charcoal. Ideally, a gas grill and a pellet grill would be the best combo for serious grillers.

Features You May Not Need or Want

Don't be seduced by all the bells and whistles you can get on a grill. Think hard about whether you really would use that so-called can't-live-without add-on. Here are some features you may be able to do without:

➤ Warming rack: I've never used a warming rack; in fact, I find it interferes with my grilling area. Many grills include one as a standard feature. I leave it off when assembling my grill.

➤ Rotisserie: I can understand why some grillers find the rotisserie feature attractive. For daydreaming recipes and the way meat looks as it rotates over the heat—well, it's hard to resist. I've had a rotisserie but rarely used it. Instead of a rotisserie chicken, I'd rather make a beer can chicken— similar texture and finish, better taste. I slow roast a pork loin instead of using a rotisserie; it comes out juicier, as does a roast beef or small turkey. I like the concept but never seem to want to bother with the hassle, especially since my alternative techniques do a better job. But this is personal preference—your choice.

➤ Side burner: Call me a dinosaur, but I find a side burner annoying, and two side burners are twice as annoying. I want plenty of room on the sides of my grill to hold utensils, marinades, meat thermometer, a stack of plates or a serving platter, a margarita. Instead of a built-in side burner, get one or two stand-alone electric warmers or hot plates for a lot less money (and for other uses as well). You can place them where you want in your grilling area, or remove them when not needed. They offer more flexibility, less cost, more convenience.

Features You Will Need or Want

Then there are those extras that will be useful and handy. Here are some features you're likely to find helpful:

➤ Built-in thermometer: A thermometer built into your grill will tell you when your grill is hot enough to use and, for slow-cooking roasts and other food, it will enable you to regulate low heat at the desired temperature. But get to know your built-in thermometer by checking with another thermometer. You don't need perfect accuracy for this type of cooking, but it is useful to know the approximate temperature under your grill cover.

➤ Remote thermometer: A remote thermometer can be a great convenience. It's like having an unpaid assistant standing by to monitor the grill while you enjoy a beer with your friends.

➤ Removable grease catcher: An easily removable grease catcher enables you to keep your grill clean and odor-free when it gets really hot.

➤ Removable ash catcher: For charcoal grills, an easily removable ash catcher is convenient and much less messy than trying to get coal ash out of the bottom of your grill any other way.

➤ Flavor bars: Flavor bars vaporize juices that drip on them, returning flavor to the grilled food. They wear out from the high heat and food residue, so you'll want to

Grilling Tech Talk

Make sure your gas grill has an accessible alternative lighting port if it comes with a push button or other automatic lighter. Those features always seem to wear out in a year or two. A handy long-nose flamer to light your burners through an easy-to-reach port is essential.

replace flavor bars every couple of years. (Burners may need replacement every three or four years; grates last five years or more, but if you chip your porcelain grates, you'll need to replace them sooner.) Make sure that parts are available over the long term.

Equipment and Utensils

You can find all sorts of utensils and other types of equipment to use with your grill. I use my favorite equipment and tools frequently for my routine family meals, as well as for more elaborate entertaining.

Grill Topper

Grill Innovations' grill topper turns your gas grill into an outdoor convection oven for roasting meat and poultry, making pizza and bread, and even baking a pie. See the website: www.grillinnovations.com.

The best inventions solve a problem simply—their elegance lies in the adage less is more. This is the best grill topper on the market because it goes beyond a sheet of flat metal. It is designed to enhance the convection effect of a closed grill, providing even temperature, roasting, and baking. It is lightweight but substantial. It replaces a heavy pizza stone, a grill pan, and flimsy aluminum foil.

In the summer, when the last thing you want is an oven heating up your house and fighting with the A/C, you can fire up your patio grill to bake anything from a loaf of homemade bread to lasagna. I don't know how I grilled without it all these years and now consider it an essential element in my grilling tool kit.

Perforated Grill Pan

A perforated grill pan looks like a metal tray or shallow flat-bottom wok with many small holes. I use it to grill small mushrooms, cherry tomatoes, and string beans or haricots verts. Some have even smaller holes or are made of closely woven wire so you can even grill peas. Yum! Tossed with a little olive oil, these veggies come out succulent and slightly smoking. Even your kids will enjoy vegetables done this way on the grill. See the resources section for online suppliers offering a good variety of styles and sizes.

One caveat, however. I don't recommend getting a nonstick grill product of any kind. It's unnecessary since you want that wonderful combination of olive oil and grill smoke. And the high heat of grilling can degrade the nonstick coating to the point where it may get into your food. We ingest enough chemicals in the normal course of our lives without adding more.

Grill Toppers

A raised rail grill topper can be very useful both for searing and for flame suppression, especially with charcoal grilling. Grillgrate makes a good product that is modular so you can fit it to your model or cover only part of the grates as desired.

Frogmats makes another kind of grill topper that protects food and promotes the healthy kind of grilling I recommend. It's slicker and very useful for fish and roasting fruit.

Grill Brush

A grill brush is essential for keeping your grates clean and free of residue that affects grilled food taste. My favorite grill brushes are from Weber and Oxo, but there are many to choose from of similar quality. Make sure they are not so stiff or harsh that they could damage the porcelain finish on your grates.

I appreciate the Grill Daddy brush. It has a built-in water tank that dispenses water onto the grates, which converts to steam when the grates are hot, and does a real nice job getting rid of previously cooked food residue. After you steam clean the grates, wipe them with dry bundled paper towel, apply neutral vegetable oil, and you'll have clean grates for grilling.

Gloves

Heavy-duty grill gloves are useful for handling hot skewers, grill toppers, and other equipment that is in contact with your heat source. Your hands are your handiest tool, but keep them protected from searing heat.

Meat Thermometer

Your meat thermometer can be as simple or as elaborate is you like. I find an instant-read thermometer is usually all I need because I've enough experience to know when my food is close to done. But if you are less sure of yourself, use a remote thermometer, either the common wire cable or a wireless thermometer. There are new apps for smart phones that are expensive but fun and accurate. The choice is yours, but don't choose to just wing it on the cooking time. A thermometer is an essential tool for grilling.

Other Essential Tools

Other tools you'll find hard to live without include the usual spatula, fork, and tongs. But there are a few other necessary tools you might forget:

➤ Flat metal skewers prevent shrimp, mushrooms, scallops, and similar foods from spinning when you rotate them on the grill.

➤ If you like to produce aromatic smoke with your gas or charcoal grill, consider getting a metal wood-chip box that nests in the coals or sits on the burners.

> ➤ A soft-bristled brush for applying marinades during cooking is an important tool. Be sure the bristles are not nylon or other synthetic material that will melt if accidently put in contact with hot grates.

Grill Maintenance

The single most important maintenance issue is cleanliness. Keep your grates well scrubbed and oiled. Use neutral, high-heat oil like canola, corn, or peanut. Extra-virgin olive oil is too precious to waste on grill lubricating and has a smoke point that is too low—it will burn and give an off flavor to foods. Don't use soap, which can leave a residue. A wire brush, a little elbow grease, and plain water does the job between each grilling session.

Make sure your grease catcher is cleaned regularly and the cup or tray is emptied often. Accumulated grease gets hot and affects the flavor of some grilled foods. And grease can catch fire.

Be sure to remove charcoal ash after each grilling session and dispose of it carefully, making certain there is no heat left. If in doubt, put the ash in a metal container, soak in water, and dispose of in a safe place. Careless handling of charcoal ash, esp____ ____ ____ estive dinner with plenty of wine and beer, can kill.

Deep Cleaning

I remove my grates several times a year and thoroughly wash and scrub them with soap—a dirty job but someone has to do it. That's my opportunity to brush the flavor bars with a wire brush, check the bars for pitting or corrosion, and make sure the burners are working properly. Check the flame on your gas grill—it should be mostly blue. If the flames are yellow, the burners may need adjustment or replacement. All these parts, grates, burners, flavor bars, and hoses can and should be replaced if not in good condition.

Grates

If you are not using your grill for a while, make sure grates are clean, oiled, and covered to protect them from the elements. This is

Grilling Tech Talk

Outdoor grills require more care and cleaning than kitchen stoves. If you're new to grilling, you have to keep this in mind and develop a routine before and after each grilling session. Just a quick scrub with a wire brush is enough to leave the grates residue-free for next time. Before you begin grilling, use a bundle of wet paper towel to wipe the hot grates clean. Then use another bundle to dry them, followed by a light spray of oil. With just a little effort, you're on your way to a tasty meal.

essential for cast iron grates, which will rust if left to the elements over a long period of time. You can, of course, wire brush the rust off, but it's so much easier to do a little preventive care.

Propane

Always store propane safely away from a heat source. Keep a plug in the valve of your reserve tank even if you know the valve is in good working order and turned off. Transport tanks carefully so they don't roll around in your vehicle. When exchanging tanks make sure the new tank is in good condition with no rust and a tight valve with a plug.

PART TWO

Healthy Grilling and Delicious Eating

CHAPTER 3

 **Beef Burgers**

> ## In This Chapter
>
> ➤ Striving for beef burger perfection
>
> ➤ The almost perfect beef burger
>
> ➤ How to grill healthy burgers, searing and roasting
>
> ➤ Burger sauces and condiments

In this chapter you'll find burger nirvana. That means the best combination of beef cuts for maximum flavor. It means learning how to grind and easily prepare beef burgers in your own kitchen without special equipment. And, most important, how to grill healthy burgers that are lower in fat yet juicy and delicious—burger perfection.

Striving for Beef Burger Perfection

There are three critical elements required to achieve the perfect beef burger. Here they are in order of importance:

1. The grilling technique: How you use the heat to achieve a low-fat burger that remains juicy and succulent

2. The beef mixture: The types of beef you use to make your burger

3. The grind and making the patty: How you chop the meat and handle it to achieve succulent burgers

Tasty Tips

If you follow my grill-roasting method, you'll get good results with common store-bought hamburger meat such as ground chuck or sirloin. Even low-fat ground round (90 percent lean) comes out juicier when grill-roasted than when grilled using other techniques. Grill-roasting gives your burger an attractive appearance with good grill marks, while using low heat. This is a healthier grilling method that retains the juicy succulence we all crave in a perfect burger.

The Meat Counter

Buying beef is the first step toward burger perfection, whether you get it already ground or grind your own. This is your opportunity to sample different cuts of meat in your burger mix—like sirloin, chuck, and brisket—or stick to a tried and true prepackaged formula. Sometimes convenience is the deciding point, although mixing ground beef cuts is convenient too. If I have a few extra minutes, I almost always buy beef cuts to grind at home in my food processor.

The Beef Mixture

The mixture of beef you choose is a matter of personal taste. Some folks like a combo of chuck and sirloin and/or other beef cut combos; others prefer just plain ground chuck or sirloin alone. I like the mixture made famous, and justly so, by the Shake Shack in New York. The exact mixture of meat is a secret. Imitation, however, is the sincerest form of flattery so many grillers have tried to reconstruct the recipe.

According to published reports, the formula is a grind composed of one-half sirloin, one-quarter boneless short ribs, and one-quarter brisket. These three beef cuts deliver a flavor balance that can't be beat. The fat produces a juicy burger even when cooked through on constant medium-high heat, as restaurants' lawyers require them to do.

The Shake Shack serves its burger on a toasted potato roll. The long lines at lunch time are proof that this recipe for ground beef produces unforgettable burgers. It is my special occasion beef burger mix.

Fat Fighters

As much as I love the Shake Shack's beef burger recipe, I must admit there is too much fat in it for me. That's one of the reasons it's so tasty. If you enjoy a grilled burger dinner often—we average about once a week with a hearty vegetable soup or mixed green salad and fresh fruit for dessert—I advise a much leaner mixture. I call that my home-style beef burger (see recipe below), and I reserve the Shake Shack–style meat mixture for special occasions as part of a more elaborate barbecue dinner.

The Grind

Once you arrive home with one or more beef cuts in your grocery bag you're ready to prepare the meat to make burgers. It only takes a few minutes to grind your own burger meat. Grinding your meat gives you complete control over the amount of fat you eat, the combination of beefy flavors you choose, and, of course the cleanliness of your own kitchen. Best of all, you don't need a meat grinder!

Use your food processor and follow these steps for the perfect burger grind.

1. Trim the beef cuts to your liking. For everyday burgers, keep the fat content low by trimming off any visible fat from the beef cuts. Trim off gristle. For a perfect special occasion burger (the Shake Shack–style mixture), keep some of the visible fat on the meat you're using.

2. Cut the beef into approximate 1-inch cubes and mix the different beef cuts together. Spread them out on a platter or baking sheet, and place it in the freezer for about twenty minutes. You want the meat very cold—stiff but not frozen.

3. Load the meat into your food processor in small batches, an inch or so above the blade, making sure you maintain the approximate proportion of each beef cut in the mixture you are grinding.

4. Pulse for two to four seconds repeatedly till the meat becomes the texture you want. I like a medium grind, usually about eight pulses. Fewer pulses may produce a grind that is too coarse; more than ten pulses may result in a grind that is too fine, like the inside of a hot dog. So carefully check the meat and err on the side of too coarse—you can always correct that with a couple more pulses. Put batches of ground meat into a bowl.

5. Using your hands (rubber gloves preferred), gently toss the meat together to mix. Season with salt and pepper and/or other spices and herbs, then form into balls about 2 to 2½ inches in diameter. Gently press the ball into a patty about ¾-inch thick or more, according to your preference. Only you know how thick you and your family like your burgers. Don't squeeze the meat. Uneven edges look attractively rustic. The last thing you want is a homemade burger looking industrial.

6. Chill in the refrigerator to allow the meat to relax. Remove from the fridge about fifteen minutes before grilling. Sprinkle both sides with salt and pepper to taste if you didn't season earlier.

Grilling Tech Talk

I've often been tempted to get a meat grinder. But once I discovered the benefits of using a food processor to chop meat and poultry (tuna and salmon too), I decided a grinder was not needed. The food processor has one big advantage over a grinder: you can control the coarseness of the chop as you process the meat and vary that simply by increasing or decreasing the number of pulses. With a little practice you can become a master meat and poultry grinder (fish burgers too), achieving results like a coarser and finer grind within the same burger or other variations that spark your creativity.

The Grilling Technique

I grill burgers, and most other meat and poultry for that matter, by searing and then roasting. Searing caramelizes the natural sugars on the meat's surface and delivers attractive grill marks, and a little crustiness, to contrast with the softer, juicier inside. But once you have seared the meat, the extreme direct heat (about 400–500°F) of a good grill begins to dry, and perhaps even burn, the outer part of the meat as the inside cooks. It's at this point that you want to move from searing to roasting.

This change of grilling method gives the inside of the burger time to cook without drying or burning the outside. Don't get me wrong; we want some crusty exterior on our burgers. Proper searing over very high heat will do this (for steaks, too). But enough is enough. To achieve burger perfection, you want an exterior sear with high heat and a balanced, juicy interior by roasting over indirect heat till done.

Follow these steps:

➤ Gently place your burgers on very hot, well-oiled grates directly over the heat source (450°F or more, or follow the two-second rule). Cook for about three minutes till the meat is seared with good grill marks and can be released from the grates—easily flipped without sticking. Sear the other side for two to four minutes. If you're using a gas grill, close the cover during each sear.

➤ If you're using a charcoal grill, flip the seared burgers and move them to the indirect heat in the center. Add cheese if desired. Close the cover and roast for about six minutes. The burgers should be medium done then, so add or subtract time as you prefer. Do not flip. Just let them gently roast over the indirect heat.

➤ If you're using a gas grill, after searing both sides turn off the middle burner(s). Flip the burgers and move them to the middle of the grill away from the remaining burners. Turn the lit burners down for a lower heat level under the cover. Add cheese if desired. Close the cover and roast for six minutes. Burgers should be medium done then, so add or subtract time as you prefer. The thermometer should register about 350°F with just the remaining burners on. Do not flip the burgers, just let them gently roast. Rest burgers a couple of minutes before serving.

Grilling Tech Talk

Use canola, peanut, or corn oil to lubricate your grill grates. Never use extra-virgin olive oil. Many burger grilling recipes instruct you to brush burgers with extra-virgin olive oil. Burgers do not need to be brushed with any oil—even lean meat burgers have enough intrinsic fat to lubricate themselves as they cook on oiled grates.

I think our love affair with extra-virgin olive oil has clouded the judgment of cooks who should know better. If you like that olive oil taste on meat or poultry, it can be sprinkled on after they are finished cooking, hot off the grill and ready to serve, or brushed on rolls or bread that you briefly toast on the grill. Extra-virgin olive oil is expensive and not a good oil for lubricating very hot grates. Use much cheaper corn or canola oil.

Home-Style Beef Burgers

A burger dinner is a healthy choice if you keep the fat content low and grill-roast your burgers. You can do this by trimming and grinding your meat or by buying freshly ground supermarket meat that is labeled 90 percent lean—usually ground round.

If you buy ground meat, make sure it was made that day by the in-store butcher staff. Better yet, if the market has a butcher operation for customer orders, ask the guy behind the counter to grind your specific beef cuts for you while you watch. That's almost as good as doing it yourself at home using your food processor.

For everyday home-style burgers, handle and grill the meat as I recommended above. By significantly lowering the fat content, however, you will sacrifice some juicy taste to the benefit of your arteries. An almost perfect burger will emerge from your grill if you use the grill-roasting method. In fact, with lower fat, this grilling technique takes on added importance to achieve the desired results.

Ignore those grilling instructions that tell you to completely cook burgers over direct heat, either flipping every couple of minutes or flipping only once. Sear the burgers on both sides, move them off the direct heat, cover the grill, and slow roast them for approximately six more minutes for an almost perfect burger, medium done.

Tasty Tips

Try to avoid buying ground meat to form and freeze burgers for grilling in the future. The same goes for previously frozen beef patties. Freezing and thawing results in a mushy mess that never tastes as good as fresh-made burgers. Buy as much as you need for that night's dinner, or for a day or two ahead, but beyond that time limit don't try to preserve burger meat by freezing it. Freezing ground meat for other uses, in sauce for instance, is certainly OK.

Mass-Produced Burgers

I do not recommend buying ground meat you know comes from some remote high-volume meat packing plant. I am not suggesting that it's dangerous to your health. Meat is generally safe in our country, but mistakes do happen and ground meat recalls do occur. Given a choice, it's always better to know the source of your food—in this case, ground beef—to actually see it being prepared right there where you are buying it.

Grill Speak

We talk about beef burgers primarily made from ground round, ground chuck, and ground sirloin. But what are they and why make these distinctions? The answer lies in the fat and flavor. The more muscle on that part of the cow, the tougher and leaner the meat. Round comes from the hip area, gets a good workout, and contains less fat than the area above that, the sirloin. Chuck comes from the front of the steer and has more fat that's easy to trim for home grinding in your food processor.

Beef Burgers Beyond Salt and Ketchup

The burger purists among us will resist adding anything to good-quality beef except salt and pepper, of course, and maybe a cheese topping and fresh summer tomatoes. They will allow ketchup to grace the meat, but venturing beyond that is sacrilegious to many burger purists. Perhaps they are right.

The beef burger is as American as it gets, unadulterated with bread crumbs, herbs, and eggs, which one encounters all over Europe. We pride ourselves on "an all-beef patty" and similar claims to burger purity. In Germany, a burger is closer to a flattened meatloaf. Nothing wrong with a meatloaf sandwich, but that's not my idea of a hamburger even if it is from Hamburg. (Frankfurters in Frankfurt, however, are wonderful, but that's another story for a sausage discussion.)

The burger non-purists like me insist on the finest beef ingredients, but we're willing, often excited, to go beyond salt and ketchup (go to Part Three for my favorite burger

Fat Fighters

Reducing the fat content of your burger is not the only way to eat healthy. Portion control really adds up over time—or I should say subtracts from thighs. Lean burger meat is about 60 calories per ounce. Meat that's 25 to 30 percent fat is about 85 calories per ounce.

If you reduce the size of a typical burger from 6 ounces to 5, you will save, on average, 65–75 calories. If you enjoy a burger dinner on a weekly basis you'll reduce your annual calorie intake by about 4,000 calories. That's like fasting for two days every year. You'll hardly notice the difference between a 5- and 6-ounce burger, but you will lose 1 to 2 pounds annually as a result. That's one small step toward weight loss and healthier eating.

recipes). One of the many reasons burgers remain an all-American favorite, and a consistent dinner winner in our house, is its versatility.

Leaner, Fitter Burger Tips

Here are some healthy ways to keep burger fat and calories low:

➤ Always buy 90 percent lean burger meat or trim and chop it yourself; for cheeseburgers, use reduced-fat cheddar or Swiss (Cabot, Sargento, Bordens, and other brands have several 2 percent or less milk fat cheese products, most with less than half the fat of regular cheese).

➤ Don't add bacon to cheeseburgers—too much fat. Use low-fat Canadian bacon if you want that salty pork taste.

➤ Use low-fat mayo either plain or as an ingredient in Russian dressing for burgers with lettuce and tomatoes.

➤ For burger rolls, use low-calorie whole grain or multigrain English muffins, sandwich rolls, or toasted low-calorie whole wheat bread. (Thomas's, Arnold, Wonder, and others make 100-calorie muffins, rolls, and bread).

Get Saucy with Your Burgers

Ketchup is the classic burger sauce and some would say the most boring. Jazz up your burgers with creative sauces that enhance the meaty flavor.

The Perfect Burger Sauce

The famous Shake Shack creation in New York City is topped with a special secret sauce. Food detectives have published this version, which I agree tastes like the real thing.

Mock Shake Shack Sauce

Ingredients
½ cup mayonnaise (use low-fat mayo if desired)
1 Tbs ketchup
1 Tbs yellow mustard
½ kosher-style dill pickle
¼ tsp garlic powder
¼ tsp paprika
Pinch of cayenne pepper

Directions

Put all ingredients in a blender until pureed.

Spread on toasted potato roll with burger.

Tasty Tips

I find nearly all barbecue sauces too overpowering on burgers. They are meant to complement hearty, smoky meats and poultry that have often been rubbed with a variety of spices and slow cooked for hours. For burgers, I like to mix my favorite barbecue sauces with an equal part of low-calorie mayonnaise, and spread this on a toasted roll. The mayo softens the barbecue sauce, creating a gentler flavor for my burgers. Or I mix in a small amount of BBQ sauce when forming the patties, less than 1 teaspoon per burger. A delicious sweet, savory, smoky background flavor when grilled.

Lower-Calorie Pesto Sauce

This sauce can give beefy burgers an extra kick. I like to make a lower-caloric variation on the classic basil pesto. Try this, or let your creativity flow with other herbs or even aromatic vegetables like arugula or spinach.

Pesto Sauce for Burgers

Ingredients

½ c low-calorie mayonnaise
½ c shredded fresh basil leaves (or other aromatic herbs or leafy veggies)
1 Tbs fresh parsley or ½ Tbs dry parsley
1 Tbs grated parmesan cheese
A little olive oil if desired

Directions

Put all ingredients in a small food processor or blender and puree. Spread on toasted rolls or grilled Italian bread with burgers.

Spicy Sauce Variations

Spices from the warmer climates of Asia and Latin America add unusual flavors to a weekly burger dinner. Your family will never find burgers boring if you spice up the sauce with these suggestions.

Asian Subcontinent Burger

Ingredients
Mild curry powder to taste
½ cup nonfat plain yogurt
1 squirt fresh-squeezed lemon juice

Directions
Mix hot or mild curry powder to taste into nonfat plain yogurt. Add a squirt of fresh squeezed lemon juice, whisk, and spread on toasted whole wheat pitas.

Tasty Tips

After you've moved your burgers from the direct heat to the roasting side of the grill, you can use the direct heat area to toast a variety of breads. Our all-time favorite is quite simple.

Buy or bake your own really good, crusty Italian bread (see Chapter 14 for baking bread). Ideally, you want an oval panna de casa bread, if available. Slice and cut bread to hamburger size. Brush one side of the bread with extra-virgin olive oil and sprinkle with kosher or sea salt to taste. Grill the bread oiled side down for just a couple of minutes to a light golden brown with a few grill marks. Place burgers between the oiled sides; the dry outer sides of the sandwich are for your hands.

Szechuan Burger

Ingredients
1 tsp sesame oil
2 Tbs light soy sauce
1 tsp hoi sin sauce
A touch of Chinese hot chili oil

Directions
Whisk all the ingredients together. Drizzle on hot-off-the-grill burgers and serve on thin sesame sandwich rolls.

South of the Border Burgers

Ingredients
1 tsp cumin
1 tsp ancho chili powder
½ tsp smoked paprika
½ c nonfat cottage cheese, ricotta cheese, or crumbled quesa fresco

Directions
Combine the ingredients and whip till smooth. Spread on toasted bread or rolls creates.

Sicilian Sauce

A Sicilian burger requires a cooked sauce.

Ingredients
1 anchovy filet
2 Tbs olive oil
2–4 chopped garlic cloves
1 Tbs tomato paste
1 handful of chopped parsley
1–2 Tbs grated parmesan or Romano cheese

Directions
Sauté the anchovy filet in olive oil. As the filet "melts," mash it with a wooden spoon and mix it into the oil. Add the chopped garlic cloves and gently sauté. Add the tomato paste and continue gently cooking, stirring the paste into the oil. Add the chopped parsley, stir, and remove from heat. Add the cheese, stir, and spread on toasted Italian bread. Serve burgers hot off the grill on the bread.

Tasty Tips

Inside out cheeseburgers are a twist on the classic cheeseburger. Start with two burgers, each about half the thickness of your usual burger. Place your favorite cheese slice (cheddar, Swiss, blue, or brie are all delicious) on top of one burger, and then place the other burger over the cheese. Carefully, tenderly, seal the two burgers together so the cheese Is not exposed. Grill-roast the burgers till desired doneness. Let the burger rest a little longer than usual because the cheese inside can be liquid and hot enough to burn a child's chin as it drips out. Take that first bite carefully to avoid discomfort.

Mideast Sauce

A Mideast burger is so simple and tasty you'll be embarrassed to tell guests it's made with (whisper) a good store-bought tabouli salad mixed into store-bought hummus, half and half, and spread on grilled pita. You can squirt some lemon or lime juice on the pita if you like.

By tasting these store-bought items, over time you will winnow out the mediocre concoctions. My favorite New York brand of tabouli and humus is Abraham's.

Burgers are so easy to prepare, and so healthy if prepared at home as recommended here, that a weekly burger dinner should be on your meal-planning agenda. In Part Three you'll see all sorts of burgers—not just beef—that we love and know you will too. Chicken, turkey, tuna, salmon, pork, and lamb are just the beginning. Veggie burgers, too. See the burger recipes in the next section of this book.

CHAPTER 4

Chicken on the Grill

In This Chapter

➤ How to buy chicken for the grill

➤ Brines, marinades, and chicken rubs

➤ The healthiest, tastiest way to grill chicken

➤ How to roast chicken on the grill

Less than a century ago, politicians would promise prosperity by invoking the phrase *a chicken in every pot*. In those days, chicken was a luxury meal, a Sunday treat. In our time, chicken is so inexpensive and convenient we prepare it several times a week. A good source of protein with little fat, chicken is the grilling artist's canvas on which to paint favorite flavors and presentations.

Chicken, the Ideal Low-Fat Grilled Meat

A boneless breast cooks relatively quickly, ten to fifteen minutes depending on thickness, and it delivers only about 25–30 calories per ounce, so a 6-ounce breast is less

Tasty Tips

We always grill more chicken than we expect to consume in the meal we're preparing. Unlike many other meats, chicken is as delicious cold out of the fridge as it is hot off the grill. Sliced chicken sandwiches for lunch is healthier than processed luncheon meats. Chicken salad recipes come in so many varieties you can make a different salad every week of the year. Cube the meat for soup, chili, or chicken hash, a quick family dinner. You and your family will enjoy leftover chicken almost as much as when it came hot off the grill.

than 200 calories. You should always have several packs in the freezer for last-minute meal planning.

A simple marinade adds flavor in less than an hour. And because of the many ways chicken can be prepared, your family will never give you that "not again" look when you announce chicken tonight, followed by chicken sandwiches or salad for lunch over the next couple of days.

Tasty Tips

When you're meal planning with boneless skinless chicken breasts don't let your creativity be limited by the size or shape of the chicken. Slice the breast in half lengthwise, giving you two thinner pieces of meat which will either grill in a flash, 3-4 minutes per side, or stuffed and rolled, are roasted over indirect heat for 12-15 minutes. You can slice these slices into strips for satays, weave onto skewers, paint with spice-infused oil and grill to perfection in a few minutes. Easy and healthy chicken dinners the family will love.

Shopping for Chicken

You can find chicken at your grocery store in a variety of forms. You also have the choice of buying prepackaged chicken or fresh chicken from the butcher. Of course, fresh chicken is the better choice for grilling, and you don't even have to worry about preparing it, if you don't want to.

Outsource Chicken Prep

One of the major attractions of chicken is that it is so convenient. Let your butcher do most of the work for any kind of preparation you need. If your supermarket does not have a custom butcher station where you can have a conversation with the people behind the counter, find one that does. Here is a short list of the chicken preparations you can buy or have the butcher prepare, and some details about their attributes:

➤ Boneless, skinless breasts and/or thighs: They grill quickly, are low in fat, marinate in a short time, can be used for kabobs, and are a dieter's delight with thighs about 10–15 calories more per ounce than breasts.

➤ Boneless breasts and/or thighs, skin on: They grill quickly, get crispy skin, have a little more fat, marinate well, and are great with spicy rubs.

➤ Breasts and thighs, bone in, skin on: They take about twice as long to grill as the preparations above but deliver more intrinsic chicken flavor; crispy skin is a vehicle for interesting rubs and marinades.

➤ Chicken drumsticks/wings: They are best with skin on, bone in, have good flavor, and are good with rubs.

➤ Whole chicken: Roast a whole chicken on the grill over indirect heat; use for beer can chicken; brines, marinades, and rubs add flavor.

➤ Whole chicken split: It has loads of flavor, use marinate or rub, and use for brick chicken.

➤ Chicken halves: Each half of a small chicken is one serving and offers white and dark meat, is juicy, has good chicken flavor, and can be used with brines, marinates, or rubs.

➤ Ground chicken: Use for chicken burgers.

Grilling Tech Talk

Each of these chicken preparations can be done by a skilled home cook, but why bother? Most of us are time-challenged enough. Ask your supermarket butcher to prepare the chicken just the way you want to put it on the grill. Butchers will truss a whole chicken for roasting, split it for brick grilling, or grind breast and thighs for burgers.

Be a Smart Chicken Shopper

Not all chicken is created equal. Here is some advice on what to look for when shopping for chicken:

➤ Always check the sell-by date on the package, especially if you are buying a couple of days ahead. Use chicken within two days of sell-by date.

➤ Always check for pink or reddish liquid in the package, which can increase the spoilage rate or impart an off taste to the chicken. A little is normal; a lot is not.

➤ Always check for the words *previously frozen* on the label. If you plan to freeze some of the chicken for future use, you will be refreezing it, which can degrade the meat quality and texture.

➤ Ignore the labels that state No Hormones Used or Raised Hormone-Free. All chickens are hormone free by law. While not really false advertising, these labels are misleading and may be used to justify a higher price.

➤ Labels that claim Self-Basting or Basted mean that butter, butter substitute, or some other solution has been injected into the meat, up to 3 percent by weight in bone-in poultry; 8 percent in boneless poultry. I avoid products that contain added ingredients like this. A simple saltwater brine, homemade, adds flavor and juiciness without additional artificial, fattening, or unpronounceable chemicals.

Factory Farming vs Free Range

Many of us are concerned about factory farming, especially in the poultry and pork industries. When we think of factory farms, we assume animal cruelty, a short life crowded inside a huge building, where everything from the diet to the atmosphere is artificially controlled for maximum growth rate.

When we see the words *free range,* we feel a little better. We picture the chickens happily clucking around a farmyard pecking at grubs and scampering over to a basket-wielding housewife who throws grain by the handful to her contented charges. Ah, were it only true. *Free range* means the chickens must have access to the outside. It does not mean they live in a meadow or barnyard, nor does it necessarily mean they spend more than a few minutes in the sunlight.

Free range is more a marketing term than a poultry lifestyle. However, there are many chicken operations that are humanely run. A little research can assure you that the chickens you buy were raised and slaughtered within the spirit of the rules governing free range. In this case a brand really does matter and, if this is important to you, it is worth the time, effort, and perhaps extra dollars, tc   ded poultry products you want to buy.

Tasty Tips

When buying chicken, always compare prices to kosher chickens. They are often on sale and priced the same or close to non-kosher chicken, especially in big-box stores like Costco. Kosher chickens are always saltwater brined, saving you that step. Brining results in a more succulent roast chicken and a juicier grilled breast or thigh.

Truth in Labeling

What about natural and organic chickens? The problem is that neither of these terms actually means what it implies. *Natural* means the chicken has been minimally processed and not dyed a different color to appear more attractive. It is often confused with *organic*, a word that means the chickens were fed organic grain, free of chemicals and other human-made ingredients. The Organic label is regulated by the US Department of Agriculture, but its meaning is still confusing. Here are some definitions of the labels:

> ➤ Chicken can be labeled organic if 95 percent of its feed was organic.

> ➤ Chicken labeled made with organic ingredients indicates that 75 percent of its feed was organic.

> ➤ If only one ingredient is organic, the label can display that single ingredient (for instance, Fed Organic Corn), giving a false impression that the chicken consumed only organic feed.

> ➤ Only 100% Organic on the label means exactly what it says. So if this is important to you, pay attention to the labeling and buy accordingly.

How to Grill Chicken

My foolproof method is simple and easy. If time and planning permit, brine chicken according to directions in brining section of this chapter. Marinate chicken according to directions in that part of this chapter. Remove chicken from your marinade to rest for a few minutes. If using a rub, follow directions from that part of this chapter. Adjust charcoal or gas grill to medium heat and lightly oil clean grates.

Charcoal

For charcoal grilling, create two cooking surfaces, direct heat and indirect heat, by banking the coals on either side and leaving a coal-free area in the middle. A disposable aluminum drip pan in the middle stabilizes your coal arrangement.

Sear chicken parts over direct heat for three to four minutes per side. Then flip chicken one more time and move to indirect heat. Roast over indirect heat for six to eight minutes (about twelve to sixteen minutes total grilling time) for boneless chicken parts, or roast bone-in chicken parts for ten to twelve minutes (twenty to twenty-four minutes total grilling time) in covered grill. Time varies by heat level and thickness of chicken parts.

Gas

For gas grills, keep all burners on high for direct heat grilling. After searing the chicken for three to four minutes per side over direct heat, flip chicken one more time, turn off the middle burner(s), and turn down the remaining lit burners. Move chicken parts to the center of the grill over indirect heat, cover, and roast for six to eight minutes for boneless parts and ten to twelve minutes for bone-in parts. Grill temperature thermometers should read about 350°F for the roasting phase of grilling.

The chicken is done when the instant read thermometer shows 165°F in the thickest part of the chicken breast and 170°F for thighs. Or if you don't have a thermometer, sacrifice one piece of chicken by gently cutting at its thickest part to make sure it is cooked through, no pink meat. Let chicken rest for a few minutes before cutting or serving.

Tasty Tips

When it comes to hot coals or gas burners, less is more. Despite its mass appeal and versatility, chicken is a fragile meat. After a relatively brief sear, treat it gently. Prolonged red-hot heat is the fastest way to ruin a chicken. Lower and slower, but don't overcook.

We have been so terrified by chicken contamination we are motivated to cook chicken too much, drying it out inside and charring the outside. An instant-read thermometer is an essential tool here, especially if you're a beginner and if cooking over charcoal where the heat can vary, affecting cooking time.

The Science of Brining

Brine is a saltwater solution—with other added herbs and spices if desired—that adds flavor and succulence to chicken. If you have time, brine your chicken. Calculate your brining time by the weight of the chicken, about one hour brining per pound for a whole bird; about one hour total for chicken parts. Here's how it works.

Saltwater moves through the skin of the chicken by a process called osmosis, and then into the cell membranes in the meat by a process called diffusion. After a while, much of the salt is expelled while some water is absorbed into the meat. This yields a juicier result when the chicken is grilled or roasted.

My Standard Brining Recipe for Chicken

There are many brine recipes but the standard saltwater brine is ¼ cup of kosher salt for each quart of water; resulting in 1 cup of kosher salt per gallon. For each pound of chicken make one quart of brine, so a 4-pound chicken gets 1 gallon of brine. Immerse the whole chicken in the brine for about one hour per pound but never exceed eight hours. This 4-pound chicken sits in the brine for four hours.

For chicken parts, brine about one hour total, no matter how many parts. Use a picnic cooler and add ice in a plastic bag to the brine, or brine in your refrigerator, if convenient. The chicken will spoil if the brine liquid warms up, so make sure you keep it iced or in the fridge. Dry the chicken after removing from the brine for a crisp skin.

Grill Speak

Kosher salt is pure salt with no additives, and no iodine or anti-caking ingredients. The crystals are typically larger than table salt so there is less actual salt by volume than the smaller, tighter-packed table salt crystals. That is why we recommend about twice as much kosher salt, by volume, as table salt in recipes.

Table salt is iodized-added iodine—an essential mineral for good health—and some people can taste this ingredient. Most of us get plenty of iodized salt in our diet. Using kosher salt in brining and grilling imparts a cleaner salt flavor to food, as does more expensive sea salt.

Brining Recipes

Infusing your chicken with flavored brines adds succulence. Once you understand how brining chicken improves flavor and juiciness, you'll want to brine the bird as often as practical.

When grilling, we'll use chicken parts more often than whole birds. These can be brined just as you would a whole chicken, only for a much shorter length of time—no more than an hour for breasts, thighs, legs, and wings as compared to a whole bird, where your brining time should be determined by weight.

To dissolve the ingredients faster, heat a portion of the liquid. Start your brine by adding the salt, sugar, and other ingredients to about a quart of water in a saucepan, and heat to dissolve. Then chill and add the rest of the liquid. So, for a 4-pound chicken dissolve 1 cup of kosher salt and 1 cup of sugar in about 1 quart of water on the stove. Chill with ice or refrigerate. Add more cold water to make 4 quarts. Immerse the whole chicken and brine it for about four hours. For chicken parts, make the same amount of liquid (4 quarts) for 4 pounds of chicken parts, and brine them about one hour.

Sugar and Spice are Nice

Add an equal amount of sugar to the salt in your brining liquid—it gives a pleasant sweetness without being overpowering. Or reduce the salt by a third and add 2 tablespoons soy sauce per quart of water if you like a background soy flavor. Add spices like cinnamon, nutmeg, cumin, or any others you like.

Other Flavors, Sweet and Crispy

Substitute honey or molasses for some of the sugar. Substitute chicken stock, beer, apple or orange juice for some of the water. Experiment with other flavors that seem interesting or unusual. Add some coffee or tea to the brine in place of some water.

Grilling Tech Talk

As you experiment with brines, stay away from anything that is significantly acidic because the diffusion of acid into the protein cells will "cook" the meat, rendering it mushy.

Brining is a background or subtle flavor influence, as opposed to marinades and rubs, which impart a real power punch of flavor. Each has its proper place, and the inclusion or exclusion of acidic ingredients are different. Marinades typically include an acidic component. Brines do not.

Herbs and Spices

Many spices and herbs go very well in a brine. Add them when you are heating the liquid to dissolve the salt and sugar. Pickling spice mix, about 1 tablespoon per quart, is a favorite. Old Bay seasoning adds good flavor too, but reduce the salt by about the same amount of Old Bay you add because there is plenty of salt in that brand. Use 1 or 2 tablespoons per quart and add two cinnamon sticks per gallon of liquid at the heating stage. This combo is another favorite of mine. Chinese Five Spice powder or Garam Masala are popular Asian accents for a brine, again about 1 or 2 tablespoons per quart. Everyone's taste preferences are different, so play around with these herbs and spices—don't follow any hard and fast rules.

The Science of Marinating

There are two very good reasons to marinate chicken:

1. When chicken and other meat are exposed to direct high heat, whether by frying, sautéing, or grilling, two chemicals develop that in high doses have been linked to cancer in lab animals. These chemical, HCA and PAH (see Chapter 1 for more detail) are reduced by about 90 percent when the meat is marinated for more than half an hour with an acid-based solution (vinegar, lemon juice, lactic acid, red wine, and similar). Grilling meat for shorter time periods also reduces these chemicals, which is why I recommend the grill-roasting method for most recipes.

2. Marinades—and rubs—add flavor. Using different marinades from every corner of the world enables you to keep your family happy at mealtime and entertain your friends in style without a lot of extra work.

My Quick and Easy Standard Marinade

This marinade is as simple as it is flavorful.

Standard Marinade

Ingredients
1 lemon
Olive oil
1 Tbs Dijon mustard
4–6 chicken breasts
Salt and pepper to taste

Directions
Combine the juice of one lemon with equal part olive oil (about 3 tablespoons each) and Dijon mustard. Whisk to emulsify. Put four to six chicken breasts in a ziplock plastic bag, pour marinade in, squeeze out most the air, seal the bag, and rub the meat around so all pieces are coated. Marinate one to eight hours before grilling. Salt and pepper to taste when the chicken breasts go on the grill. This marinade packs good flavor whether chicken is boneless, skinless, or any other style.

Fat Fighters

Boneless, skinless chicken breasts are among the lowest fat and lowest calorie meat products, which is why they can dry out on a grill if not carefully monitored. Many professional cooks insist that chicken should always be grilled with the skin on to insulate the outer part of the breast while the inner part gets thoroughly cooked to 165°F degrees—you never want medium-rare chicken. But the chicken skin is where most of the fat resides.

To avoid that fat, grill the boneless chicken breast with the skin on and remove the skin once the breast is served. The chicken benefits from the insulation, it's juicier, and some of the marinade or rub seeps through into the meat. You are also removing any HCAs and PAHs there may be.

A World of Marinades

Because chickens thrive everywhere in all sorts of climates, they are probably the most versatile source of protein. Almost every culture sparks marinades for chickens, so you can add flavor to your chicken with marinades from around the world.

The basic marinade consists of an acid, oil, and other kinds of flavorings. The acid typically comes from vinegars, citrus fruits, or yogurt (lactic acid). The oil can be strongly flavored such as sesame oil, lightly flavored such as olive oil, or neutral like canola or peanut oil. Other flavors are as widely varied as your imagination allows.

These marinade recipes can be used on all styles of chicken, from boneless, skinless breasts to chicken halves or quarters. Whole chickens, however, are more suited to a rub than a marinade—but that's just an opinion and you should be guided by your creativity and experimentation.

Here is a sample of my favorite marinades. The ingredients are for six to eight chicken pieces. Always marinate boneless, skinless chicken breasts, both for flavor brightness and to suppress the formation of HCA. Marinate at least an hour—more as noted in specific recipes.

Italian Chicken

Ingredients
¼ cup red wine vinegar
¼ cup olive oil
1 tsp dried basil

1 tsp dried parsley
½ tsp dried oregano
½ tsp dried rosemary
½ tsp garlic powder

Directions
Combine the red wine vinegar and olive oil. Whisk in the rest of the ingredients.
When chicken is done, sprinkle with freshly chopped basil and parsley.

Southwestern Chicken

Ingredients
¼ c store-bought medium hot salsa
¼ c canola oil
2 Tbs fresh squeezed lime juice
1 tsp cumin
½ tsp garlic powder

Directions
Combine all the ingredients.

When chicken is done grilling, sprinkle with freshly chopped cilantro leaves.

Jamaican Jerk Chicken

Ingredients
3 scallions
4 garlic cloves
1 medium onion
2–4 scotch bonnet chilies (careful when handling, especially the seeds, they are very hot)
¼ c fresh-squeezed lime juice
2 Tbs soy sauce
2 Tbs canola oil
1 Tbs brown sugar
1 Tbs allspice
1 Tbs thyme
1 tsp black pepper
1 tsp salt
1 tsp grated nutmeg
½ tsp cinnamon

Directions

Chop aromatics—scallions, garlic cloves, onion, and scotch bonnet chilies. Combine lime juice, soy sauce, and canola oil, then add brown sugar, allspice, thyme, black pepper, salt, grated nutmeg, and cinnamon. Put all ingredients in a blender or food processor and emulsify.

Indian Spiced Yogurt Chicken

Ingredients

½ c plain yogurt

¼ c chopped onion

1 Tbs chopped garlic

1 Tbs chopped fresh ginger

1 chopped Serrano chili (optional)

1 Tbs canola oil

1 Tbs white vinegar

1 tsp garam marsala

1 tsp medium curry powder

½ tsp turmeric

½ tsp cayenne

½ tsp salt

Directions

Combine all the ingredients and emulsify in a food processor.

Moroccan Chicken

Ingredients

¼ c olive oil

¼ c red wine vinegar

1 Tbs ground cumin

1 Tbs ground coriander

1 tsp ground cinnamon

1 tsp sugar

½ tsp salt

½ tsp cayenne

freshly chopped mint and parsley

Directions

Whisk all the ingredients into the olive oil.

When chicken is done grilling, sprinkle with mint and parsley.

Peruvian Chicken

Ingredients
⅓ c soy sauce
2 Tbs canola oil
2 Tbs fresh squeezed lime juice
4 garlic cloves
2 tsp ground cumin
1 tsp paprika
½ tsp oregano

Directions
Combine all the ingredients and emulsify in a blender. This needs at least twelve hours to marinate—twenty-four is even better. This is best with bone-in chicken parts.

Vietnamese Chicken

Ingredients
3 Tbs canola oil
3 Tbs rice vinegar
3 Tbs soy sauce
Finely chopped fresh ginger
Finely chopped garlic
2 Tbs sugar
2 tsp turmeric
1 tsp Chinese Five Spice
1 tsp ground star anise
½ tsp salt
Fresh-squeezed lime juice

Directions
Combine the canola oil, rice vinegar, soy sauce, finely chopped fresh ginger, and finely chopped garlic. Whisk in the sugar, turmeric, Chinese Five Spice, ground star anise, and salt. Marinate for four to six hours. Squeeze fresh lime juice on chicken a minute or two before it is done grilling.

Tropical Chicken

Ingredients
½ c canola oil
1 Tbs fresh-squeezed lime juice

1 Tbs fresh-squeezed lemon juice
1 Tbs tequila
1 tsp grated lemon zest
1 tsp triple sec
½ tsp salt

Directions
Whisk the lime juice, lemon juice, and tequila into the canola oil. Add lemon zest, triple sec, and salt.

Barbecued Chicken

Ingredients
¼ c canola oil
¼ c apple cider vinegar
½ tsp salt
½ tsp cayenne pepper or to taste
Barbecue sauce

Directions
Combine the canola oil, apple cider vinegar, salt, and cayenne pepper. Marinate at least half an hour. Sear chicken for three to four minutes each side, as per my standard grill-roasting directions. Brush your favorite barbecue sauce on upper side of the chicken, flip, move to indirect heat, brush chicken with barbecue sauce, and allow to roast for six to eight minutes till done for boneless; ten to twelve minutes for bone-in chicken.

A World of Rubs

Add flavor with dry spices and herbs. Rubs are dry spices and herbs that, as the name suggests, you massage on chicken for extra flavor. I generally marinate skinless chicken parts and use a rub for skin-on parts or whole chickens (see beer can chicken recipe in Part Three).

The technique for applying a rub couldn't be easier. Gently lift the skin and work your fingers under it against the meat, freeing much of the skin from the meat. I like to wear rubber gloves when I do this; it prevents contamination.

Pour some rub mixture onto your fingers and massage it onto the meat beneath the skin. When you've added enough rub, gently press the skin back down against the meat. If you're planning to eat the skin you can add more rub on the outside. Or better yet, I recommend a plain olive oil and lemon juice or vinegar marinade brushed onto the skin about half an hour or more before grilling. Think of chicken skin as a natural insulator that enables the meat to cook more slowly than a skinless part. The heat melts any fat beneath the skin and enables the rub to infuse the meat. Most of the fat drips away. The result is a more succulent chicken, packed with the flavor of ~~~~~~~~~~

Tasty Tips

Just as grilling makes everything taste better because the dry heat intensifies the innate flavor of the ingredients, so does toasting whole spices. Heat reduces moisture in dry spices, concentrating the spiciness and boosting its effect. Pour a few weeks' worth of the whole spice into a dry frying pan and gently toast till the aroma makes everyone smile—generally five minutes or so. Let cool, and then grind the spice in a coffee grinder that you've dedicated for spices. Store in a clean container, away from heat and sunlight.

My Basic Rub

This rub is designed to enhance the flavor of chicken on the grill without overwhelming it. I use it lightly under the skin, combined with a lemony marinade that I mop on the skin. Or I apply it heavily all over the outside of the skin for whole or split chickens. My basic rub mix is a marriage of Asia with our American South. The result is my all-purpose, quick and easy rub that tastes complicated but could not be simpler to prepare. There are only two ingredients:

1. Old Bay seasoning: Salt tempered by celery seed, sweet red pepper, and paprika. The proportions are secret and I could not improve on it if I tried. But I wouldn't. The Old Bay folks nailed it.

2. Store-bought garam masala: Garam masala is to Indian cooking what Five Spice is to Chinese and Herbes de Provence is to French cooking—a standard combo of spices and/or herbs that add the fundamental flavors we've come to associate with each cuisine, delivered conveniently. You'll find it in the Asian food aisle or in a well-stocked spice section of your supermarket. Garam Masala is a mixture of cumin, pepper, cinnamon, cardamom, cloves, and mace. The proportions vary by brand, so experiment till you find your favorite.

When you combine these two spice mixtures in equal parts, you've achieved a really good all-purpose rub with the least amount of fuss.

For more of an Indian accent in your rub, add 1 teaspoon medium or hot curry powder to

Tasty Tips

Heat it up. If you like heat in your rub, add ½ teaspoon of cayenne pepper or ½ teaspoon white pepper to ½ cup of the basic rub. White pepper has more heat than black pepper, so treat it differently.

the basic rub.

Chinese Influence

For a more Chinese accent to your rub, substitute Chinese Five Spice powder for the garam masala and add 1 teaspoon ginger powder to ½ cup of the rub mixture.

South of France on Your Grill

I love the aroma of Herbes de Provence as it melts into the chicken. Pretend you're in the Côte d'Azure by rubbing this herb mixture under the skin, then paint the skin with olive oil and lemon juice, let it sit for half an hour, and then grill gently. Bone-in breasts and thighs never tasted this good.

Zesty Citrus

Add a citrus punch to the basic rub. To ½ cup of the basic rub add the zest of two lemons, a lemon and a lime zest, the zest of two limes, or the zest of two oranges. Mix well and massage this citrus rub under the skin. Then paint the skin with the juice of whichever fruit you used, mixed in equal proportion with olive oil. Let rest half an hour or more and grill gently according to my grill-roasting directions.

Grilling Tech Talk

Here's a kitchen rule I always try to follow: never get a gadget that does just one thing. A zester looks like a little curved fork and does a pretty good job raking the skin off citrus. But it does only that. Instead of using a zester, I use a microplane—gently because you don't want the white pith beneath the skin. Not only do the zests come out exactly like I want them, short and thin, but I can also use the microplane for grinding fresh ginger, nutmeg, or cinnamon sticks.

Southern Italian Accents

To my store-bought Herbes de Provence, I like to add an equal amount of finely chopped fresh mint and basil, plus some fennel seed to taste. If using dried mint and basil, I add those two ingredients as half the rub, and Herbes de Provence as the other half, and then top it off with a little fennel seed. If, like me, you love fennel, increase the amount.

Southwestern Flavor

For a southwestern accent, use Old Bay for half the rub and Anaheim chili powder—or a hotter variety to taste—for the other half.

Bring Out Your Inner Scandinavian

Dried dill loses much of its heft so try to use fresh, which is usually available year-round, and chop it finely. To ¼ cup of fresh dill, add ½ teaspoon mustard seed, ½ teaspoon celery seed, and ¼ teaspoon poppy seeds, massage under the skin of breasts and thighs. Paint the skin with lemon juice and olive oil and gently grill according to my grill-roasting method.

I like bone-in parts for this recipe because it needs to cook longer and the flavors, more subtle than some of the others listed here, improve with longer, gentler grilling.

Tasty Tips

All of these rubs work just as well massaged beneath the skin of whole chickens roasted in the oven or on a grill. When rubbing a whole chicken, be sure to get the rub inside the cavity as well for extra flavor.

How to Roast a Chicken on the Grill

Roasting a chicken on the grill requires indirect heat for the entire time. Beer can chicken is my preferred roasting method (see Part Three for recipe), but you can certainly cook a great-tasting bird using this standard method.

Massage your rub under the skin of the chicken as described above, and then lightly coat the

Fat Fighters

Busy folks like us are often confronted with a last minute dinner dilemma. How did the day go by without a thought to the evening meal? This is when we pile on the calories with delivered pizza or a trip to the fried chicken store. Instead, take individually packed chicken breasts out of the freezer and immerse them in hot tap water. In a few minutes they are thawed. Marinate in the fridge for half an hour, pop them on the grill, steam some frozen broccoli or spinach, and enjoy a nutritious low-calorie dinner. You're back in control of your diet.

skin with olive oil and freshly squeezed lemon juice, or other juice, to help crisp and flavor the skin. I like to put the squeezed lemons inside the cavity. Mop the skin with this light marinade several times through the cooking process—every fifteen minutes or so.

Grilling Tech Talk

If roasting on a grill topper or stone, don't truss the chicken. Allow the thighs to spread out a bit on the hot surface so they get more of the heat sooner. Thighs take longer than legs or breasts to reach their done temperature (175°F) so contact with the hot stone or topper gives them a jump-start. For roasting directly on the grates, it's a good idea to truss the bird so the thighs don't burn, but always make sure the chicken is getting indirect heat.

Use a Grill Topper

On a gas grill, heat the grill topper to very hot over all burners on high for about ten minutes. Place the chicken, breast side up, in the middle of the topper and turn down the burners, close the cover, and roast for about an hour for a 4-pound bird. Your grill thermometer should stay close to 400°F, so monitor your burners to maintain this temperature. Use an instant read thermometer to check the breast meat, done at 165°F. I like the grill topper design from Grill Innovations (see Resources) because it creates a convection oven effect, resulting in an evenly done bird.

Use a Pizza Stone

It will take a while to get the stone as hot as you need it to be, so let it heat up for at least twenty minutes. Then follow the directions for the grill topper roasting, about an hour for a 4- pound chicken.

Tasty Tips

Grill-roasting a chicken allows you to introduce your favorite wood smoke to enhance the flavor of your rub and mop. I like to soak hickory or mesquite chips in water, place them in loosely wrapped aluminum foil or a small aluminum disposable pan on the coals or burner plates beneath the bird. This will get the wood smoking in a few minutes. Have a spray bottle of water handy to prevent wood flare-ups.

On the Grates

For both a gas and a charcoal grill, you can roast a chicken directly on the grates. If using charcoal, once the coals are glowing, rake them to both sides and place the chicken breast side up on the center of the grill. Roast over indirect heat for about an hour. If using gas, keep the front and rear burners on medium to achieve a grill thermometer reading of about 400°F and roast the chicken in the middle over indirect heat for about an hour.

Grilling Tech Talk

You can easily truss a whole chicken to ensure even roasting. You don't want body parts hanging out getting scorched and overdone. Use about a yard of cotton butcher twine—nothing artificial that will melt into the chicken. Cotton twine may darken but won't burn if not exposed to direct flames. Wrap twine around the ends of the drumsticks, draw them together, and then pass the twine across the breast toward the other end of the chicken, across the wing, and under the front of the chicken, then across the wing and breast on the other side. Pass it across the thigh, under the rear of the chicken, and across the thigh on the other side. Tie it off on top of the breast bone in the center of the chicken. This is a rough rendition of a figure eight.

Chicken Kabobs

Chicken is so inexpensive, even if you buy organic as I recommend. There is virtually no waste in boneless breasts, the fat and calorie counts are well within your safe range, and there are enough creative ways to grill this healthy food that you can serve a chicken dinner often. These breasts make perfect kabobs and satays on bamboo or metal skewers. Simply cut into cubes or strips (or thaw chicken tenders from your freezer), marinate for half an hour in my standard marinade or choose one from the world of marinades. They grill quickly, about six to eight minutes total grilling time, and make a welcome change from boneless, skinless chicken breasts. A perfect last-minute meal for hungry kids.

Grilling Tech Talk

Roasting a chicken, whether using this standard method or the beer can method, will require you to hold and lift the chicken. As you mop the bird with more marinade while it's roasting, you'll need to stabilize it with your hands. And when the chicken is done, the easiest way to take it off the grill is by using your hands—especially if there's a beer can sitting inside partly full of very hot beer. So get yourself a pair of insulated rubberized gloves specially made for grilling. This equipment is as essential as your two hands.

Chicken Burgers

There are a few important handling and preparation techniques that make chicken burgers better:

➤ Mix one egg into each pound of the ground chicken meat as a binder. This isn't necessary, but if you like a firmer burger this works real well. The higher the moisture content, the more the need for an egg binder.

➤ Add extra flavor with chopped red peppers and sweet onions, cooked or raw.

➤ Herbs such as thyme and sage enhance the flavor of ground chicken breast.

➤ If you are grinding chicken at home in a food processor, be sure to chill the cubes of chicken meat in your freezer till very firm but not frozen. A mix of mostly breast with some boneless thigh meat makes a flavorful chicken burger.

➤ If you're buying already-ground chicken, be sure to check the calorie count on the label. If the grind is all breast meat, the count should be about 25–30 calories per ounce. If your store-bought ground chicken is significantly more calories per ounce, you may want to look for alternatives or ask specifically for a grind mix you prefer. There's nothing wrong with skin and other parts in the grind, but it's good to know what you're eating.

➤ After forming ground chicken balls, gently flatten into burgers, rest the burgers on a lightly oiled platter in the fridge for half an hour or more, and then grill-roast the burgers on clean oiled grates.

See Part Three for delicious chicken preparations in the Chicken Recipes section; and in Burger Recipes, you'll find crowd-pleasing chicken burgers.

CHAPTER 5

 # Grilling Beef the Healthy Way

This chapter explores the perfect culinary marriage—beef and heat, whether from wood, charcoal, or gas. Since caveman days, it's been love at first bite. Nothing surpasses that sizzling goodness. But like all good marriages, steak and the grill need perspective, some wisdom, and, of course, compromise.

➤ Perspective: The reason a grilled rare steak marbled with fat tastes so good is exactly why it's not so good for you.

➤ Wisdom: You should not eat meat every day, especially fatty, juicy steaks, and you shouldn't eat much of it when you do. Spending a little time apart makes the heart grow fonder—and healthier.

➤ Compromise: But don't start throwing your lyin', cheatin', heard-it-all-before chunk of beefy bad boy out of the house forever. There's still hope for this union.

Steak is just too good to banish from your menu, and there are plenty of ways to enjoy grilled beef. By recognizing and dealing with the downside, steak can keep its honored place on the grates.

Reducing HCA and PAH

Like all meat, poultry, and fish, the longer and hotter you grill steak, the more it will form the possibly harmful chemicals known as HCAs and PAHs. In high doses, these chemicals have been linked to cancer in lab animals (see Chapter 1 for details). There are three ways to reduce the formation of these chemicals, and fortunately each method results in a great-tasting steak.

Marinate for Health and Taste

Marinating steak, poultry, other meats and fish in a marinade using oil and acid such as wine vinegar, citric juice, tomato juice, yogurt, or other acidic ingredients is the key to reducing these undesirable chemicals. Marinating for at least an hour before grilling reduces the formation of HCA by as much as 90 percent.

Prevent Flare-ups

When you cut off all visible fat, you not only get rid of needless calories, you also prevent flare-ups. Flare-ups from fat dripping onto coal or burner covers can produce PAH if the flames reach your meat. So a heart-healthy steak can also be an overall healthier piece of meat if you keep flame away from it.

Grilling Tech Talk

You'll notice that I often state grilling times using terms like *about* or as a range of minutes. All grills, whether gas fired or charcoal, differ in their heat output. Factors such as the brand and type of charcoal, the type of gas (natural or propane, which burns nearly twice as hot), and gas pressure, even the air temperature around your grill, affect the BTUs and the heat hitting your food. The more you use it, the more you'll know your grill's heating nuances. Adjust your cooking times after a little practice.

Grill-Roasting Steak

The shorter time you grill over high heat, the fewer HCAs and PAHs are formed. Grilling over lower heat reduces or eliminates the formation of HCAs. Eliminating flare-ups eliminates PAHs. So this requires a two-part gas or charcoal arrangement: one that's hot and sears the meat, the other that uses much lower indirect heat that roasts the meat.

> ➤ For gas grills, you sear directly over the burners for about two to three minutes per side. You want attractive grill marks and easy release from the grates. Then turn off the rear and middle burners, leave the front burner on high, flip the meat once more, and move the meat to the rear part of the grates. Cover the grill and roast about six more minutes for medium-rare (about ten to twelve minutes total cook time for a 1-inch-thick steak).

By grilling over high heat for a few minutes you impart caramelized flavor and those attractive grill marks, but the relatively short duration inhibits the formation of these chemicals.

> ➤ For charcoal grills, arrange charcoal along the outer part of your grill, leaving space in the middle with no coals. Placing an aluminum drip pan in this space is a good idea. Sear the meat for about two to three minutes per side directly over the hot coals. Then flip the meat one more time and move the steaks to the center of the grill over indirect heat. Close the cover and roast about six minutes for medium-rare.

For both gas and charcoal, the roasting phase temperature should be at around 350°F. An instant-read thermometer inserted sideways in toward the center of the steak registers about 135°F for medium-rare. Rest the steaks a few minutes before serving or slicing.

Grilling Tech Talk

Don't use a fork to flip your steaks. Piercing the meat during the cooking, or even while it's resting after grilling, allows juice to escape. Juice is precious—especially in leaner cuts of beef. You want that juice inside the meat, not on the bottom of your grill. Use tongs. Let the steak rest a few minutes before slicing to preserve juice inside the meat.

Tasty Tips

Add a little sugar to your salt. Stop laughing, I'm serious. Here's why this boosts the flavor of steak and other grilled meats. Caramelized sugar is a flavor enhancer. Sprinkle kosher or sea salt on the meat right before grilling (if you do this too early, it draws out moisture). If you mix a pinch of sugar with the salt, it will caramelize on the grates. Meat has natural sugars that caramelize in high heat—you're just giving it a little jump-start with the added sugar. You get attractive grill marks, deeper flavor, and even shorter high-heat grilling.

Grill Speak

A persistent sirloin steak myth is that the word *sirloin* evolved from the medieval respect for this King of Beef, resulting in the affectionate nickname Sir Loin. Actually, it's from the French denoting its location above (*sur*) the *loigne* (loin) on a beef carcass. *Sur loigne* became *sirloin* in English.

How to Choose a Healthier Steak

Conventional wisdom suggests that a traditional steak dinner should feature a thick, well-marbled sirloin as the centerpiece. Because it's from the top of the loin area on a steer, the sirloin gets very little exercise, resulting in more fat and tenderness than in some other cuts of beef.

Healthy grilling, however, suggests that we often need to rethink conventional grilling wisdom and meal planning. Many leaner steak cuts are tasty, and with marinades they can deliver flavor as good as or better than fattier beef.

Steak Mythology

The idea that no other beef cut compares to sirloin and its siblings, New York strip and shell steak, because you need good marbling, meaning intrinsic fat, to achieve great flavor is a myth. These fattier beef cuts are all between about 75 and 90 calories per ounce. Compare that to a leaner tenderloin that weighs in at about 50 calories per ounce, more than a third fewer calories, and almost all of those eliminated fat calories are saturated fat. We want to reduce that fat for good health. Other lower-fat beef cuts include flank steak, top round—also known as London broil—well-trimmed rib eye and T-bone, and super tender filet mignon, a cut of the tenderloin.

You will not be disappointed eating any of these healthier steaks, especially if you use the tasty marinades described in this chapter. You can achieve great flavor and texture in a lower-fat steak if you marinate and grill it properly.

Serving Size

Another key to a healthy steak dinner is serving size. A 6-ounce serving of the leaner beef cuts described above will deliver 300–350 calories, or about 100–150 calories more than a boneless, skinless chicken breast. As part of a daily 1,800–2,200-calorie food program, which along with exercise is a sound weight-loss strategy for the long haul, a steak dinner is hardly an extravagance. There's no reason why beef lovers can't eat grilled steak several times a month as long as they stick to lower-fat beef cuts and reasonable serving sizes.

Fat Fighters

I've discovered that some people have a serious mental health condition when we limit the serving size to 6 ounces of steak. I've named this serving size disappointment syndrome (SSDS) and it's characterized by whining and sometimes even fist-pounding demands like, "Why can't we have more steak?!" My solution is lots of portabella mushrooms brushed with olive oil and finely chopped garlic, grilled with the steaks, sliced and served alongside them in the steak juice.

Beef and portabellas complement one another in flavor and texture (portabellas even look like steak) and best of all, they satisfy those people who would otherwise suffer from SSDS. The calorie and fat count of these 'shrooms are negligible while the beefy flavor cures the cravings for too much steak.

Types of Beef and Their Uses

Depending on where they were located on the steer, steak cuts have different textures, taste, and best cooking method requirements. Here are a few popular steak cuts to consider when planning your grilled beef dinner:

> ➤ Sirloin: As stated earlier, this is located in the upper hind quarters, gets little exercise, which results in a tender and fattier meat. Bone in or out, sirloin grills beautifully but should be consumed in moderation due to its higher calories and fat. More of a special occasion steak—and if you're going to splurge, try for USDA certified prime for a little more marbling and tenderness.

Grill Speak

The USDA grades beef based on intramuscular fat, commonly called marbling, the appearance of health, and other aesthetic factors at the request of the producer. This is not a safety inspection, which is also done by the USDA and is required for all meat and poultry. For most of us, only three grades matter: prime, choice, and select. Only 2 percent of beef is prime with marbling at 8–11 percent, and it's difficult to find that in supermarkets. Choice is the choice of most retailers, and it's fine, about 6–8 percent intramuscular fat and overall in good condition. Select won't hurt you, but I wouldn't grill a steak with that grade. Remember, these ratings are only valid if they are displayed with the USDA shield. If that shield is absent, the rating is meaningless, a marketing ploy.

➤ Tenderloin: As the name implies, the most tender steak cut, also called filet mignon and short loin. You can buy a whole tenderloin at bargain prices during peak grilling season and prepare it yourself by removing the tough outer "silver skin," or pay a little extra to have your butcher do it. Cut into 1- to 2-inch-thick pieces to make luscious filets that should be grilled over lower heat relatively briefly and done rare for maximum flavor and texture.

➤ T-bone and porterhouse: From the middle and rear of the short loin, these bone-in cuts are very tender and flavorful. The more tender side of the T is the filet mignon when it's removed from the bone. Left intact, these two cuts nestled against their bone deliver great flavor and texture. They should be grilled medium-rare to rare.

➤ Rib eye and rib steak: These cuts from the rib area are tender and juicy, a little on the fattier side but can be easily trimmed to lower the calories. When left on the bone, it's a rib steak; when boned, it's a rib eye. Both are terrific grilling steaks. Get them cut 1 inch thick or more, and always grill to medium or rarer.

➤ Flank: A favorite in our family, this flavorful meat can be on the tough side but marinades, care in grilling, and slicing the meat across the grain result in a healthy, succulent beef dinner, low in fat, with great texture. When handled correctly, this moderately priced steak is a good choice. Marinate for several hours, grill medium-rare, and slice thin are my recommended methods for getting the most out of this steak.

➤ Chuck: From the forward end of the steer, this shoulder beef gets plenty of exercise, resulting in a tougher and quite flavorful meat. A long marinade will tenderize it some, but most grillers use this as the centerpiece of their burgers, either all chuck or mixed with other cuts to achieve a favorite composition. Chuck is among the least expensive pieces of meat.

➤ Round: This is a leaner and slightly tougher cut of beef. Top round is the more tender cut but still best suited to make lean burgers. Round is recommended for lower-calorie/lower-fat burgers that can be flavor-boosted with rubs, or mix in a little barbecue sauce. Low-sodium soy sauce adds a nice accent as well. A healthy choice if, like us, you enjoy frequent burger dinners.

➤ Hanger steak. From the front part of the steer below the diaphragm, this used to be called butcher steak because no one wanted to buy it. So knowing butchers took it home for their families. It's not terribly attractive, kind of grainy looking, but the flavor can't be beat. The problem is you have to grill it just right. Too rare and it has a mushy texture; too much over medium and it toughens up. So it's critical to grill hanger steak just on the pinker side of medium for perfect texture. Mexicans prefer this cut for fajitas and the French order *onglet* whenever available. There are only two rather small pieces on each steer.

As popularity of this cut has increased, butchers can no longer afford to keep it for themselves, but it's still one of the more economical cuts of beef. Always marinate for at least four hours before grilling to get maximum flavor and to break down some of the fibers.

➤ Brisket: Whether pot roast, pot-au-feu, or corned beef, this is a delicious meat to braise or boil, but it's unsuitable for grilling. Except, I like to cut off the thinner end to keep my pot roast a more uniform thickness, and use it later as a burger ingredient. Brisket freezes well for future use; chop in the food processor to make a very flavorful additive to your burger mix.

Grill Speak

Porterhouse steaks are bigger T-bone steaks, and T-bones are named for their appearance. The bone really is shaped like a *T* that separates two different steak cuts, the tenderloin and the strip steak—sometimes called New York strip. This is a favorite of steakhouses and is the traditional choice for steak Florentine in Italian cuisine. No one knows how the large T-bone became porterhouse. Conjecture is the name grew out of the nineteenth-century alehouses where porter, a dark beer, was often served with this steak. A juicy porterhouse is enough beef for two or three people who enjoy sharing the two cuts of steak.

Healthy Beef

There are healthy concerns about beef that go beyond just fat and calories. Fortunately for us, just as we can use beef cuts that are healthier for us, so we can affect the cattle-raising practices that increasingly appear to be detrimental to us and the environment.

Beef is a delicious and healthy food, loaded with essential nutrients, especially B vitamins, in a form that is most easily utilized by our bodies. Not only is beef good for us, it's a part of our cuisine that is thousands of years old and in its natural state, one of the purest food items.

Antibiotics and Feedlots

There is good reason to be concerned about the factory farming of chicken and pork, and, sadly, raising cattle also has a dark side that should concern those of us who take healthy grilling seriously.

Cows are a ruminant grazing animal. They have different stomach chambers that turn grass, their natural food source, into the nutrients they need to stay healthy. In order to fatten them up for market as quickly as possible—time is money after all—most steers spend the last weeks of their lives in a feedlot, where they consume large quantities of corn and other grains and grain byproducts that pack on the fat.

There are significant problems with this practice. They are eating food that as ruminants they are not designed to process efficiently, so they produce an abundance of methane gas, a pollutant that contributes to climate change. Some of them get sick from this unnatural diet. The solution is to feed them antibiotics to prevent or reduce illness. In fact, most of the antibiotics produced in this country, by a wide margin, are used in animal feed. We humans end up consuming traces of these antibiotics. Bacteria, like all other living creatures, evolve, and the result is an ever-increasing bacteria population that is becoming antibiotic resistant. This means when we get a hospital-borne infection or other bacterial illness, we, especially kids and older folks, can be in greater danger.

The bottom line here is that this is all about the bottom line. Big pharma profits, big agriculture profits, and we are increasingly at risk of contracting a bacterial infection that can't be cured by antibiotics. Recently the government has begun putting pressure on the beef industry to give antibiotics only to sick steers, not as a preventive measure but to treat illness. We will see if this initiative has the desired effect. In most European countries, mixing antibiotics into feed is banned, and we can ban it too if consumers demand it.

Organic Beef

There is plenty of organic beef around, and although it is more expensive, many of us choose to pay more because it's healthier. An organically raised steer gets antibiotics in its food only if sick, eats 100 percent organic food, and its mom ate organic food during most of her pregnancy.

The USDA inspects growers' records, and the enforcement is dependable. More than that, the vast majority of organic beef growers are serious about both the scientific and philosophical principles that support organic practices. But organic beef still can be fattened on grain, as long as the grain is organic, of course.

Grass-Fed Beef

Even if grass-fed beef is not labeled organic—although most of it is—it is my choice when buying steak, chops, and burger meat. The extra time that the steers need to reach market weight can be double the feedlot-fattened steers, resulting in about twice the price at the meat counter. But the extra cost seems worth it to me.

These cows are grown the same way they were 8,000 years ago when first domesticated. They eat their natural food, they graze in open pastures without anything artificial entering their bodies, or ours when we consume them. The meat is often branded so you can go online and read all about how the animals were raised and the dedication of the producers to improve the quality of beef.

By voting with our dollars for beef that is high quality, great tasting, and produced with pride, we are fostering changes in the beef industry that benefit everyone.

Truth in Labeling

Beginning in March 2012, the USDA instituted new labeling requirements for ground beef, poultry, and other meat products, as well as forty popular cuts of beef, poultry, pork, and lamb. The labeling lists fat content, type of fat, and other nutritional information that consumers need to make informed choices.

In ground beef, the label must state the percentage of lean and fat in the product, such as stating a burger grind is 80 percent lean, 20 percent fat, and it must state the percentage of fat that is saturated and unsaturated. Fat must come from the same cut as the lean, so in ground round that is 90 percent lean and 10 percent fat, the fat must be from the beef round, not some other part of the steer. The lean-fat statement is for raw meat measured by weight.

Different Measurements in Fat Labeling

For whole cuts, such as sirloin and chuck, and for brisket and eye round roast, for instance, the retailer must either display the label facts in the store or on a label attached to the meat. The calculation of fat content in whole meat is based on an average of the amount of fat by weight that would be left in the meat after cooking—not raw as with ground meat—and the cooking methods are averaged as well. So you would see the fat content in a chuck steak based on a 3-ounce serving after cooking, by averaging the fat left after braising, roasting, and grilling or broiling. A ground chuck burger fat content is measured before cooking. The significance for you is that the cooking method will affect the amount of fat in the meat. Grilling eliminates more fat than pan frying or braising, for instance.

Grill Speak

Food products can be labeled lean only if they have less than 3 grams of fat. Virtually all meat and poultry have more fat than that, which is why some producers and retailers voluntarily put the lean to fat ratio on the label. This use of the word *lean* was exempt from the food product labeling requirement because it was used in the context of lean to fat. The lean-to-fat ratio could not be used to designate a particular meat as lean because all meat exceeds the fat grams that allow the word *lean* as a descriptor. By expanding from voluntary to required, and by requiring lean-to-fat ratio labeling on forty popular meat products, the USDA has helped consumers choose their food more wisely. Now it's up to us.

Comparing Fat Measurements

It's easy for consumers to compare fat content in various beef burger mixes (such as a ⅔ sirloin, ⅓ brisket grind versus a ½ ground chuck, ½ sirloin grind) and single beef burger grinds (such as ground sirloin versus ground round), and to compare ground beef to ground chicken or ground turkey. With all of these grinds, and more, the way you cook your meat affects how much fat is left.

Grilling lets much of the fat drip away as it's emulsified by the heat. When you grill-roast burgers, you end up with less fat than you do with any other cooking method. When you grill-roast steaks, you end up with a lower fat content than the label says because that calculation is based on the fat remaining after cooking by an average of several cooking methods.

Grilling Tech Talk

The medical jury is still out on conjugated linoleic acids (CLA), despite claims by Dr. Oz and others. Grass-fed beef is a rich source of CLA, so if you're interested in getting more into your body, this is the way to go. Our bodies are designed to absorb nutrients from the foods they are present in. A good rule of thumb is to eat those products rather than try to get the nutrient through the use of supplements. The weight management and cancer inhibiting claims of CLA are not proven. What is proven beyond reasonable doubt is that some media-savvy doctors have found a cash cow in CLA supplements. It's better, cheaper, and tastier to eat the real beef, especially if it's grass fed.

Steak Marinades

Here are a couple of my favorite marinades for steak.

My Favorite Steak Marinade

Ingredients

¼ c olive oil
¼ c red wine vinegar
1 Tbs Dijon mustard
1 tsp Worcestershire sauce
1 tsp (or more) fresh garlic, minced—or rub a cut piece of garlic on each steak for a gentler garlicky background
Salt and pepper to taste

Directions

Whisk together all of the ingredients except the salt and pepper. Place four to six 6-ounce lean steaks, each about 1 inch thick, in a resealable plastic bag, pour in the marinade, squeeze out most of the air, and massage marinade to completely cover the meat. Marinate one to four hours; more is OK too. Remove from the marinade when ready to grill, pat with paper towel to remove excess marinade, and salt and pepper to taste.

Bloody Mary Steak Marinade

The basic recipe is inspired by the cocktail minus the vodka, which has no flavor anyway (but I've seen vodka added as well and it does no harm). Surprisingly, the meat does not end up tasting like tomatoes—the marinade just adds a background flavor that enhances the beefy taste. You can use canned tomato juice, V8, or Spicy V8 for a bigger kick. No need to salt the meat—the juice has plenty of salt. Rub the meat with garlic before marinating, if desired. This recipe is for six steaks, such as London broil, tenderloin, flank steak, rib eye, or other leaner beef, about 6 ounces each.

Ingredients

6 ounces canned tomato juice or V8
1 Tbs prepared horse radish
1 Tbs Worcestershire sauce
1 tsp fresh-squeezed lemon juice
3 Tbs light olive or canola oil
½ tsp celery seeds
Dash of Tabasco or other hot sauce, or to taste (or use Spicy V8)

Whisk together all of the ingredients. Marinate steaks for one to four hours, remove from bag, and pat dry. Sear for two to three minutes per side on well-oiled grates, then flip and roast over indirect heat for about six to eight minutes till medium-rare.

Tasty Tips

It's fun to experiment with variations on the Bloody Mary marinade. Creative bartenders push the limits of this classic cocktail—you can too. Vodka doesn't add flavor, but some liquors can give the marinade another dimension. Add 2 ounces of one of these beverages:

➤ Peaty, smoky Scotch whisky (Bloody Scotsman)

➤ Irish whisky (Bloody Molly)

➤ Red wine (Bloody Cab)

➤ Guinness stout (Bloody Maureen)

➤ Dark rum (Bloody Pirate)

➤ Bourbon whiskey (Bloody Kentucky Colonel)

Steak Tonight

The key to a healthy steak dinner starts with selecting the best beef for you and your family. A leaner cut, a smaller portion, and organic grass fed is the prime steak for overall health and weight control. Grill-roast steaks to virtually eliminate HACs and PAHs. Let steaks rest at room temperature, lightly salted and peppered (or with a favorite rub) for fifteen to thirty minutes before grilling.

A 1-inch-thick London broil or filet should be seared about two to three minutes per side over direct heat, and then flipped once more and roasted over indirect heat at 350°F for about six to eight minutes for medium-rare. Flank steaks and hanger steaks are thinner, so the roasting phase should be about four to five minutes for medium-rare. An instant-read thermometer should read about 135°F. Always rest steaks for about five minutes before slicing.

In Part Three, you'll find many ways to make steak dinners a much-anticipated meal that's good for everyone.

CHAPTER 6

 # Grilled Pork

There are so many ways to grill pork that entire books and websites are devoted entirely to this versatile meat. We'll cover the highlights here, and stir your creative juices with recipes in Part Three. Here are my recommended techniques for preparing and grilling different pork presentations, from whole roasts to kabobs and a lot in between. The single most important grilling technique is this: respect your pork.

How to Grill Pork—the Healthy, Tasty Way

It's easy to ruin pork on the grill. Pork chops are usually low in fat, so even slight overcooking turns a tender chop into an unpleasant, leathery turnoff. Pork can be surprisingly fragile. I use the word *surprisingly* because you can literally cook some pork cuts for hours, improving the meat as the day wears on, while other cuts from the same animal can be destroyed in minutes. So treat your pork with the respect it deserves. Knowing your pork varieties is essential. Different pork cuts require very different treatment on the grill.

There are four basic ways to cook pork on your charcoal or gas grill—roasting, slow roasting or barbequing, braising then roasting, and grill-roasting. Each of these is appropriate for one or more cuts of pork.

Fat Fighters

Pork cuts vary in their recommended cooking methods because their fat content (and therefore calories) is different. Tenderloins, for instance, are about 30 calories per ounce, whereas pork butts—the preferred long- and slow-cooked pulled pork BBQ—is about twice that calorie count. In the middle, at 40–50 calories per ounce, are center cut pork chops—the ideal grilling choice. So a very satisfying grilled pork chop weighing 4–6 ounces is less than 300 calories. Eating a grilled pork chop for dinner is a smart weight loss strategy. It's not dieting; it's celebrating nutritious low-fat food.

Roasting Pork

Roasting over indirect heat is the method for cooking pork loins and tenderloins:

➤ Pork loin, bone in or boneless, and tenderloins, are grilled over indirect heat on a covered grill, at about 350°F for about twenty minutes per pound. Reduce the time for tenderloins, which are thinner than loin roasts. An instant-read thermometer is essential to prevent overcooking.

➤ Sear first over direct heat for a couple of minutes per side, then move to indirect heat and leave meat alone to gently roast till done.

➤ Brining and rubs improve flavor, tenderness, and juiciness. You can also brush on barbecue or other sauce or marinade once you move to the roasting stage because the indirect heat won't burn the sauce.

➤ Roast the loin or tenderloin till the internal temperature reaches 145°F—a faint pink color at the very center is ideal.

➤ Always let the roast rest for ten to fifteen minutes before slicing, so juices redistribute.

Grilling Tech Talk

News flash: The FDA recently lowered the recommended safe cooking temperature for pork from 160°F to 145°F. Most of us have been grilling to that lower temperature anyway, especially for the leaner "other white meat" cuts like chops and loins. But this makes it official and assures you that saying *medium* for pork doesn't mean you're eccentric.

Grill Speak

Trichinosis, a parasitic disease that can be fatal, was a real pork problem many years ago and still is in parts of the world where hogs eat meat. It is passed from animal to animal by eating the meat of an infected host.

In the old days, pigs were the garbage consumers on farms and as a consequence could carry trichinosis, which was passed on to humans in undercooked pork. Not any more. Hog farming is carefully monitored by the USDA, and pigs are fed a strict diet to maximize health, taste, and low fat—an entirely vegetarian diet. The approximately forty human trichinosis cases a year in our country are almost entirely contracted by eating wild game, such as bears and raccoons, or privately raised hogs. Commercial pork is wholesome, safe, and among the healthiest kind of meat, low in fat, and rich in nutrients such as phosphorus, thiamine, and B vitamins.

Slow Roasting or Barbecuing

Cooking over indirect heat is the method used for pork shoulders, also called butts:

➤ Pork shoulders—butts—are higher in fat and connective tissue, or collagen, so require slow cooking at temperatures below 300°F over indirect heat for at least forty-five minutes to one hour per pound on a closed grill.

➤ Adding wet seasoned wood chips to the heat source for smoke, and mopping with your favorite sauce throughout the cooking process, boosts the flavor of this classic pork feast.

➤ Barbecue rubs are another flavor booster.

➤ Low and slow is the rule for pork butts, with a grill temperature of around 275°F–300°F over indirect heat. An internal temperature of 170°F is the goal, and patience is a virtue here.

➤ Let pork butt rest for at least fifteen minutes before serving, and keep it warm for the entire time it is being served; never serve cold. There is not much fat left in the roast, but what is there will congeal at cool temps. Ugh!

Grill Speak

Yes, I can hear you. Why is a pork shoulder called a pork butt? This is one of the many mysteries of life—accept it and move on.

Braising then Roasting

Use indirect heat for pork ribs, the foolproof method for baby back ribs and center cut ribs:

➤ Precook the ribs in liquid, either in water or a stock of your choice, in a tightly lidded pan. Simmer ribs till the fork easily pierces the meat, an hour or so. (This can be done ahead of time and refrigerated.)

➤ Pat the ribs dry, use your favorite rub and a little oil, and sear over direct heat for a few minutes.

➤ Move to indirect heat and roast on a covered grill at 350°F for about thirty minutes or longer till meat is very tender. Then paint with your favorite sauce and flip two or three times as needed. Sauce won't burn over indirect heat.

Grill-Roasting

Here is the method for bone-in or boneless pork chops, tenderloins, and kabobs:

➤ Marinate for about one to four hours, or according to directions, in your favorite marinade, or brine and use a rub.

➤ Sear tenderloins, chops, and kabobs over direct heat about two to three minutes per side for attractive grill marks and good color.

➤ Flip and move chops and kabobs to indirect heat and grill-roast for about six to eight minutes for 1-inch-thick chops, about two minutes less for 1-inch-cubed kabobs, till the internal temperature is 145°F, a light pink center. Sacrifice one kabob cube instead of inserting a thermometer, which is difficult on a little piece around a hot grill—check for doneness with a knife cut. (Total time is about ten to twelve minutes for chops, a couple of minutes less for kabobs.)

➤ Flip and move tenderloins to indirect heat and grill-roast, flipping one more time, for twelve to sixteen minutes till the internal temperature reaches 145°F, pink at the center. (Total time about eighteen to twenty-two minutes or more, depending on thickness and heat.)

➤ Chops, kabobs, and tenderloins can be brushed with your favorite sauce at the roasting stage, when the sauce won't burn, but always check, especially with charcoal fires which can vary.

➤ Serve chops and kabobs hot off the grill. Give tenderloins a few minutes rest before slicing.

More Healthy Grilling Info

The USDA recommends the following internal cooking temperatures for pork and the number of minutes that pork should be held at those temperatures to remove any risk of trichinosis. Commercial pork is not of concern here. We're talking about pork you are not sure about. This is important if you buy pork from a local farm or are gifted it and can't be absolutely certain it was raised according to strict USDA standards. Freezing pork below 20°F also eliminates trichinosis parasites. Err on the side of more heat longer—160°F to be sure.

°F	°C	Minimum Time
120	49	21 hours
122	50.0	9.5 hours
124	51.1	4.5 hours
126	52.2	2 hours
128	53.4	1 hours
130	54.5	30 minutes
132	55.6	15 minutes
134	56.7	6 minutes
136	57.8	3 minutes
138	58.9	2 minutes
140	60.0	1 minute
142	61.1	1 minute
144	62.2	Instant

How Did Pork Get So Healthy?

The answer is that we caused it. As American consumers became more conscious of the perils of a high-fat diet, the hog farmers responded with marketing savvy. Instead of trying to convince folks that bacon is good for you (it's easy to argue bacon is good, but stop short of *for you*), the pork producers bred a nutritious, delectable product that delivers the texture of steak with low fat, a worthy rival to a chicken breast. In the last twenty years, pork has lost 30 percent of its fat. Eat plenty of pork and you will too. Best of all, pork tastes great on the grates!

Fat Fighters

The leanest pork cuts have the word *loin* or *round* in them, as in pork tenderloin or pork round. You can see that these products are not riddled with fat. If there is any fat, it's around the sides, and it can be easily sliced or grilled away.

We already know that grilling is one of the lowest-fat methods for cooking. A typical center-cut pork loin chop is about 50–60 calories per ounce. A 4–6-ounce chop makes a very satisfying dinner entrée, delivering approximately 300 calories with 10–14 grams of fat. That's less than 20 percent of the recommended daily fat allowance for a 2,000-calorie diet.

Fat Fighters

I'm not being deliberately vague when I give a range of calories per ounce in these pages. The reality is that the same pork cut (and all other meats and fish) varies somewhat in calorie counts. A pork chop can be 40 calories per ounce, or 60, depending on breed, feed, and farmer. The only thing you can be certain of is how much you're eating. Eat moderate amounts of pork, serving sizes 6 ounces or less, and you'll be living a sensible weight-control program, and feeling satisfied.

Tasty Tips

Brining makes pork juicier. By a process known as osmosis, the brine is absorbed through the cell walls and then, by diffusion, the flavored liquid is spread through the meat. After several hours, much of the salt is expelled. The liquid that has been absorbed not only flavors the meat—more subtly than a spicy rub or acidic marinade—but it also soaks the meat. By weight, this liquid can add 15 percent. Instead of melted fat giving the pork a juicy texture, the absorbed water results in a moist, luscious roast, as juicy as if it were loaded with saturated fat calories. Brining this lean meat really pays off.

Not All Pork Is Low Fat

Pork loin roasts and tenderloins are low in fat and calories. But when it comes to ribs, they are double the calories and the fat. Save them for a special occasion. Pork ribs will stick to more than your ribs if you eat them with any regularity. Same holds true for barbecued butts. A 1-cup serving of pulled pork weighs in at about 400 calories and twice the fat of a pork loin chop. Healthy grilling does not mean you can't ever eat these delicious pork dishes. But limit portions and frequency. Besides, there are too many scrumptious ways to enjoy the lean pork cuts.

My Basic Flavor-Booster Pork Brine

Immersing pork in a saltwater-flavored solution for several hours will enhance your enjoyment of pork. It's worth the small effort and planning ahead. A good technique is to heat a smaller portion of the water to boiling, and then dissolve all the flavoring elements such as salt, sugar, spices, whatever. Then add the rest of the cold water to the amount you need, and chill before brining the pork.

Basic Pork Brine

Ingredients
1 qt water
1 c kosher salt
½ c sugar
½ c whole peppercorns
1 tsp allspice
Ice

Directions

Heat about 1 quart of water to boiling. Add kosher salt, sugar, whole peppercorns, and allspice. Stir and dissolve. Combine this with ice and cold water to make 1 gallon of brine in total. Chill the brine.

Completely immerse the pork roast in the brine for at least eight hours, up to twenty-four hours. For chops, brine about four hours. Pat meat dry before rubbing and grilling.

Grilling Tech Talk

Brines must be kept cold so your meat doesn't spoil, especially a long brine over two hours. If you can't keep the brining meat in a refrigerator, place it in a picnic cooler packed with ice bags. If you can't do that, put a plastic bag of ice right into the brine, enough to keep it cold. Adding ice cubes directly to the brine dilutes it and retards or eliminates the brining action, which requires enough salt to facilitate absorption and diffusion of the brine flavor. Brining doesn't make meat taste saltier because the salt is expelled over time—a minimum of four hours is required for this to occur in chops, at least twice as long with roasts.

Variations on the Basic Pork Brine

To bring extra flavors to your brine, and to your pork roast or chops, add the following ingredients to the basic pork brine:

⅓ cup honey dissolved into the boiling water instead of sugar
Then add to the cold brine:
2 Tbs fresh thyme or 1 Tbs dry
2 Tbs crumbled bay leaf
2 Tbs dry parsley

For a New England brine with a Chinese accent, add the following ingredients to the basic pork brine:

⅓ cup maple syrup dissolved into the boiling water instead of sugar

Then add to the cold brine:
1 c low-sodium soy sauce
8 cloves
2 Tbs crumbled bay leaf
1 Tbs ground thyme

A savory Spice Islands brine can be created by adding the following ingredients to the basic pork brine:

½ c brown sugar dissolved into the boiling water instead of sugar

Then add to the cold brine:

¼ c whole cloves
2 Tbs ground nutmeg
3 cinnamon sticks

Other brine flavors can be created for the basic pork brine. Here are some suggestions:

> ➤ 1 cup or more crushed and squeezed fresh or canned cherries added to the brine

> ➤ Substitute 1 quart apple cider or natural apple juice for half (2 quarts) of the water

> ➤ Add the zest of three limes, and squeeze the juice of one lime into the brine

> ➤ 1 quart dark beer instead of 1 quart water

Use your imagination and instincts to add zest to your pork brine.

My Basic Pork Rub

Whether or not you take the time to brine, rubbing the meat with an assortment of dry spices and herbs adds flavor depth to your roasts and chops. Each of the following recipes is enough for a 3- to 4-pound roast or for six to eight 6-ounce chops.

Basic Pork Rub

¼ cup Old Bay seasoning (contains salt and good paprika flavor)
1 Tbs dried thyme
1 Tbs dried oregano
1 tsp ground black pepper
½ tsp cayenne (or less/none if heat is not desired)
1 Tbs each dried garlic and onion

You can increase all the measurements and make a big batch, store in a jar for several months, dark and cool. (I keep mine in the back of the fridge.)

Variations on the Basic Pork Rub

To bring different flavors to your pork rub, add the following ingredients to the basic pork rub:

For a smoky rub with a Southwestern accent add the following ingredients to the basic rub:

Substitute smoked paprika for half of the Old Bay and add 1 tablespoon ancho chili powder and 1 teaspoon ground cumin.

All you need to do to add a flavor of Indian to your rub is add the following ingredients to your pork rub:

¼ c Garam Masala
1 Tbs turmeric
1 Tbs medium or hot curry powder
1 tsp ground ginger
½ tsp ground nutmeg

Coffee gives the meat a rich chocolate undertone, and there are many variations on the use of coffee in rubs. Here's one variation:

Use coffee right from the can or your coffee grinder.

¼ c ground coffee
2 Tbs grated lemon or orange zest or a combination of the two
1 Tbs ground cinnamon
1 tsp garlic powder
1 tsp sugar

This rub uses the Mexican flavor theme of cumin and chili powder. Again, many variations on this basic recipe encourage you to have fun and experiment:

3 Tbs chipotle or other medium-hot smoky chili powder, or ancho for milder taste
1 Tbs cumin
1 tsp dried oregano
1 tsp grated orange zest
1 tsp grated lime zest
Salt to taste

Tasty Tips

I like to finish my rubs by massaging some oil onto the pork after I'm done with the spice mix. Pork doesn't render fat when it roasts—there just isn't much in the loin and tenderloin. The same is true for grilled loin chops. So a little oil helps the meat brown as it roasts or grills, and it boosts the flavor of the rub into a sort of glaze, liquefying some of the ingredients as they heat. I don't use full-flavor oil like olive or sesame because I want to enable the rub to achieve greatness on its own. So use a neutral vegetable oil such as canola or corn.

My Basic Pork Marinade

When you marinate grilling meats you achieve two important goals:

1. You're reducing the formation of the possibly carcinogenic chemicals HCA and PAB by as much as 90 percent

2. You're adding lots of flavor

There are as many marinade recipes as there are cultures multiplied by creative cooks. So we will focus on just a few that are perfect with pork and serve as departure points for your own culinary creativity.

There is something about that union of pork and apples that is not only a time-tested classic combination, but also happens to be a marriage made in pig heaven. Flavors like this go together so well because they make each other taste better than either one does alone.

Apple Pork Marinade

This is enough for a 4- to 6-pound loin roast or six to eight 6-ounce loin chops

Ingredients
Whisk together or use a blender:
½ c apple cider or fresh natural apple juice
¼ c apple cider vinegar
2–3 Tbs olive oil
1 Tbs Dijon mustard
1 Tbs tart apricot, peach, or raspberry jam
1 tps sugar (can use honey if desired)
Salt and pepper to taste

Directions
Marinate the roast for four to six hours, chops two to four hours. Use marinade as a mopping sauce, especially on the roast as it cooks on the grill (make additional marinade and reserve for mopping during grilling).

Other Rubs for Pork

Normandy Pork Marinade

Ingredients
Continuing the apple and pork theme, whisk or blend together:
½ c hard apple cider
2 Tbs calvados
1 Tbs Dijon mustard
1 Tbs Herbes de Provence
1 tsp ground black pepper
¼ c olive oil

My grilling guru Ed Hamlin of grillinnovations.com makes a tasty garlicky marinade that works perfectly with pork tenderloins, another example of simplicity as the best solution.

Ed's Pork Tenderloin Garlic Marinade

Ingredients
½ c olive oil
¼ c balsamic vinegar
3 Tbs fresh rosemary leaves, crushed
3 Tbs fresh garlic, crushed
1 tsp kosher salt
½ tsp black pepper

Directions
Ed strips the leaves off of fresh rosemary and crushes garlic cloves, and then whisks all the ingredients together. Then he marinates the tenderloins for four to six hours and mops with the reserved sauce as the meat roasts on the grill.

Citrus Garlic Marinade

Pork loves citrus, especially lime juice. This works best on grilled pork chops and kabobs.

Ingredients
Whisk together or use a blender:
½ c fresh squeezed lime juice
¼ c olive oil
2 Tbs fresh chopped cilantro leaves
1 Tbs grated lime zest
½ tsp cayenne or hot pepper flakes
Salt to taste

Directions

Marinate chops or kabobs about two hours and grill without mopping.

I agree with those who argue that no culture has refined pork cookery to equal that of the Vietnamese. Try this marinade on chops or kabobs.

Vietnamese Pork Marinade

Ingredients
Whisk or blend together:
½ c neutral vegetable oil
3 garlic cloves, crushed
3 large shallots, chopped
2 Tbs Chinese rice vinegar
2 Tbs fish sauce (available in the Asian food section of supermarkets)
1 Tbs sugar
1 tsp sesame oil

Directions
Marinate chops and kabobs for two to four hours and grill without mopping.

Pork Kabob Marinade

This is for about 2 pounds of pork loin cut into 1-inch cubes

Ingredients
¼ c wine vinegar
¼ c canola or other neutral oil
2 Tbs soy sauce
2 Tbs smooth natural peanut butter
1 Tbs sesame oil
1 Tbs lime juice
1 Tbs fresh garlic, minced
1 tsp or less, hot pepper flakes

Directions
Marinate pork cubes for one to two hours. Grill-roast kabobs for ten minutes total, but monitor carefully to make sure they don't overcook and dry out.

We love pork on the grill because it's so versatile. You can serve it weekly for months and never bore the family. For entertaining, you can dress up this economical meat and even serve several different tasting chops or loins at the same time with virtually no extra work. See Chapter 18 for a bounty of pork delights, including succulent tenderloin, loin roast, chops, and kabobs. For pork burgers, see the burger recipes in Part Three.

CHAPTER 7

 # Grilling Fish

In This Chapter

➤ How to buy fish for the grill

➤ Fish-grilling techniques

➤ Marinades and rubs recipes

➤ Fish kabobs and more

When it comes to grilling various types of food, many of us seem to have the most trouble with fish on the grill. It is true that grilling fish takes some practice, and certain fish are really not suitable for cooking this way. We'll discuss that, along with how to select, buy, and handle fish, some delicious marinades, and other grilling tips and tricks for tasty grilled fish.

Fish are low in calories and high in heart-healthy omega-3s. Some fish are abundant and should be a part of your regular weekly meal planning. Avoid fish that are being overfished or under environmental pressure. Aquaculture is delivering an excellent seafood product, especially the salmon operations in Canada and northern Europe. When deciding what fish to grill, it's a good idea to consider all these factors—the environment, the overall health and diversity of our planet, and the right types of fish for the grill.

The Right Fish for Grilling

Most fish is the perfect healthy grilled food, but not all, and that's a problem for some of us. We try to grill the wrong fish, and then we blame that cooking method for our failure. Don't grill fish that you should sauté—it's like microwaving a steak and then complaining that it's gray and flabby. Simply put, the best sautéed fish you ever ate should never see a charcoal or gas grill. I'll go further: any really good sautéed fish should stay in the pan, not on the grates.

The sea gives us wonderful fish that seem custom designed by nature for our grill. It makes no sense to try to grill less suitable species. We should grill whole red snapper and whole porgies, fillets from fresh-caught bluefish, striped bass, mahimahi, and always-available salmon. We should grill steaks from salmon, tuna, swordfish, mako, and other meaty denizens of the deep. The best grilled fish I ever ate were fresh sardines splashed with lemon juice and olive oil, cooked on a rusting charcoal grill on a beach in Portugal.

All these species are easy to grill and taste better from the grates than from any other cooking method. So avoid grilling delicate trout, flaky flounder or cod, or even farmed tilapia and catfish. They deserve a pan; you deserve the ease of preparing them that way. After all, occasionally you have to justify that stove in your kitchen.

Tasty Tips

Aquaculture operators have been paying attention to consumers. The quality of farmed salmon is much improved and the negative environmental impact reduced. Farmed salmon from the United States, Norway, Canada, Scotland, and other northern European countries is highly regulated, carefully nurtured, and improving year by year. Wild Alaskan salmon, a sustainable fishery that provides a high-quality product, is often my first choice. Even the frozen fresh-caught wild Alaskan salmon is excellent. Let's reward these responsible fishermen and aquaculture operators with our purchases.

Buying Fish for Your Grill

Here are a few simple tips for buying and preparing whole fish such as snappers, porgies, striped bass, or coho and other medium-size salmon:

➤ Buy whole fish that have a spine and bones that will peel out intact in one easy pull when done cooking. If you're not sure what to buy, ask the fish guy, "Will all the bones come out easily when I grill these whole fish?"

➤ Check the gills on whole fish. They should be red and smell fresh, not fishy. If gills have been removed, there are other telltale freshness indicators such as smooth non-slimy skin, very intact scales, clear eyes, flesh firm to the touch, and no fishy odor. Always ask the counterman to hand you the fish in the paper before he wraps it so you can sniff to check freshness.

➤ Buy only from fish sellers with a high turnover of product—if you have to take a number at the counter that's a good thing.

➤ No matter how busy the fish sellers are, they should be happy to do the work for you. Whole fish should have the gills, fins, and scales removed before you take them home.

➤ Before grilling whole fish, take a sharp knife and cut several diagonal slashes across the fish, from behind the gills to the tail, about halfway into the flesh. These will help keep the fish from curling as it cooks, help the olive oil, marinade, or mop flavor the meat, and speed up the grilling process.

➤ Store whole fish for no more than a day in the lowest, coldest part of your fridge (fresh-caught fish can be stored this way for two to three days, but make sure they are gutted and cleaned first).

Here are a few simple tips for buying and preparing fish fillets or steaks for grilling:

➤ Buy fish fillets and steaks that are about 1 inch thick and have firm, meaty flesh. Don't buy fish that easily flake when cooked—that's for the sauté pan or oven. If you are not sure, ask the fish guy, "Is this a good piece of fish for our charcoal or gas grill?"

➤ Check for freshness. Smelling is the key here. Fresh fish has no odor except a slight hint of the sea. If it smells fishy, don't buy it. The flesh should be firm to the touch.

➤ When buying fillets, try to select pieces that are relatively uniform in thickness. You may be better off buying a big fillet and cutting it into several smaller pieces of approximately the same thickness. You can always serve guests a couple of small fillets instead of one unevenly done larger piece.

➤ When buying salmon steaks (not fillets), you can ask your fishmonger to remove the bone. Good fish guys know how to use the longer side pieces of the salmon to create an attractive and easy-grilling salmon steak. Discuss your grilling intentions and ask for suggestions.

➤ When buying tuna steaks, always make sure it is sashimi-grade tuna. Cheap tuna can be old or frozen more than once, and it toughens when it's being grilled. If the bargain-price tuna seems too good to be true, it is. Frozen tuna is usually very fresh, as is frozen wild salmon from Alaska.

➤ When you unwrap your salmon fillets, run your fingers along the center of the meat from the tail (narrower) end, feeling for leftover pinbones. Remove them with needle-nose pliers. This is easy to do and avoids bone problems later.

➤ With both tuna and swordfish steaks, remove any dark areas along the edge of the meat before grilling. Most people don't enjoy the taste of this dark meat.

➤ Keep wrapped fillets and steaks in the coldest bottom part of your fridge for no longer than two days.

Grill Speak

What is sashimi-grade tuna? We use quality-defining terms like prime and choice for beef, and grade A for poultry and other products. These terms are regulated by the USDA. But there are no official terms for fish quality. Sashimi-grade tuna is a marketing device rather than a regulated quality grade. Always buy sashimi-grade if you trust the retailer because it means the fish has been immediately killed after being caught and therefore no lactic acid has been released, which hastens spoilage.

In Japanese cuisine, sashimi is thinly sliced raw fish, so by definition it must be the highest quality and very fresh. Most sashimi in the United States comes from frozen fish but is still very high quality, as is sashimi-grade frozen tuna from a reliable seafood purveyor such as Costco.

Grilling Tech Talk

Both tuna and salmon steaks and fillets hold up quite well when comparing the frozen product to the fresh ones. Often flash frozen within hours of being caught or harvested, these two fish arrive at your freezer in excellent shape. Thaw the individually wrapped fish in warm tap water. If not sealed in a pouch, wrap the frozen fish tightly in a plastic bag and immerse in warm water to thaw. In less than half an hour your fish is thawed, ready to marinate, grill, or prepare later. Just be sure to refrigerate immediately any fish you're not grilling because it will spoil unless promptly chilled.

Fish and the Environment

Smart consumers who are concerned about health—for both the environment and our own bodies, should consult the Monterey Bay Aquarium website at www.montereybayaquarium. org/cr/SeafoodWatch. I know of no organization that so comprehensively and authoritatively covers the entire seafood spectrum with up-to-date ratings on sustainability, toxic issues like mercury and PCBs, nutrition information, aquaculture practices and issues, and catch methods with their impact on the environment. If you want to be an informed seafood consumer, this is the place to go. Plus it offers lots of recipes, handling advice, and tips on buying and preparing every fish you can think of.

Be a Responsible Consumer

It's easy to love seafood and be a responsible consumer at the same time. Salmon and other aquaculture operations have made vast improvements in both product quality and the environmental impact. American tuna and swordfish fishermen have adopted sustainability practices that enabled species like yellowfin tuna and swordfish to rebound after decades of decline. Alaskan salmon and halibut are thriving, thanks to responsible fishing.

Not all the world's fishermen are as committed to the long-term viability of wild fisheries, however. We should avoid Chilean sea bass, for example, a most threatened species. Perhaps reverting to their original name would help, the Patagonian toothfish. It is irresponsible to consume bluefin tuna, in my opinion, especially since other tuna species are plenty good and plentiful.

We consumers can make a difference in the long-term viability of wild fisheries. Grill only fish you are proud to serve your friends and family.

Tasty Tips

The mistake most of us make, trying to grill the wrong kind of fish, is often compounded by erring on the side of grilling fish too long. Many people are turned off by underdone fish, and this is understandable. With the exception of tuna and salmon, most fish tastes better when cooked through. However, overcooking fish gives seafood a bad reputation because it becomes a dry, leathery, or mushy mess. So time your grilling carefully and check the fish for doneness. Don't overcook. Cut into a salmon or tuna piece to make sure there is some pink inside for tenderness. Cut into white flesh fish to make sure the middle is opaque, a sign it's done to perfection. You'll get the timing down pat with a little practice. You don't have to rest these fish after grilling, as you would beef.

Marinating Fish

Fish marinades, in my experience, are best when they follow a formula using citrus for the acid and a neutral vegetable or olive oil, along with herbs and spices, but there are many variations on this template. As you gain fish grilling confidence, you'll explore many marinade recipes.

It's a good idea to marinate fish because it inhibits the formation of the possibly harmful chemicals HCAs and PABs. Marinating in an acid oil solution can reduce the formation of these substances by up to 90 percent and that along with the grill-roasting technique I recommend, virtually eliminates the possible problem. See Chapter 1 for details.

Marinating Fish Is Different

Grilled fish tastes better with a marinade. The marinade serves a dual purpose by inhibiting the fish from sticking to the grates. But marinating fish is different from marinating meat or poultry. Fish seems to absorb the marinade much faster. Most fish have a more delicate flavor to begin with—you don't want to overpower the intrinsic fish taste that we pay dearly for. With a short shelf life and more sensitive handling considerations, the fish itself is the real star of the dinner show. The marinade is an accent. This is especially true for white fish, which are even more delicately flavored than darker, oilier fish. Those fish have a bolder intrinsic flavor that can handle a spicier or more robustly flavored marinade.

Here are a couple rules of thumb to keep in mind when marinating fish:

➤ Marinate most fish for approximately half an hour.

➤ Choose your marinade ingredients depending on the species of fish you are grilling. There is no standard one-size-fits-all marinade.

Grilling Tech Talk

Be aware when using lemon- and lime-based marinades that these citruses are the key ingredients for ceviche recipes, the lovely raw fish concoctions from south of the border. The citric acid "cooks" the fish chemically, but you don't want to do that to fish you are going to really cook. So be judicious in the amount of citrus you use in your marinade and especially the amount of time you marinate—always less than an hour, and even less for white fish.

Fish Marinades

Because dark- and white-fleshed fish are so different in taste and texture, you need to marinate with those considerations in mind. I have explored dozens of different marinades over the years, and when planning a cookout that's a bit special, it's fun to use a more exotic marinade with side dishes that build on that theme. But for routine, healthy family dinners,

I have two marinade templates that are easy to assemble, provide lots of flavor, and enable me to get the fish on the grates in way under an hour. That makes all the difference on a weeknight after working all day.

A Marinade Template for White Fish

These more delicately flavored fish need a lighter marinade.

Ingredients

For 2–3 pounds of white fish such as halibut, striped bass, mahimahi (dolphin fish), snapper, or porgies, whether whole fish or fillets, whisk together:

¼ c neutral oil such as canola or corn
¼ c fresh-squeezed lemon juice
1 tsp lemon zest
1 tsp grated fresh garlic or to taste
1 tsp fresh-grated ginger or more if you only have dried
½ tsp salt
½ tsp pepper

Directions
Marinate fish about half an hour in a nonreactive bowl or sealed plastic bag in the fridge.

Variation: Use lime juice and zest, and instead of garlic and ginger, use 2 Tbs or more chopped fresh cilantro

A Marinade Template for Darker Fish

Ingredients

These bolder-flavored fish can handle a stronger marinade.

This is for 2–3 pounds of darker, oilier fish such as salmon, tuna, mako, swordfish, bluefish, mackerel, and sardines.

Whisk together:

¼ c olive oil
¼ c white wine
3 Tbs fresh-squeezed lemon or lime juice
1 Tbs lemon or lime zest
1 Tbs grated fresh garlic or more to taste
1 tsp salt
½ tsp pepper
Red pepper flakes to taste

Directions

Marinate 2–3 pounds of fish about half an hour or up to an hour in nonreactive bowl or sealed plastic bag in fridge.

Variation: For an Asian accent, substitute ¼ cup neutral oil and 2 tablespoons sesame oil for the olive oil. Substitute ¼ cup soy sauce for white wine, and add 1 tablespoon grated fresh ginger (eliminate the salt). Substitute cayenne for red pepper flakes if you like some heat.

Vietnamese Marinade

There are many variations on this basic theme, but try this one to get a sense of the flavors. Then you can vary the ingredients and experiment. My Vietnamese marinade is real simple and tastes authentic.

Whisk together:

¼ c neutral oil
¼ c rice vinegar
2 Tbs Vietnamese fish sauce
1 Tbs grated fresh garlic
1 Tbs lemon zest
1 tsp hot chili powder
1 tsp sugar

Directions

Marinate about 2–3 pounds of fish for half an hour for white fish, a little longer for darker fish, in a nonreactive bowl or sealed plastic bag in the fridge.

Mediterranean Marinade

This is for about 2–3 pounds of darker fish, especially good for swordfish and tuna.

Whisk together:

¼ c olive oil
¼ c red wine vinegar
1 Tbs herbes de Provence
1 tsp dried oregano
1 tsp lemon zest
½ tsp salt
½ tsp pepper

My Favorite Salmon Marinade

Ingredients
This is for about 2–3 pounds of fillets or steaks.
Whisk together:
¼ c olive oil
2 Tbs Dijon mustard
2 Tbs white wine
¼ cup finely chopped fresh dill or less if you only have dry dill
1 tsp salt

Directions
Marinate for about half an hour. Salmon, mustard, and dill are an ideal family of flavors.

Ed's Tuna Marinade

Grilling guru Ed Hamlin of grillinnovations.com is not only a grill master and inventor, he's also an accomplished Florida sports fisherman who lands his fair share of tuna. Here's his marinade for four to six tuna steaks:

Ingredients
Whisk together:
½ c teriyaki sauce
2 Tbs light soy sauce
2 Tbs pickled ginger, chopped fine with its juice
1 tsp honey
½ tsp sesame oil

Directions
Marinate tuna steaks about half an hour, then set the steaks on a plate with a little olive oil to coat right before grilling. Grill for two to three minutes per side for very rare or rare steaks; grill-roast another few minutes for medium. Well-done tuna is like well-done sirloin, a crime against nature.

Fat Fighters

Yellowfin tuna is about 40 calories per ounce. Halibut is around 40, and salmon averages 50–60 calories per ounce. Much of the calories come from the omega-3 heart-healthy oils. A 4- to 6-ounce serving of these grilled fish, most of them under 300 calories per serving, satisfies a hungry dieter because of their rich flavor. So eat fish often if you are on a weight-loss program, guilt free, right off the grill.

Grill Speak

Fish steaks and fish fillets refer to how the fish is cut. A fillet has been cut along the backbone, head to tail, just above the spine and ribs and (hopefully) contains no bones at all. Salmon filets, however, often contain tiny pinbones that you can feel by running your finger tail end toward the head end, and are easily removed with a needle-nose pliers.

A steak is a portion cut across the fish through the backbone and often contains that cross section of the spine. When left in the fish, it's easy to eat around without chomping on bones. Typically, swordfish, tuna, salmon, and other large fish are cut as fish steaks. A good fishmonger can remove the salmon steak bone for you and prepare this fish for the grill.

Grilling Fish: My Foolproof Method

Always start with clean grates that are well oiled. The right kind of fish, meaty and steaky, will not stick after a few minutes of direct heat. These fish steaks and fillets behave like beef steak and chicken on the grill. If you are having a sticking problem and you've got clean, well-oiled grates, you are probably grilling the wrong fish. And don't try to grill large fillets. Cut them into smaller pieces of approximately the same thickness so that they're easy to lift with a spatula and cook evenly. In other words, grill fish that in size and texture are made for the grill, not for the pan or oven.

Here is some advice on the best way to grill fish:

➤ Set up your charcoal fire for indirect grill-roasting with the coals along the sides and a disposable aluminum pan in the middle to catch drippings. For gas grills, light all burners till the grill is hot enough to sear fish, about 400–500°F.

➤ For charcoal grills, sear fish over direct high heat for two to three minutes on each side, until the fish lifts off easily without sticking. (Thin fillets will probably be done at this point.) Then flip and move fish to indirect heat, roasting in the center of the covered charcoal grill over the drip pan for about six minutes for fish approximately 1 inch thick, about ten minutes total cook time. Fish are done when the thickest interior is opaque.

If skin on, start the searing on the other side, then flip to skin side down and place fish over indirect heat. Roast an extra two to four minutes, about twelve minutes or slightly longer total time.

➤ For a gas grill, sear fish for two to three minutes over direct high heat until fish lifts off easily without sticking. Flip and sear the other side of the fillet or steak. (Thin fillets will probably be done at this point). Then flip and move fish to the center of the grill over indirect heat, having turned off the center burner, leaving the front and rear burners on medium to low at a temperature of about 350°F. Close cover and roast about six minutes more for fish about 1 inch thick till interior is opaque. For salmon and tuna steaks, reduce the roasting time, or for really rare fish don't roast at all.

Grilling Tech Talk

For medium tuna and salmon, reduce roasting time to about three to four minutes. For skin-on fillets, sear fish on the other skinless side for about two to three minutes, then flip and roast skin side down about eight minutes. Use a spatula to slide between skin and meat when you remove it from the grill—a quick and easy skinning method—and the skin left on the grates flake right off when cleaning the grill later.

Monitor Fillets and Steaks

To check for doneness, look for an opaque center (except for tuna and salmon) by inserting a knife halfway into the flesh, giving it a slight twist, and lifting it to see into the fish. After some experience, you will know the fish is done by the elapsed grilling time, especially on a gas grill where the heat is well regulated, or by how it yields to the touch.

Whole Fish Grilling

Whole fish may take longer if they are thicker, and you may want to flip again during the roasting phase. This takes some practice, but the taste rewards are worth it. Like many other meats, grill-roasting fish

Tasty Tips

When grilling fish, keep it simple. Most fish absorb ambient flavors, so a little grill smoke really comes through, and along with olive oil and lemon juice an almost unbeatable flavor combination emerges. Salmon, bluefish, mackerel, and other oilier fish can handle bigger flavors, marinades, and sauces. But for the lighter, whiter kinds of fish like snapper and bass, less is more.

on the bone adds flavor and preserves moisture. Give yourself time to learn and understand that mistakes are inevitable until you have some experience.

Tasty Tips

Tuna is a special case. Many folks prefer tuna just seared with a bright red center—rare or very rare. This means grilling 1-inch-thick tuna steaks for two to three minutes at most per side over medium-high direct heat, then removing them from the grill and serving. And tuna is one of the few kinds of fish that is as delicious chilled in a salad as hot off the grill. Grill more tuna than you'll consume in one meal for tasty leftovers.

Grilling Tech Talk

Here's a salmon grilling technique I find very user friendly. Buy your fillet with the skin on and don't oil the fish the way you would a skinless fillet. You actually want it to stick to the grates. Get the grill very hot—over 400°F—and then place the salmon skin side down on clean, oiled grates at the center of the gas grill. Turn off the middle burner and reduce the heat coming from the front and rear burners. Close the cover and grill-roast over indirect heat for about ten minutes for 1-inch-thick fillets (less time for thinner) without moving the fish. Inside the grill cover the temperature should be about 350°F. Check for doneness. Most folks like salmon medium to medium-rare.

For a charcoal grill, roast the salmon over a drip pan in the middle with coals banked on the sides and cover closed. Insert a spatula between the skin and meat and lift the salmon off its skin. Remove the skin from the grates later when you clean your grill—it flakes right off.

Grill-Roasting Salmon

Roasting salmon skin side down is such a reliable method you'll be tempted never to grill salmon any other way. Because you don't move the fish for the full ten minutes it's roasting, you have an opportunity to sauce the salmon while it's cooking. I recommend whisking lots of finely chopped fresh dill into fat-free yogurt—a little Dijon mustard as well—and spreading it on the salmon with a spoon just after placing the fish on the grates. The yogurt sauce melts into the salmon as it roasts. Or cover the salmon in thinly sliced lemons or limes and sprinkle with triple sec or curacao for a tropical flavor theme.

Grilled Swordfish Steaks

You can eat swordfish guilt-free these days, thanks to sustainable fishing practices that have resulted in a rebound of the population. Like all large predatory fish, however, swordfish have elevated mercury levels, so consume them once a month or so as a tasty treat. In moderation they are not a health hazard.

Marinate swordfish in a simple olive oil, lemon juice solution—add a little Dijon mustard for a more zippy flavor. Grill steaks about three minutes per side over direct medium-high heat, then flip and move to indirect heat and grill-roast for another four to six minutes till center is opaque.

Swordfish are so easy to grill, so mistake proof, they're as easy as grilling a beef steak. They are perfect as kabobs too, where you can vary the marinade using North African or Indian spices in keeping with this presentation.

Grilled Tuna Steaks

As noted earlier, only buy high-grade tuna. Ask your fishmonger for the best cuts. Marinate the steaks for half an hour in an Asian accented marinade, using sesame oil, rice vinegar, and ginger, or a simple olive oil, lemon juice solution.

Grill tuna directly over very high heat for two to three minutes per side. Tuna is best served rare or medium-rare. And unlike many other fish, leftover grilled tuna is delicious in a salad of fresh greens or sliced on toasted Italian bread with a splash of fine extra-virgin olive oil.

Wood Plank Grilling

Salmon and some other fish are delicious when grilled on wood planks such as untreated cedar or apple intended for grilling. This technique was developed by Indian tribes in the Pacific Northwest, the beneficiaries of huge salmon runs that spurred creative salmon cooking ideas. See the recipes on plank-grilling fish in Part Three.

Eat Fish Every Week

There are hundreds of grilled fish recipes on the web and in printed cookbooks. We eat grilled fish on a weekly basis year-round and have developed some family as well as entertaining favorites. In Part Three, you'll see a selection of fish recipes that are easy to prepare and quite tasty for a weeknight family dinner. There are also a few donated by friends who are master fish grillers. These take a little more time and are worth it.

Grilling fish can be a daunting challenge if you've never done it. Select the right kind of fish, handle and grill it as recommended here, and you'll soon develop the skill to grill fish with the same relaxed confidence as you have when you grill a burger or pork chop.

Keep a bag of frozen salmon, tuna, and mahimahi in the freezer. All three are great grilling fish. Remove your serving size from the freezer a couple of hours before dinner time, thaw in warm tap water for about thirty minutes, marinate for an hour, and you'll have a delicious, healthy main course on the dinner table with very little work.

CHAPTER 8

Shrimp on the Grill

In This Chapter

➤ Health benefits of grilled shrimp

➤ How to buy and prepare shrimp

➤ How to grill shrimp

In this chapter we discuss American's best-loved seafood. Hot or cold, grilled whole or used in sauces and stuffing, shrimp are everywhere and are so popular for very good reasons. Some people, however, avoid shrimp because they believe the cholesterol levels are too high.

If high cholesterol is a concern, only your doctor or nutritionist can tell you whether you should eat these crustaceans and how often. But recent medical research suggests that eating food higher in cholesterol is not a cause of human high blood cholesterol levels. In fact, studies have shown that shrimp consumption can actually improve the LDL (bad) cholesterol to HDL (good) cholesterol ratio, and a diet rich in shrimp can lower blood triglyceride levels, reducing fat in the blood and inflammation in the arteries. Shrimp have omega-3 oils, a heart-healthy fat, and they are rich in selenium, an essential mineral many of us don't get enough of.

Fat Fighters

Large shrimp are only about 20–25 calories each, meaning you can eat a 6- to 8-ounce serving for under 200 calories. Even when you add some oil to the shrimp as a marinade or mop, you are not ruining your weight-loss program because most of the oil drips onto the coals or flavor bars. And olive oil is an essential ingredient in a healthy diet.

Buying Fresh and Frozen Shrimp

Shrimp "on the barby" is a cliché for good reason. No seafood is more bountiful, more readily available, and simpler to grill. Just about the only way you can ruin shrimp is by grilling them too long. Aside from that, grilling shrimp is as easy as heating hot dogs over charcoal or gas.

Unless you live close to shrimp ports, you're better off buying shrimp frozen. They spoil relatively quickly, so shrimpers must ice them as they are caught and process them daily in port. There is no reason for shrimp to taste like iodine if they are kept cold and used within a day of thawing.

Wild shrimp are very sweet and flavorful when handled carefully. If you have a reliable source, always buy wild shrimp or American farmed fresh shrimp. If you don't, buy frozen farmed shrimp from a quality retailer, your friendly fish store, or a supermarket where you know they monitor the aquaculture operations.

You may want to avoid farmed shrimp from China, which in recent years has been plagued by food adulteration scandals. See the Monterey Aquarium website in the resources section to ensure you are buying healthy, safe shrimp.

Buy the larger sizes for grilling (the smaller shrimp are fine for soups, salads, and in rice or pasta, but are too small for the hot grates). Thaw in the fridge overnight. For a quick thaw, immerse frozen shrimp in warm tap water. They will be ready to marinate and grill in half an hour. Always use shrimp within a day of thawing. If you quick thaw in warm water, you should immediately chill or grill the shrimp to prevent spoilage.

Grill Speak

Shrimp size is expressed as the average number of shrimp per pound. For the grill, I prefer shrimp labeled 21–25, meaning 21–25 shrimp to the pound. You'll find shrimp as big as 8–10, oxymoronically called colossal shrimp. Shrimp that are really shrimpy can be labeled 100. Deliciously sweet Maine shrimp, available fresh only in winter, are this tiny size, about 100 to the pound, and are best for a creamy New England-style shrimp chowder.

Grilling Tech Talk

I've seen expert grillers in heated arguments about whether to grill shrimp naked, that is peeled, or in the shell. The argument for in the shell is the insulation factor, the protection a shell gives the meat, preventing scorching or drying out. The argument for peeling is ease of handling when the shrimp are done. Who wants to painstakingly peel hot shrimp, sometimes with the shell adhering to the meat if scorched on a hot grate? I firmly come down on the side of peel before grilling. Just be careful when you cook. Let's face it, shrimp are delicate and can overcook in a moment. But the rewards are worth it if you grill with care. Peel ahead. You and your family will be happier.

Preparing Shrimp for the Grill

Keep it simple. Life is hectic enough without making extra work for yourself by having to peel and devein shrimp. Whenever possible, buy peeled raw fresh or frozen shrimp, tail on for ease of handling. Or, if you're serving the shrimp in a dish such as pasta, rice, or a salad, get rid of the tail before grilling. No one likes to pick up shrimp covered in salad dressing or a pasta sauce and have to wrestle with removing the tail. In other words, if you know your guests are going to eat their shrimp with a fork, make them fork-friendly. If using fingers, the tail is the utensil. To de-tail, simply squeeze the remnant shell just in front of the tail fin, and with your other hand gently tug the shrimp out. Voila—ready to marinate and grill. Use the same technique to remove the cooked shrimp from the tail when eating them, gently squeezing with one and hand and pulling with your teeth.

Grilling Tech Talk

Shrimp are perfectly done when they appear white throughout the flesh, not opaque at all. Underdone shrimp are slightly limp. Don't try to re-grill them—it won't work. It's best to use underdone shrimp in a soup, chowder, or pasta sauce, where reheating won't turn them into rubber. Overdone shrimp are rubbery and dry. You can make them into shrimp paste for stuffing calamari or as an ingredient tossed into a seafood soup or chowder just before serving. Chop them small enough to be an accent rather than a key ingredient.

Hover over shrimp on the grill for perfect doneness–practice makes perfect.

My Foolproof Grilled Shrimp

We eat this grilled shrimp so often I don't have to measure ingredients. This is my favorite rushed dinner concept, so easy to prepare, and the grilling time is just a few minutes.

A pound of shrimp, about 21–25 pieces, is plenty for two people, with cold leftovers for snacking the next day or served with seafood sauce and evening cocktails.

Grilling Tech Talk

Skewers keep shrimp from falling through the grates and make flipping a one-step instant process. This is important because shrimp cook so quickly. Flat metal skewers prevent rotation of the shrimp as you flip them, but if they're not available, use two bamboo skewers. This will convince you to invest a couple bucks in flat metal ones. Always remove shrimp from metal skewers before serving because the skewers retain the heat. Use grill gloves or a thick wad of paper towel to handle metal skewers.

Grilled Shrimp

Ingredients
Freshly squeezed juice of one lemon
Zest of that lemon
¼ c olive oil
1 tsp Old Bay seasoning or 1 Tbs favorite jarred barbecue sauce
1 Tbs hot sauce
¼ c canola oil

Directions
Whisk all ingredients and marinate shrimp for up to half an hour. Remove from the marinade but don't rinse or wipe. Thread shrimp onto flat metal skewers or pairs of bamboo skewers. Grill on well-oiled grates over medium-high heat for about two minutes per side depending on size and heat (experiment to get your grilling time precise—this is critical for perfect shrimp).

Foolproof Shrimp Variations

You can get creative with different marinating ingredients on the general theme of acid, oil, and a flavoring accent. Marinate each of these variations for half an hour:

➤ Using lime juice instead of lemon juice, and adding ground coriander seeds, add a Mexican flavor, and a little cumin emphasizes that south-of-the-border touch.

➤ For a Cajun flavor, add store-bought Cajun spices to the Old Bay seasoning, use less Old Bay, and you can heat it up with a dash of cayenne.

➤ Substitute 1 tablespoon honey added to the oil and lemon or lime juice mixture. You'll love the deep sweetness of the slightly charred honey background. This is a family favorite.

➤ Infuse canola or other neutral oil with a generous heap of chopped fresh dill, use apple cider vinegar instead of lemon juice, and an abundance of ground black pepper.

➤ Chinese-inspired grilled shrimp is easy. Use sesame oil instead of the olive oil, but about half the amount because sesame oil is so assertive. Add seasoned rice vinegar and 1 tablespoon soy sauce. You can make it very spicy by adding 1 teaspoon of Chinese hot oil or a little sweeter with a dash of plum wine—or both for a hot and sour touch.

Tasty Tips

A general rule in grilling is not to use barbecue sauce until the last couple of minutes for meat, poultry, or fish. Barbecue sauce has sugar and tends to burn if used on food over direct heat. But shrimp are different. A little barbecue sauce in the oil you're using plus the brief shrimp grilling time inhibits burning and adds a nice smoky sweet accent. The same goes for a little honey added to the marinade oil.

Tasty Tips

Shrimp are smaller than most other grilled main courses, so they have a comparatively greater surface exposure to the marinade. As long as you don't marinate them for too long, about half an hour is right for most marinades, you can introduce unusual flavors that friends and family may find very appealing. Some recipes, however, call for a longer marinating time, so go ahead and build in lots of flavor. Follow recipes the first time and then take chances and experiment.

Shrimp, Hot or Cold

Everyone likes shrimp and most of us love it, especially hot off the grill. Something about the smoke, the caramelized sugar—grill lines—and the sweet meat itself. A combination of flavors that even seafood haters seem to enjoy. In Chapter 20, you'll find shrimp recipes from around the world, from the simplest straightforward recipes to more complicated and worth the trouble preparations.

Shrimp are so low in calories and fat that we all can enjoy them, one of the few foods you can eat too much of and still not feel guilty. The other guilt-free aspect of shrimp is if you make too much, the leftovers are just as good as the original. Cold shrimp with cocktail or remoulade sauce is a great way to start a festive evening. Or just add them to a salad for a light lunch or dinner.

CHAPTER 9

 **Grilling Shellfish**

> ## In This Chapter
>
> ➤ How to buy and prepare shellfish for the grill
> ➤ How to grill shellfish
> ➤ Shellfish flavorings and sauces

In this chapter we grill shellfish, from oysters to lobsters, from the simplest technique to more elaborate culinary delights. Shellfish have a natural insulation—their shell—which makes grillers a bit overconfident at times. Shellfish need attention, but the little extra effort is well worth it. for a great start, it's important to know how to approach buying shellfish.

Buying Shellfish

Buying your shellfish alive or frozen is key, and only a busy fish emporium should become your supplier. If there is a line at the counter and you have to take a number, you're in the right place. If you're lucky enough to live by the sea, it's relatively easy to find a reliable shellfish seller. But even in the heartland, you can enjoy reliably fresh or thawed shellfish from high-volume supermarket fish counters and big-box retailers like Costco.

Buying and Preparing Lobsters

No one ever called lobster boring, but if you've spent many summers on the Maine coast, as our family has, and bought those sweet, tasty crustaceans from a lobsterman neighbor right off his boat—well, even we got a little tired of steamed or boiled lobsters. So I learned to grill them. We never boil lobsters now because the grill produces a taste and texture that no other cooking method can equal—if you do it right. Before we get to lobster-grilling techniques, we should discuss buying and preparing lobsters for your grill.

Buy 1¼- to 1½-pound lobsters for the grill. These are the ideal sizes because the tail meat and claw meat will cook within the same time frame. They should be lively when you bring them home. Store them in the coldest part of the fridge in the bags your fishmonger gave you, or on a bed of ice in a cooler chest. Keep them out of fresh water—melting ice should be removed. Fresh water is poison to lobsters.

The outer limit for keeping live lobsters under refrigeration is about one day. But check frequently after twelve hours and cook immediately if they are dying. In that case, drop the lobsters into boiling water and half cook them, about six to eight minutes. Then cut them open, rinse out the intestines, etc., and store them up to another twelve hours in the coldest part of the fridge or wrapped and buried in ice before grilling.

Grill Speak

When we northerners say *lobsters*, we mean the clawed kind, famously the Maine lobster. Southerners mean the spiny lobster that's commonly found in Florida and the Gulf Coast. They are not related, don't look the same, and don't come to market in a similar state.

Typical clawed lobsters are sold alive and spiny lobsters are usually sold frozen, unless you're lucky enough to be in the Keys during the brief late summer lobster season for divers or have access to local commercial lobster retailers. When it comes to the grill, however, they are both easy to cook, and each provides a delicious low-calorie main course.

Buying and Preparing Spiny Lobsters

These clawless crustaceans are mostly from Florida and are almost always available frozen. Imported spiny lobsters from Africa, Australia, and as langoustines from Italy and the Mediterranean are all excellent grilled food.

Thaw them in cold water for an hour or so, or in the fridge for about a day—it will take that long for them to thaw. They are perishable, as are all shellfish, so use them within a day after they thaw.

Buying and Preparing Crabs

In my experience, it just doesn't seem worthwhile to grill crabs. It's too much work getting them ready for the grill and picking the meat afterwards. But there are two exceptions. Alaskan king crabs ("the deadliest catch") are available frozen and are not outrageously expensive when you consider the shell-to-meat ratio. They're often on sale at big-box stores. Thaw them in the fridge overnight or in cold water for an hour or so. They are wonderful on an aromatic charcoal and mesquite or gas and soaked woodchip fire.

Soft-shell crabs are the other exception. They're delicious and easy to grill. You eat the whole thing, so they're very rewarding. Once you've tasted grilled soft-shell crabs, you'll never eat deep-fried ones again. Have your seafood seller prepare them for cooking, and grill them within a few hours of purchase. West Coast grillers like Dungeness crab, but like all crabs they take some work. Get your fish guy to prepare them for the grill.

Buying and Preparing Oysters

Buy oysters only from a reliable source, and store them in a deep bowl at the bottom of the fridge for one to two days. If they are gaping, they are dead and useless. Easy to grill, oysters absorb flavored smoke and are an unforgettable treat for oyster lovers and a terrific choice for a grilled dinner party appetizer. Even folks who shy away from raw oysters can enjoy them grilled.

East Coast and Gulf Coast oysters are briny, metallic, and sweet. West Coast oysters are usually plumper and have a more muted flavor (this is East Coast prejudice talking, so you be the judge). Don't open them except if directed to by a specific recipe.

Buying and Preparing Clams

Like oysters, get your clams from a reliable fishmonger or gather them yourself if it's a safe and legal tidal area. Clams come in several sizes. The smaller ones are too delicate for the grill and the large quahogs or chowder clams are too tough.

Buy approximate 1½-inch diameter clams known as littlenecks or slightly larger cherrystones. Store them in a bowl in the bottom of the fridge for up to two days. Gaping clams are dead and useless. Don't open them except when directed to by a specific recipe.

Buying and Preparing Mussels

Despite that many expert grillers share their mussel recipes, I have an aversion to treating them this way. To me, the joy of mussels is the combination of a plump, succulent meat with a variety of exciting sauces and broths—and the bread mopping when you're done.

Mussels actually shrivel when grilled (as they do when they're baked, them by the way), the opposite of what you want to happen. And the sauce or broth becomes an afterthought rather than an integral part of the dish. Just like certain fin fish, not all shellfish are best grilled. With so many other shellfish possibilities, why ruin a delicious mussel with the intense dry heat from your gas or charcoal grill?

But if you insist—mussels are available in supermarkets, bagged and cleaned, and keep for two to three days in the fridge. Grilling recipes abound on the Internet, but none, in my opinion, produces a dish as good as mussels Provencal, Thai-flavored mussels, or mussels Posillipo from a stove top pot.

Buying and Preparing Scallops

The larger sea scallops that are about 1 inch thick are ideal for grilling, but you must pay careful attention. Remove the little muscle on the side, the abductor, which becomes chewy when grilled. Thoroughly dry scallops before grilling, using paper towels and pressing them gently. Scallops are best grilled briefly over direct high heat; too much time on the grill renders them rubbery and dry.

Grill Speak

To prevent too much loss of moisture, scallops are soaked in sodium tripolyphosphate (STP), which is a safe food additive but the enemy of effective grilling. STP enables scallops to add and retain water, as much as 40 percent more water by weight, and scallops are sold by the pound. Some chefs feel STP dilutes the sweet, delicate flavor of scallops. The extra moisture prevents scallops from searing and browning on the grill. Pay the extra cost of dry-packed or day boat scallops that have not been treated with STP. They feel drier and are sticky instead of wet. After grilling, you may end up with more actual scallop meat than you would with the wet-packed product.

Grilling Shellfish

It is easy yet quite impressive to grill shellfish. You'll find they are a perfect show-off dish for dinner parties because most grillers ignore these simple, natural appetizers or tasty main courses. No prep work at all is needed for clams and oysters, and only a little for most of the other shellfish. But it's easy to overcook shellfish so make sure you get your timing perfected for lobsters and crabs, and pay close attention to clams and oysters since the juice can boil off in seconds after they open, leaving a dried out tasteless morsel to weep over. Let's start with the more complicated and tastiest grilled shellfish, lobsters.

Grilling Tech Talk

Splitting a lobster for the grill is easy. Lay the lobster on a cutting board, feet side down. Kill it by cutting through the first carapace hinge just behind the head with your knife point. Then line the knife up with the direction of the lobster and work from the head section down to the tail, pressing the point of knife all the way through the shell, and then push down the blade through the back and tail until the lobster is split open. Clean out the intestines, etc., in cold running water. Don't worry about rinsing in cold water, you won't lose flavor. It's just a quick, easy way to get out the stuff you don't want cooking with your meat.

How to Grill Lobsters

Some grilling gurus invite us to treat lobsters as if we're baking them by simply placing them on the grates, closing the grill cover, and roasting whole for twelve to fifteen minutes. That will work, but what an opportunity you're missing. My foolproof, flavor-packed grilled lobsters are a little more work, but well worth the effort—just follow these steps:

1. Split the lobsters in half lengthwise with a sharp, heavy chef's knife or cleaver. You can leave the end of the tail attached, not split, or totally separated into two halves.

2. Combine olive oil and fresh-squeezed lime juice in equal proportions in a bowl.

3. Twist off the claws with their arms and crack the claws with the back of the knife or cleaver. Dip them in the olive oil and lime juice mixture.

4. Break or cut off the tail section from the main body. You can freeze the bodies and legs for making lobster broth later. Generously paint the tail meat with the olive oil and lime juice solution and rub a light coating of olive oil on the entire tail shell.

5. Place the lobster tails shell side down on the grates over direct medium-high heat and cook for about six to eight minutes on a covered coal or gas grill at about 350°F–400°F under the hood. Baste once or twice more with the olive oil and lime juice mixture.

6. At the same time, place the claws and arms on the grates and cook for about four to six minutes per side, flipping once.

7. Flip the tails. Grill meat side down for about two to four minutes more till meat is gently charred. The meat should be white in the center, but be careful not to overcook—lobsters get rubbery just like overcooked shrimp. Practice getting your grilling time right because each grill is slightly different, especially charcoal grills. If you find that the claws and tail meat are not getting done at the same time, start grilling the claws sooner or later for the timing they need.

8. Remove lobster pieces from the grill and place on a platter. Serve with more of the olive oil and lime juice mixture and melted butter for those who prefer that flavor.

Grilled Lobster Tastes So Good!

This combination of olive oil and lime juice, along with the light smoke from the hot oil on the shells, results in a luscious lobster that surpasses the boiled or steamed cooking method. The olive oil on the shell also helps transmit the heat.

If you and your guests prefer butter, you can substitute that for the olive oil and lime juice mixture—some fresh-squeezed lemon in the butter is a good touch.

Grilling Tech Talk

Lobster killing is no fun, even if you're not the least bit squeamish. Make it easy. Briefly plunge the lobsters into boiling water, about three minutes, and then let them cool before cutting them in half as described here. Or if you buy lobsters where they offer to cook them, ask the counter guys to cook your lobsters briefly, just enough to kill them. You can store these parboiled lobsters for a day in the fridge.

Keep It Simple

The key to easy lobster grilling is keeping it simple. By separately grilling the claws and tails, you're accounting for the time differences on the grates that these two body parts may require. By parboiling, either at the store or at home, you're eliminating the need to kill the lobsters with a knife, an unpleasant and difficult task for many of us. And using a basting liquid while you grill adds a flavor punch to the sweet meat.

Tasty Tips

No one disputes the grilling time for lobsters, which is about ten to twelve minutes total for split lobsters. But there is some controversy about which side down you start with. I'm a shell side down guy because whatever you're basting with—my favorite olive oil and lime juice mixture, for instance—you are going to grill the lobster longer on the insulated side, meaning the shell down side. More insulation, longer on the heat. This gives the basting liquid more time to flavor the meat since it's facing up, getting basted a couple of more times. Then flip and sear the meat for two to four minutes, sealing in that delicious olive oil and lime juice solution, and caramelizing the natural sugars. You're boosting the flavor when you grill this way.

Tasty Basting

You can have fun experimenting with basting mixtures. Here are some ideas:

➤ How about scampi? Melted butter, garlic, and lemon juice. Or a healthier version with olive oil instead of butter.

➤ For an Asian accent, try sesame oil, soy sauce, and ginger, or heat it up with a touch of Chinese hot oil.

➤ We like a pesto, olive oil and finely chopped basil or parsley processed with walnuts or pine nuts into a paste, then spooned onto the tail meat. In this version, I grill the lobster for the entire time shell side down for about ten to twelve minutes over indirect heat—roasting the split lobster tails. Or you can sear the meat first, then flip and grill for about six to eight minutes more after spooning the pesto onto the meat.

➤ For a touch of Cajun, try canola oil with Old Bay, and sprinkle hot sauce to taste.

Crabs on the Grill

As mentioned earlier, I'm not enamored of crabs as grilled food. Just too much work and not enough reward for all that effort—killing them, cleaning them, grilling, and then picking the meat. But king crabs are different, as are soft-shell crabs, both of which are favorites around our place.

King Crabs

Like lobsters, these large, meaty crustaceans do really well on the grates. Rub the shells with oil. If some of the larger pieces have exposed meat, you can brush them with an olive oil and lime juice mixture.

Break the legs into sections—the smaller ends need less time on the heat. Larger, thicker sections cook in about eight minutes, flipping once halfway through the cooking period, less time for thinner pieces. Be careful not to overcook because crab meat gets flaky when too well done, and it loses flavor as it changes in texture. You want silky meat with a hint of the oil-produced smoke.

Flavored wood chips such as apple and other fruit woods impart a subtle accent to this sweet crab taste. Keep it healthy with an olive oil and lemon or lime brushing and dipping sauce instead of using butter.

Soft Shell Crabs

You can buy soft shell crabs frozen, cleaned, and ready for cooking, or when in season, fresh at your better fish stores. The spring and early summer are when blue crabs shed their shell and briefly wear a paper-thin exoskeleton that will harden in a few days to protect the crab. This is when you can eat the entire crab, provided of course the unpleasant innards and carapace shell have been removed. You can do that yourself—but why? Let your fishmonger prepare your crabs for cooking or buy frozen, fully cleaned soft-shell crabs. Thaw them in the fridge for about eight hours or in warm water for less than an hour.

Like all shellfish, soft-shell crabs spoil rather quickly after they are killed, so grill them within eight hours after bringing them home from the fish store. It's hard to improve on the flavor of the crabs themselves, but grilling is better than sautéing. Brush them with olive oil and lemon or lime juice, grill over medium heat for about three to four minutes per side, and enjoy.

Tasty Basting

Here are some basting ideas to add special flavors to your soft shell crabs:

➤ Soft shell crabs are a Cajun country classic, so basting them with flavorings like Old Bay and filé, a sumac herb, infusing with a neutral oil like corn or canola.

➤ Grill Chinese soft-shell crabs brushed with sesame oil, Chinese Five Spice, and a touch of soy sauce.

➤ Add herbes de Provence to the olive oil and lemon juice mixture for a southern France theme, or finely chop in fresh basil and parsley for an Italian accent along with a little balsamic vinegar.

➤ Mix canola oil with a touch of your favorite barbecue sauce for a southern theme.

Never overpower the delicate taste of these crabs with too much of a good thing—let the crab be the star.

Clams and Oysters on the Grill

It's hard to improve on the taste sensation of raw clams and oysters. If you enjoy slurping these mollusks right out of the shell, you may not easily convert to grilling them. But there is good reason to do so. A flavored wood chip smoke like apple or cherry wood imparts a delicious undertone to clams and oysters. Grilling entices folks who may not like them raw to give them a try. And with a hint of smoke and a squirt of fresh squeezed lemon juice, oysters and clams on the grill are hard to beat.

Use tongs to gently remove them when done, which takes about six minutes over direct medium-high heat. Don't cook them too long, just till they open. A few minutes more and their juices will evaporate along with their flavor. Oysters should be grilled round or cup side down. Cooked oysters are safe to eat and very low in calories, so consume many without guilt or worry.

Grilling Tech Talk

Oysters and clams right off the grill are very hot, and their shells retain heat longer than you might think. So use tongs to remove them to a platter, and then while continuing to hold the lower shell with the tongs, use regular household pliers to remove the top shell. It will twist off easily. Then, still holding the shell with the tongs, slip a sharp knife beneath the meat to separate it from the shell. Your guests will appreciate this prepping for them, and with a little practice you'll get each oyster and clam ready to serve in seconds.

Tasty Tips

Open oysters before grilling and use the oyster knife to separate the meat from the shells. Create recipes using ingredients that please you and your guests, bits of bacon or prosciutto, minced garlic or shallots, and a creamy fresh mozzarella or Fontana cheese placed over each oyster. Put the shells on hot grates and grill for a few minutes till the cheese is melted. Warn your friends to be careful—the shells stay hot.

Scallops on the Grill

Sea scallops are large enough to grill without worrying they'll fall through the grates. You want dry-packed scallops. Ask your fishmonger or check the packaging for frozen scallops to be sure. Wet-packed scallops are soaked in STP, a harmless water retention agent, but they have so much moisture they don't brown and caramelize the way we grillers expect. Scallops cook quickly, about two minutes per side over direct high heat. Make sure your grates are clean and well oiled.

Simple Grilled Scallops

This preparation could not be easier. Mix 3—4 tablespoons olive oil and lime or lemon juice in equal amounts, salt and pepper to taste, and marinate scallops for a few minutes. Either place the scallops on the oiled grates with tongs or thread them onto bamboo skewers. Grilling for about three minutes per side is all you'll need—any longer and the scallops get rubbery. Scallops are thick enough to continue to cook off the grill, so err on undercooking till you become proficient. There is no need to soak the bamboo skewers—they won't burn during the short grilling time.

Tasty Tips

Scallops wrapped in bacon are a traditional variation, but I much prefer thin slices of prosciutto, Serrano, or similar aged hams. The reality is that bacon will not cook through, especially since it is side cooking, in the same time frame as the scallops. The cured hams are ready to eat and combined with the sweetness of the scallop make the perfect balance of salty and sweet. Much less fat, too.

Rosemary Scallops

For a crowd-pleasing meal, use rosemary sprigs as skewers, instead of bamboo, and add a touch of herbes de Provence to your olive oil and lemon juice mixture. Thread the scallops onto the rosemary sprigs after removing most of the leaves and side shoots, sliding the scallops with the grain of the leaves so you are not breaking them but rather enabling them to fold through each scallop. Don't crowd the sprigs with scallops so there is room for browning between each. Grill about three minutes per side and serve immediately.

Shellfish Celebrations

We never tire of lobsters and other shellfish on the grill. All are low in calories, low in fat, and full of nutrients we need for a well-rounded diet. They are a tasty treat as part of a weight-loss program. For recipes and more grilling ideas, turn to Chapter 20, where I've gathered our favorite ways to make shellfish—a family dinner treat and often the centerpiece when we entertain.

CHAPTER 10

 Shell-less Shellfish on the Grill

In This Chapter

➤ Health benefits of grilling squid and octopus

➤ How to buy and prepare squid and octopus

➤ How to grill squid and octopus

Both squid and octopus are underappreciated in American cuisine. If we have any familiarity at all with squid, most of us encounter it as fried calamari rings in pub food. Which means fried onion rings or French fries with a slight, and I mean perhaps a very faint, taste of the sea. Usually it has no taste at all except salt and oil. Octopus? Forget about it, an "ick" food if there ever was one.

What a shame. Squid is a deliciously versatile shell-less shellfish, and octopus is a succulent appetizer or main course for even timid eaters—if prepared correctly. Both are easy low-fat, high-protein ingredients that your friends and family will enjoy as a change of pace from shrimp and lobster. And they are among the most economical foods you'll find at the fish counter. Forget about fatty frying. These tasty sea creatures are made for your grill.

Nutritious Shell-less Shellfish

Squid and octopus are good sources of iron, potassium, and B vitamins. Octopus also provides plenty of zinc, an essential mineral often missing in our diet. Best of all, these two grilling treats are very low in calories. Here are the stats:

➤ Squid (calamari) are about 25 calories per ounce, giving you a generous 8-ounce serving of grilled squid for about 200 calories. A dieter's delight.

➤ Octopuses weigh in at about 30–35 calories per ounce, and, as with squid, nearly all those calories are protein, not fat.

➤ When you grill squid and octopus, you are adding very little to the calorie count because the oil you use in a marinade drips down into the coals or flavor bars in a gas grill. Compared to frying or sautéing, grilling is significantly lower in fat and calories—good for all, no matter what their waist size.

Grilling Tech Talk

Squid are widely available already cleaned, fresh or frozen. You can buy octopuses frozen at many supermarkets or fresh at good fish retailers. Your fishmonger will thoroughly clean them and get them ready to grill. You will not find a more convenient main seafood course for a quick grilled dinner.

Buying and Preparing Squid and Octopus

Squid are widely available already cleaned, fresh or frozen. You can buy octopuses frozen at many supermarkets or fresh at good fish retailers. Your fishmonger will thoroughly clean them and get them ready to grill. You will not find a more convenient main seafood course for a quick grilled dinner

Squid

Although cleaning squid is easy, I always buy them cleaned. This saves a little work at virtually no extra cost. Squid are quite inexpensive, usually under $5 a pound.

Thaw frozen squid in warm water in less than an hour, or overnight in the fridge, and grill the next day. The big, thick California squid make a succulent calamari steak dinner, whereas the East Coast squid tubes, smaller and thinner, can be grilled in a flash or stuffed and grill-roasted. Squid should be grilled briefly or they become rubbery.

Octopus

Always buy cleaned octopus or get your fishmonger to prepare it for the grill. Octopuses are somewhat difficult to clean, and it's not worth the effort to learn unless you are very motivated.

Older large octopuses have to be braised for a considerable time, at least an hour, to become edible. Use only the tentacles. Simply marinate them in olive oil and lemon juice. Give them a quick searing on the grill to create an octopus lover's dream come true. I usually buy baby octopuses, which can be grilled without braising (although I always braise them anyway for flavor enhancement and tenderizing), and marinade them.

Braise baby octopuses for up to an hour, and marinate them for one to four hours, according to recipes. You can braise a day or two in advance and store the octopuses, ready to grill, in the coldest part of your fridge. A good fishmonger will fully prepare them for your grill and advise on braising.

Grilling Tech Talk

If you are well organized and plan ahead, you can thaw squid and octopuses overnight in the fridge. Place them in a bowl and cover with plastic wrap.

But I'm usually not that well organized. I thaw them in warm tap water. If they are individually wrapped in plastic, I just immerse them in warm water. If not, I run warm water over the frozen bundle and gently pry apart the individual pieces and immerse them in warm water.

As long as you check frequently, and chill the squid or octopus immediately after thawing, this method is safe and will not promote bacterial growth. The thawing time is so short you will not risk spoilage. Then, if you are marinating, keep the squid or octopuses in the fridge till ready to grill.

How to Grill Squid

Next to lobster, my favorite grilled shellfish is squid, in part because it's a shell-less shellfish and, even better, it's so versatile. You can grill it like a steak, grill it on skewers, in the tube shape, or in strips. Best of all, grilling stuffed squid offers a world of flavor and texture possibilities.

Have your fishmonger clean the squid for you and keep the tube and tentacles whole. Unlike most other fish and shellfish, squid should marinate about an hour or even more due to their dense texture. Simple marinades are best: olive oil, lemon juice, and herbs for a Mediterranean theme; or sesame oil, rice vinegar, and soy sauce or Vietnamese fish sauce for an Asian accent. Adding other flavors in keeping with the country cuisine or hemisphere, east or west, is certainly appropriate.

The tasting possibilities for squid are as plentiful as their enormous schools in every ocean. Almost all cuisines on the planet include tasty squid preparations, so you have a world of possibilities.

Grill squid tubes, tentacles, or strips for two to three minutes per side, no more than four or five minutes total over direct high heat. They taste rubbery if cooked less or more. If the squid are stuffed, you must cook the ingredients you're inserting so they don't require more than a total of four or five minutes to reach eating temperature. If you are stuffing way ahead and refrigerating before your guests arrive, I suggest you put the squid in the microwave for a minute to warm the stuffing. Then grill for the normal two to three minutes per side. But be sure to practice with one or two squid ahead of time, all microwaves and grills are slightly different. Thread tentacles or squid strips and rings onto skewers for ease of turning and for keeping them on the grates. Tubes need not be skewered.

Marinated Grilled Squid

Ingredients
¼ c fresh-squeezed lemon juice
¼ c olive oil
1 tsp crushed dry rosemary
½ tsp fennel seeds
½ tsp kosher salt

Directions
Mix all ingredients and marinate squid for at least one hour—two or three is fine. Then follow one of these variations:

> ➤ Grill whole squid bodies or steaks for about two to three minutes per side, flipping once

> ➤ Thread squid strips or squid rings onto bamboo skewers and grill for two to three minutes per side

> ➤ Slice thick West Coast squid into steaks, score the meat with shallow cuts in a crosshatch pattern, and grill for three to four minutes per side, flipping once. Grill tentacles separately on bamboo skewers for about two minutes per side till achieving a char.

Fat Fighters

Squid are healthy and satisfying in a weight-loss program. They are a good source of phosphorus and B vitamins and are only about 25 calories an ounce. That means you can grill a half pound of squid and eat a delicious, filling main course for around 200 calories. Even most stuffings will add only 100 or so calories per serving. The oil you apply in a marinade or brush on is mostly gone through the grates when the squid are ready to eat. Grilled squid on a bed of lightly dressed arugula and fennel salad makes dieting a pleasure, not a task.

Grilled Squid Variations

These recipes are usually quite simple because in many cultures squid are an everyday, plentiful source of good protein. You'll find several easy and creative ways to deliver this wholesome goodness to your family.

Figure about half a pound of squid per person and buy squid whole with tentacles attached. All you need to do is grill them just as they are, or you can pull off the tentacles to grill separately (or chop up for stuffing). It's easy to slice the body into rings, strips, or steaks. All these preparations below are for four diners.

Asian Grilled Squid

Keep tubes and tentacles whole or cut tubes into rings and skewer

Ingredients
¼ c honey or brown sugar
¼ c soy sauce
¼ c rice vinegar
1 Tbs minced garlic or to taste
1 Tbs minced ginger
A dash of hot pepper flakes or cayenne
1 tsp salt

Directions
Whisk the first three ingredients together to fully blend, then mix in the rest of the ingredients. Marinate the squid for one hour. Thread tentacles and rings onto bamboo skewers—no need to soak the skewers because they'll only be briefly exposed to high heat. Grill over direct high heat for about two to three minutes per side, flipping once.

Tasty Tips

Barbecued squid are to Koreans like burgers are to Americans—street food, restaurant fare, and essential in a festive family cookout. You can make authentic Korean grilled squid by brushing Asian marinated squid with gochujiant just before placing them on the grates. This Korean chili paste in a jar is available in all Korean grocery stores and most well-stocked Asian sections of supermarkets. It adds a spicy accent that most folks enjoy.

Barbecued Squid

One of the more interesting taste idiosyncrasies of squid, at least in my mind, is that it is terrific in an Italian red sauce over pasta, your basic old-fashioned tomato sauce, however it does not seem to do well with a tomato-based barbecue sauce. But I love grilled squid brushed with Carolina-style mustard and vinegar barbecue sauce.

Ingredients
Standard olive oil and lemon marinade (leave out the herbs)
1 tsp Old Bay Seasonings or black pepper to taste or both
Squid
Carolina-style barbecue sauce

Directions
Add seasonings to the standard olive oil and lemon marinade. Marinate the squid for one to three hours. Place whole squid bodies or steaks on a hot grill, brush with Carolina-style barbecue sauce, grill for about three minutes, then flip. Brush again, grill, and serve.

Squid Overload

A few years ago while fishing in the Gulf of Maine, I ran into a huge school of squid. I'd been jigging for cod but suddenly found my jig covered with squid. Again and again. A kind of feeding frenzy overcame me and I loaded the floor of my boat with far too many squid, a memory I'm not proud of. As penance, I decided to use these squid in every meal for the next few days, as long as my family and friends could stand it. But instead of this becoming a chore, an apology to nature for my thuggish behavior, we all increasingly enjoyed the variations and creative challenge.

I grilled the bodies, stuffed the bodies, combined squid with other fish, made seafood salads, pasta sauce, and risotto. The point here is that squid is so versatile, so user-friendly for the creative cook, that you can use this inexpensive shell-less shellfish often to the delight of friends and family.

How to Grill Octopus

Buy cleaned, ready-to-cook baby octopuses, fresh or frozen. If frozen, thaw overnight or for about an hour in warm tap water. Braise them in red wine and water, half and half, for an hour, then rinse, pat dry, and marinate in olive oil and lemon juice for one to three hours. Grill over high heat for three minutes per side till nicely charred. Cut the tentacles off and serve only those, discarding the head. The braising can be done a day or two ahead.

Marinated Grilled Octopus

If your grill timing is off on either side of five or six minutes, it won't really matter. You've already tenderized the octopus so it won't be rubbery from a few minutes of under or overcooking. You can do the two cooking methods hours or even a day apart, keeping the braised octopus tentacles in the fridge till ready to marinate and grill. Some kids love the concept of eating octopus. It gives them bragging rights. It is very nutritious and low in calories. It is delicious served cold in a salad too.

Ingredients
¼ c fresh-squeezed lemon juice
¼ c olive oil
1 tsp crushed dry rosemary or 1 tsp dried oregano instead for a Greek accent
½ tsp fennel seeds
½ tsp kosher salt

Directions
After the octopus has braised for at least one hour and cooled, marinate it for one to three hours. Grill the tentacles over high heat for three to five minutes per side till nicely charred. Serve with a squeeze of lemon and a splash of olive oil.

Large Octopus

Octopuses weighing over 2 pounds are edible only after braising for at least an hour in salted or flavored water—flavors like bay leaf, wine, cinnamon, or other favorite herbs or spices. No rules here. This is rustic fisherman food. After braising for at least one hour or more, depending on size, remove the tentacles and use paper towel to remove most of the purple skin. Marinate the tentacles in olive oil and lemon juice, or marinades using other oil and acid ingredients, for an hour or two, or more up to eight hours. Grill over high heat on well-oiled grates for four to six minutes per side till nicely charred. Serve with a splash of your best olive oil.

Grilling Tech Talk

Let's face it, octopus is an unfamiliar food to many of us, but don't let that frighten you off. The cooking is not really done on the grill—it's the braise that does that. Braising couldn't be easier. Partly immersed in simmering liquid in a covered pot on the stove or in the oven, the octopus cooks flawlessly. You can't mess this up.

Later, when grilling the tentacles, you are not really cooking them. Instead, you're giving them a nice char, heating them through and flavoring them with the marinade ingredients and smoke. It's hard to mess up that part too.

Korean Grilled Octopus

Korean cuisine always has some hot ingredient, in this case chili powder, and garlic. After you've braised 2 pounds of baby octopus (to serve six people) for up to an hour in water, remove the tentacles and discard the head.

Ingredients
½ c minced onion
½ medium-size sweet red pepper, minced
4 garlic cloves, minced
2 Tbs soy sauce
1 Tbs sesame oil
1 tsp hot chili powder or ½ tsp Chinese hot oil to taste
½ tsp black pepper

Combine all the ingredients. Marinate braised octopus tentacles in this mixture for an hour. Grill over high heat for two to three minutes per side for no more than eight minutes total, till octopus is charred.

Grilled Italian Octopus

After tenderizing 2 pounds of octopus in a braising liquid of red wine and water, about half and half, for at least an hour, remove the tentacles, discard the head, rinse, and pat dry.

Whisk together:

¼ c olive oil
¼ c balsamic vinegar

2 Tbs freshly squeezed lime juice
2 Tbs fresh Italian parsley, minced
1 Tbs fresh rosemary, crushed
Salt and pepper to taste

Marinate octopus for an hour. Grill over high heat for two to three minutes per side till octopus is nicely charred, no more than eight minutes total. Garnish with more chopped parsley.

CHAPTER 11

Grilled Vegetables

In This Chapter

➤ The nutrition in vegetables

➤ How grilling boosts the flavor of vegetables

➤ Grilling surprise vegetables

➤ Spicing up ordinary vegetables

In this chapter we explore the world of grilled vegetables—not just why they are good for us, we all know that, but how to make them good to eat. Nothing else we eat has as much of the essential nutrients we need as vegetables, and most veggies are composed of the soluble fiber that enables us to digest this food efficiently.

Fiber slows our digestion and helps regulate the way our body converts fructose and complex sugars to glucose, the form we need to fuel our muscles. Fiber helps our bodies do this without packing on fat calories. In the same way, a high-fiber diet also tends to protect us against diabetes by regulating insulin production.

Losing weight, or maintaining a desired weight over the long term, is a struggle for many of us. A diet rich in vegetables can make that battle a lot easier. Best of all, when you grill veggies, you're creating the healthiest, tastiest food for your loved ones—with a minimum of extra work for you. One thing doctors, nutritionists, and the rest of us all agree on—eating more vegetables is really good for you, your family, and your weight-control diet.

Fat Fighters

Experts agree that a safe and effective weight-loss strategy should be long-term. It's important to include moderate exercise as part of any weight-loss diet to ensure gradual weight loss over many months. This gradual weight-loss principle suggests that we should consume an average of 1,800–2,000 calories a day for most women and 2,000–2,200 for most men, understanding, of course, that individuals vary in metabolism and other weight-affecting factors. When you achieve your weight goal, you can then increase this caloric intake slightly, about 10 percent, to maintain your weight. Consuming more of your daily calories in fruit and vegetables will keep you feeling good and even your sweet tooth can be satisfied.

Vegetables—the Cornerstone of a Healthy Diet

No single food category is more essential to maintaining your ideal weight than vegetables. Not only are they necessary for our overall health, they also make weight control easier because vegetables are low in fat and calories, high in fiber, and they come in so many delicious varieties. But when you mention vegetables in your menu planning, it is not uncommon for family members to frown or, worse, toss off that ugly word *whatever*, meaning not interested—don't even try. And you can't blame them. Many of us learned to eat vegetables at a school cafeteria or were served a tasteless fresh vegetable boil at home. Boiling, even steaming, tends to wash out the flavor along with some of the nutrients. Grilling concentrates both.

Highest Nutrition at the Lowest Calorie Cost

Vegetables are packed with essential vitamins and minerals, and they deliver this nutrition at the lowest calorie cost. You can eat all the veggies you want and still stay within your caloric budget. The problem is most of us don't want to eat lots of vegetables, so we take exactly the wrong strategy—we try to hide them under sauces or inside other foods.

Stand in front of a supermarket freezer display, and you are overwhelmed with cheesy, creamy, buttery sauces that suppress the clean, sweet, or savory natural taste of fresh veggies. Those sauces are an easy way to gain weight. Vegetables, treated with love and respect, need no disguise. They can be the stars on your dinner plate.

Tasty Grilled Vegetables

The taste of just about any fresh vegetable is improved by the grill. The dry heat of charcoal or gas burners quickly reduces the amount of moisture in the vegetable. Less moisture, more flavor. A light coating of olive oil produces a bit of smoke as it drips to the coal or burners, and these earthy flavors are absorbed by the veggie. Grill marks appear after a few minutes. These are produced by a combination of the oil in contact with the grates and the natural sugars caramelizing on the surface of the vegetables. The sweetness of veggies is enhanced by this process.

Tasty Tips

More often than not we boil or steam vegetables, especially when we're trying to lose weight. But think about what this does to the flavor. You are actually adding moisture, in this case neutral-tasting water, diluting the vegetable's flavor. In contrast, grilling concentrates the natural flavors of veggies by reducing the moisture and intensifying the sweetness through caramelization.

Grill Vegetables with Care

Be careful not to overcook vegetables when you're grilling them. They should end up firm but cooked through. You'll know when your veggies are overcooked when they are limp and often have a slightly bitter taste. If you've brushed them with a little olive oil, which is highly recommended, remember olive oil begins to burn at about 450°F. So keep the heat at medium and pay attention to the cooking time.

Overcooked vegetables get mushy and too brown. You want your

Tasty Tips

Salt brings out the best in most vegetables, but it's more than just a flavor enhancer. For those veggies with a high moisture content like tomatoes and eggplant, sprinkle lightly with salt and leave them in a colander for about half an hour before grilling. Salt draws the excess moisture out of the veggies—you'll see it in the bowl beneath the colander. This prevents steaming on the grates and helps caramelize the natural sugars. You need only brush lightly with olive oil and grill for the best-tasting vegetables.

veggies *al dente*, meaning they slightly resist as you bite through them. The grill marks are attractive, but they should be marks, not a dark brown patina across most of the vegetable's surface. As a general rule, grill your veggies over medium heat so they cook internally without burning on the outside.

Grilling Tech Talk

Be sure to keep your grates clean when grilling vegetables. This is a good practice any time, but for veggies it's especially vital. Most vegetables have a rather delicate flavor and the residue of previously cooked foods can ruin their taste. Salmon, for instance, is a lovely grilled fish but old burned salmon bits stuck to the grates and flavoring your zucchini is a real turnoff.

Tasty Tips

Instead of salt, you can use Thai fish sauce (or Vietnamese, which is a little stronger). Fish sauce is a glutamate that does magical things to the innate flavors of meat, poultry, Asian noodles, and grilled veggies. Although it is made from fermented fish, usually anchovies, it has no fish taste and should not be confused with the anchovy fillets most of you don't want on your pizza but are a required ingredient in Caesar salad dressing and the basis of a good Sicilian-style tomato sauce. The Japanese call fish sauce *umami*, slang for yummy, and you'll agree when you add just a little, a teaspoon or less in place of the salt, to the olive oil you paint on grilled zucchini, summer squash, sliced onions, and similar grilled vegetable favorites.

Salty Advice

When grilling vegetables, always use kosher salt, and not just because a rabbi might be dropping by for dinner. The reason serious cooks prefer kosher salt for most grilled dishes is the style of the salt rather than its relationship to the Almighty.

Kosher salt is coarser than table salt and is free of the added iodine that is an important dietary supplement (like vitamin D added to milk). Since we get iodine from the salt added to processed foods, and from our table salt shaker, most of us don't need more.

Like sea salt, which almost always is more expensive because it's processed differently, kosher salt adds a hint of crunchiness to grilled veggies. Both salts are composed of larger crystals and are therefore less "salty" per teaspoon than table salt. In other words, finer-grained table salt has more salt per volume measure. Consider this when salting to a volume, not weight, measurement. Always taste when using different kinds of salt because, in fact, they are different. Kosher and sea salts add an important taste dimension to most grilled foods, especially to veggies.

Keeping It Simple

Especially in the beginning of your vegetable grilling experimentation, treat your vegetables gently and minimally. You need to get to know them, unadorned, without spice.

Start with veggies you know and trust like zucchini, summer or yellow squash, asparagus, and mushrooms. They're easy to grill, usually plentiful, and inexpensive enough to waste if you make some mistakes in your early grilling days. All you need is olive oil, salt, and perhaps a splash of lemon juice—and the hot grates to sear in the attractive grill marks, caramelize the natural sugars, and deepen the flavor without adding any cover-up or fattening adornments. Fresh, natural, and healthy.

Mushroom Magic

Grilling big portobello 'shrooms is as simple as it gets. Give them a quick rinse to remove any dirt, air-dry on a towel, brush with olive oil, and sprinkle on some kosher salt. Grill as you would a burger over medium heat for three to five minutes a side. You'll know they're done by gently pressing—when the mushroom feels soft and yielding, it's time to eat.

Grilling Tech Talk

Professional chefs are always instructing us to carefully clean mushrooms with a soft bristle brush or damp paper towel; they say never wash them or immerse them in water. I disagree. I clean 'shrooms by gently rubbing them with my hands under cold running water. It's quick, effective, and easy. I then place them on a kitchen towel and let them air-dry before grilling or cooking them in a pot. I've never had a problem—they taste exactly the same as the painstakingly brushed ones, but I cleaned them in a quarter of the time. After all, in their wild state they grow in rainy forests.

Squash Magic

Slice yellow squash and zucchini the long way into ¼-inch-thick slabs. Lightly sprinkle kosher salt on them and if they seem very moist to you, leave them in a colander for about half an hour to lose some of their moisture. Brush them with olive oil, perhaps add a little more salt and pepper to taste, and grill for two minutes over medium heat. Turn the slices same side down for another two minutes to sear in some grill marks in an attractive crosshatch pattern. Flip and repeat. Make sure you don't overcook these. They should retain some *al dente* mouthfeel. Mushy grilled squash is unappealing.

Tasty Tips

One of the nice things about grilled zucchini, yellow squash, and similar vegetables is that you can serve them hot off the grill or later at room temperature—they're delicious both ways. If I'm serving vegetables later, I like to add good-quality roasted Italian sweet peppers right from the jar and thinly sliced sweet onions to create a pleasing grilled salad. Add a few shakes of balsamic vinegar over this appealing plate of vegetables. This makes a good after-school snack for kids or a low-calorie take-to-work lunch for adults.

Carrot Magic

There are two ways to grill carrots, and both produce sweeter, tastier results than boiling or steaming. Use the biggest carrots you can find, and the fresher the better—look for leafy green tops attached. Cut into 4- to 6-inch lengths and then carefully cut about a ¼-inch slice off one side. Roll the carrot onto its new flat side for stability, and continue cutting ¼-inch slabs. Or you can use a vegetable peeler and slice the 4- 6-inch carrots into paper-thin strips. For both styles, brush on olive oil and then salt to taste.

Grill the ¼-inch slabs over medium-low heat for about eight minutes, flipping every few minutes till carrots are golden with some brown grill marks—cooked through but not mushy. Don't let them get dark brown. Serve right off the grill or at room temperature later.

Grill the peeler slices briefly over medium-high heat for one to two minutes per side, and remove while they still have a bit of crunch. Serve immediately or later. Add them to your antipasto for more varied tastes on that beautiful plate of grilled veggies. Either way, the natural sugars are concentrated and caramelized, resulting in carrots that excite the taste buds.

Tasty Tips

An assortment of grilled vegetables makes a wonderful antipasto. It can also be served to the family as a side vegetable or in place of a salad, especially in winter when fresh lettuce can be expensive and not very fresh. You can't beat this for convenience because you can make it a couple of days ahead and refrigerate until an hour or so before serving.

And for entertaining, you can really dress up a grilled vegetable antipasto by arranging the veggies on your most festive platter, then sprinkling on fresh herbs, edible flowers, and coarsely grated pecorino or parmesan cheese. Finish off with a light drizzle of fine extra-virgin olive oil and a splash of fresh lemon juice or balsamic vinegar. Serve at room temperature for maximum flavor.

Vegetable Magic

After you've perfected the more common grilling vegetables, it's time to move out of this new comfort zone. I can't think of a vegetable you can't grill—even thawed frozen peas in a perforated grill pan are sweet and succulent hot off the grill. As I've stated several times, keep it simple. Grill veggies regularly, mix and match, grill veggies in season when they are inexpensive and delicious, grill them out of season to improve their flavor. If you desire, use your favorite soaked hardwood chips on the burner for a smoky accent (a chip box is very useful, be sure to keep one with your gas grill accessories).

Here are some ideas for grilling vegetables that are less commonly seen on the grill.

Tomatoes

Slice beefsteak or other large tomatoes about ½ inch thick, or cut wedges from smaller tomatoes. Lightly salt both sides and arrange on a grate to drain into a sink or sheet pan. After about thirty minutes, the tomatoes have lost enough juice to prepare for the grill.

Brush the tomato slices or wedges lightly with olive oil, place them on oiled grates over medium heat, and grill for about three minutes per side till tomatoes are slightly charred but still retain their shape. Serve hot or at room temperature. You can add a splash of balsamic vinegar later or brush on mayonnaise while they're still hot.

Cherry Tomatoes

Thread cherry tomatoes onto bamboo or thin metal skewers with a little space between each. Brush with olive oil and salt. Grill for three to five minutes over medium heat, turning as needed till tomatoes are blistered but maintain their shape. Serve hot or at room temperature with balsamic vinegar if desired. Add fresh herbs—basil, parsley, mint, or others.

Grilling Tech Talk

When grilling vegetables, always make sure the grates are clean, have no residue from previously cooked foods, and are oiled just before cooking with canola or other neutral high-heat oil (not olive oil). There is no need to soak bamboo skewers since your burner heat will usually be set on medium and grilling time is relatively short, so the skewers won't burn. But if you're using butcher twine to tie a bunch of vegetables, soak the twine in water first.

Eggplant

Cut eggplant crosswise into ¼-inch slices, lightly salt, and place on a grate over a sink or sheet pan. After about thirty minutes, much of the juice will have drained, and the eggplant slices will be ready for grilling. Brush with olive oil and grill for about ten minutes over medium heat, turning and flipping as needed to achieve attractive grill marks, cooked through but not mushy. Serve hot with a sprinkle of fresh lemon juice or at room temperature with a dash of fine extra-virgin olive oil. Fresh chopped oregano leaves added on the plate when serving adds another flavor dimension.

Fennel Bulbs

For a smaller fennel, cut the bulb lengthwise in half with stems attached to hold the fennel in place (cut off stems when done and freeze to flavor soups).

For larger fennel, cut across the bulb and secure the rings with slim bamboo skewers or strong wood toothpicks to prevent slices from separating during cooking. Brush with olive oil and sprinkle with kosher salt. Grill for about ten minutes over medium heat, flipping two or three times till grill marks appear and fennel is cooked through. Serve warm or at room temperature with a dash of extra-virgin olive oil.

Leeks

Cut off the green tops then slice lengthwise in half. Gently peel back the layers and rinse leeks as you normally would but keep the layers intact. Arrange cut side down on a towel to dry for about thirty minutes. Push through two or three strong wooden toothpicks across the layers so that the leek is kept together during cooking. Brush lightly with olive oil, sprinkle with kosher salt, and grill over medium heat for eight to ten minutes, flipping two or three times till cooked through. Serve hot or at room temperature, adding a splash of balsamic vinegar if desired.

Sweet Peppers

Cut an attractive assortment of green, red, yellow, and orange peppers into quarters, removing ribs and seeds, rinse, and gently flatten. Pat dry, sprinkle with kosher salt, and grill over medium heat for about six to eight minutes, flipping several times. Peppers should be soft and flexible when done. Serve at room temperature with a splash of extra-virgin olive oil and add balsamic or red wine vinegar if desired.

You can also grill-roast whole red peppers. Place them on the grates over medium-high heat, rotate them every three minutes or so as they char, and when soft and blistered remove and slice. Serve these with a splash of olive oil and a sprinkle of salt and pepper.

Asparagus

You've seen them adorning antipasto platters in upscale Italian restaurants, and they couldn't be easier to make at home. Trim the asparagus, removing the woody bottom part of the spear. If they're too fat, use a vegetable peeler to even out the thickness of the remaining lower part of the spear. Brush with olive oil and salt. Grill over medium heat for about six to eight minutes, turning as needed several times. Asparagus are done when attractive grill marks appear and the spear is wilted but still *al dente*. Serve hot or at room temperature. Sprinkle balsamic vinegar and a fine extra-virgin olive oil just before serving.

Grilling Tech Talk

Prevent layered and some leafy vegetables from falling apart and through the grates by pushing a toothpick or two through the layers from the side. But only use round hardwood toothpicks that will stand up to the heat and not splinter in the veggie. Never use plastic. The same goes for twine, which is useful for holding a small bunch of green onions, arugula, or similar veggies. Use only natural cotton butcher twine, soaked for a couple of minutes, not elastic or synthetic twine, which will melt.

Radicchio

Use the smallest heads you can find and cut in half lengthwise, retaining the root end to keep the layers together. Push a toothpick sideways through the leaves near the other end. Brush all over with olive oil. Grill uncut side down for two minutes over medium heat, then flip and grill cut side down for about four minutes till soft but not mushy. Serve warm or at room temperature, or cut into pieces and spread over other grilled vegetables in an antipasto or grilled salad. This smoky, slightly bitter veggie gives blander vegetables a good flavor kick, and grilling radicchio seems to soften its bitterness a bit.

Green Onions (Scallions)

Trim root ends of two or three bunches of green onions, and tie the bunches with butcher twine at the middle of the green ends. Fan out the bulb ends of the onions, sprinkle with olive oil and kosher salt, and grill over medium heat for about six to eight minutes, flipping several times till onions are slightly browned and cooked through. Cut off the green parts according to your taste. Serve hot with steak or chicken, or at room temperature as part of an antipasto or side salad.

Romaine Lettuce (or Other Large Leafy Lettuce)

Remove, rinse, and dry the larger outer leaves. Sprinkle with olive oil and kosher salt. Grill briefly, a minute or less, till seared over medium heat, flipping once. Serve at room temperature as a base for a summer tomato salad, or tear pieces into a mixed grilled vegetable salad.

You can also grill the inner, lighter green leaves as a single bunch kept intact by the root end. Oil and salt the outer leaves, grill a couple of minutes on each turn of the lettuce, just until you get nice grill marks, but be careful not to burn the leaves. Serve warm with a little more olive oil and lemon juice or balsamic vinegar.

Vidalia Onions (or Other Sweet Onions)

Peel and cut crosswise into ¼-inch slices, or thicker if desired. Secure with a toothpick so layers don't separate. Brush with olive oil, sprinkle with salt, and grill for about six to eight minutes till grill marks appear and onions are softened. Or you can brush with sesame oil and a splash of soy sauce for a hint of China.

Sweet onions are great grilled medium-rare, just a couple of minutes per side, retaining much of their crunch. When we grill a steak we always include these onions, placed on the grates over direct heat when the steak moves to the indirect heat part of the grill for the roasting phase.

Grilling Tech Talk

An essential tool for grilling vegetables is a perforated pan, somewhat akin to a shallow colander, or a flat, holed, rectangular grate topper that is designed to grill smaller vegetables while preventing them from falling through the grates. These are perfect for grilling small mushrooms such as button, cremini, oyster, shitake (stems removed), and others.

Does your family hate string beans? Not if they're grilled. Use a grill pan for these—and even for peas. Sprinkle with olive oil and herbs or spices when grilling.

Mushrooms

Wash and dry button mushrooms, cremini (baby bellas), oyster mushrooms, or other smaller mushrooms. Thread top to bottom on bamboo skewers, brush with olive oil, salt, and grill for about six to eight minutes, turning as needed till 'shrooms are cooked through. Or you can use a vegetable grill pan or grate topper, grilling the mushrooms whole or sliced. For a Chinese variation, brush with sesame oil and sprinkle with soy sauce.

String Beans, Sugar Snap Peas, Wax Beans, or Other Long, Slim Beans

Arrange whole beans on the vegetable grate topper, sprinkle olive oil and salt over the beans, and grill for three to five minutes. Using a spatula, gently flip the beans in batches—don't worry if you miss a few—and grill for another two to three minutes. Use the spatula to remove the beans when slightly charred and cooked through.

Chickpeas (Garbanzo Beans)

This is one of our family favorites. Use rinsed, canned chickpeas, or cook them from dried in simmering water according to package directions. Spread them out on a baking sheet to air-dry.

Toss chickpeas in a bowl with a little olive oil and salt, just enough to give each a light coating of the oil. One tablespoon of oil is enough for a whole can of chickpeas. Spread the oiled, salted chickpeas on the baking sheet. Grill-roast over low indirect heat with the grill top closed for forty-five minutes to an hour. Your grill thermometer should read about 300°F. Add soaked mesquite or other aromatic wood in the grill for smoke. Every fifteen minutes or so, give them a shake so they roast evenly. Chickpeas are done when they have roasted to a nutty consistency with virtually all their moisture gone. Chickpeas are a nutritious lower calorie alternative to peanuts, and have an earthy, smoky flavor.

Cool and store in a container in the fridge for handy, healthy snacking. You can do this in your kitchen oven when the weather turns cold, but the grill is better when you have the AC on in your home.

Grilling Tech Talk

You can add flavor without calories to many grilled vegetables by using aromatic wood in your grill. Soak a small handful of mesquite, apple, pecan, or similar wood (see Resources section) for thirty minutes. Bundle the wood in aluminum foil, poke some holes, and lay the bundle directly on the flavor bars or charcoal away from the vegetables you are grilling. Better yet, buy a wood chip box for convenient wood smoke whenever you want it. When the wood begins smoking, you can begin grilling. Delicious! (Keep a water spray bottle handy to douse any wood chip flames. Always water-spray chips till extinguished after grilling.)

Tasty Tips

For all the vegetable treatments above, always grill with the cover closed, whether using charcoal or gas. The closed cover ensures that the smoke flavor caresses the vegetables in the short time you are grilling them. And the surrounding heat helps cook the inside of the veggies while the outside is caramelizing.

Vegetable Marinades

Vegetable marinades are flavor boosters limited only by your imagination. My everyday veggie marinade is as simple as it gets, and we never tire of it. It's the classic Mediterranean treatment, just some very good olive oil, kosher or sea salt, and a splash of freshly squeezed lemon juice. When the vegetables are seared with grill marks and the sugars caramelized, it's time for another light drizzle of olive oil. You can consume them hot, cold, or at room temperature, and they are great in salads later or as a sandwich garnish. As tasty as this marinade is, occasionally we like to experiment with other flavors or vary the taste for guests.

Before grilling, marinate your favorite vegetables for about half an hour.

Tropical Marinade

Ingredients
2 Tbs orange juice
1 Tbs orange zest
1 Tbs olive oil
1 Tbs fresh cilantro or 1 tsp dried cilantro
1 Tbs tequila

Directions
This tropical marinade is very tasty with carrots and sliced sweet potatoes. Grill them for about eight minutes total.

Down by the Bayou Marinade

Ingredients
2 Tbs soy sauce
2 Tbs bourbon
1 Tbs brown sugar
1 Tbs Louisiana hot sauce

Directions
This marinade is very tasty with onions, sweet onions, and fennel.

Southwestern Marinade

Ingredients
2 Tbs canola or other neutral oil
1 Tbs ground medium-hot chili powder
1 Tbs fresh squeezed lime juice
1 tsp lime zest
1 Tbs tequila

Directions
The southwestern marinade is very tasty with onions and large portobello mushrooms.

Caribbean Marinade

Ingredients
2 Tbs canola or other neutral oil
1 Tbs jerk sauce
1 Tbs lemon juice

1 Tbs dark rum
1 tsp brown sugar

Directions
The Caribbean marinade is tasty with sliced sweet potatoes, yams, and all sorts of mushrooms.

Mediterranean Marinade

Ingredients
2 Tbs olive oil
2 Tbs red wine vinegar
½ tsp herbes de Provence
½ tsp dried basil leaves
½ tsp dried oregano

Directions
The Mediterranean marinade is tasty with onions, radicchio, and fennel.

Grill-Roasting Vegetables

Unlike meat and poultry, you can grill veggies over direct heat for a long time and no HCA formation takes place. But roasting vegetables is a time-honored preparation having nothing to do with the HCA issue. Almost any vegetable you roast in the oven can be grill-roasted to perfection, so on hot summer evenings there's no need to add more heat inside your kitchen. We enjoy grill-roasted potatoes occasionally, and grill-roasted sweet potatoes more often.

CHAPTER 12

 **Grilling Corn**

In This Chapter

➤ Why grilled corn tastes best

➤ My foolproof grilled corn techniques

➤ Buying, storing, and preparing corn for many uses

In this chapter we treat corn with the adulation it deserves. Corn is the single most popular grilling vegetable. There is a good reason why corn grows on every continent except Antarctica. It is agriculture's most versatile vegetable, a staple food for people and their livestock. It can be dried and ground into flour for bread and tortillas, or made into a cereal product, served as grits and polenta. It can be picked fresh and boiled, steamed, roasted, or, best of all, grilled. No other vegetable exemplifies the bounty of summer like sweet corn on the cob. Locavores enjoy the long harvesting season, and environmentalists celebrate corn's ability to grow in low-till or no-till soil. We love it for flavor and nutrition, hot off the grill.

Boiling Corn Is OK, But . . .

The most popular cooking method for corn is boiling. Simply drop the cob into boiling water for a few minutes and serve it with salt and butter. We all grew up on this; there's nothing intrinsically wrong with boiling corn. But we can do better—much better.

The downside of boiling corn is that you are diluting the flavor. The flavor of corn is subtle, slightly sweet with a nice mouthfeel—that pop followed by the milky liquid mixed with salty butter as you bite into the kernels.

Grilling corn on the cob, in contrast, adds other complimentary elements as the dry heat of the grill concentrates the corn flavor. The hot steaming husks intensify that flavor and add a little smokiness as they char. Layers of flavor come from brines and rubs. Spiced or herbed oils and butter add richness and complexity. Grilling corn, simply in the husk or naked on well-oiled grates, is so much better than boiling that you will never again be tempted to fire up your kitchen stove to boil water on a hot summer evening.

Corn on the Cob

Grilling corn is almost foolproof if you use my method. Follow these simple directions for perfect results every time:

1. Use scissors to remove extra silk at the top of the cob and any loose husks from the corn, but leave the husk intact—don't peel it back or try to remove silk before cooking as some grilling instructions advise. You want to leave about two layers of husk if possible. The husk is both an insulator and a transfer agent for smoke and steam.

2. Immerse the corn in cold salted water (as you would salt pasta cooking water) for at least fifteen minutes. Make sure the husks are thoroughly soaked.

3. Set the gas or charcoal grill on medium heat (thermometer reading of 350°F-375°F)— spread the coals out to give even, moderate heat.

Tasty Tips

I call this my foolproof corn-grilling technique because it really, truly is. It's nearly impossible to mess this up. Even if you get distracted and forget to turn the corn a couple of times or grill the corn too long, it will still be better than just edible. The key element is well-soaked husks— and that's it. So if you know this cookout is going to be boisterous, convivial, impossible for the cook to concentrate real well, grill corn in the husks.

4. Place the corn on the grates, close the grill cover, and turn corn every five minutes for about fifteen to twenty minutes till the husks are brown and the edges are charred in places, but do not let the corn husk actually burn.

5. Remove with tongs. Use a kitchen towel or potholder in one hand to hold the corn. Peel the husks down the cob and then wipe with a damp paper towel to remove any remaining silk. There should only be a few strands of silk left to wipe off; most comes off as you peel back the husks.

6. Butter and salt the corn and eat immediately. Cover any extra corn with foil to keep warm. Substitute extra-virgin olive oil for butter if desired.

Other Grilling Techniques

As you explore corn-grilling recipes, you'll see over-complicated, even silly grilling techniques. Some recipes instruct you to strip off the husk leaves until just one thin layer remains before soaking and grilling. When you do that, however, you're just exposing the corn kernels to more heat, requiring you to pay stricter attention to the timing and heat levels on the grill. There are times when you want to char the kernels but for straightforward grilling, my foolproof method is the easiest technique, no heavy lifting for the griller. The husk is an insulator and a flavor enhancer plus a steam generator when thoroughly soaked. You want that husk on the corn to make grilling stress-free and flavorful.

Another common and unnecessary recipe instruction advises you to peel back the husk before grilling, remove the silk as best you can, refit the husk back over the corn, and tie it with string to secure it. Then soak the corn in cold water. Whew! By the time you've performed these complicated surgical procedures on a dozen ears or more, you're ready to relax with a margarita instead of man the grill.

Grilling food is supposed to be fun. So take my advice—just go ahead and soak the corn, grill it, and then peel the husks off. The silk will easily peel away with the husk. But don't forget to protect your hands—the corn will be very hot and very moist, just the way we love it.

Corn Facts You Can Use

Here are some interesting facts about corn that may come in handy:

> ➤ A cup of corn kernels is about 130–150 calories (corn varieties and other factors affect calorie count).

> ➤ One large ear of corn yields about 1 cup of kernels, so figure 140 calories on average.

> ➤ Corn is a high-fiber food at about 4.2 grams per cup and is naturally low in sodium and has no cholesterol.

Grilling Tech Talk

Credit goes to America's Test Kitchen—my all-time favorite cooking teacher and authority on all things food-practical. For this magical way to husk corn, see www.youtube.com/watch?v=35TsFXYfpB0. Everyone hates husking corn, but now they'll fight for that job.

1. Cut through the corn and the husk 1 inch up from the stalk end, a few rows up into the kernels.

2. Microwave for three to four minutes to build a little steam between the husk and the corn.

3. Grab the corn husk on the other end, just below the silk and leaves. Squeeze and shake till the corn slides out from its husk, free of silk and ready for the grill.

I said it's magic!

➤ A tablespoon of butter is 100 calories, olive oil is about 120, so use sparingly.

➤ A pound of corn equals about 1,300 kernels.

➤ Each year the average American corn farmer grows enough to feed 129 people.

Grilled Corn Techniques and Recipes

Grilled corn recipes fall into two main categories, taking us on a culinary voyage to many regions, countries, and ethnic cuisines:

1. Corn on the cob, spiced up with a variety of flavors, grilled in the husk or charred naked over the heat.

2. Corn on the cob grilled, and then stripped off the cob, served hot or cold in savory cakes, soups, stews, salads, or salsas.

Let's not miss the opportunity to spice up our simple, foolproof grilled corn in the husk. Let the soaking liquid spur your creativity. What flavors do you like that will go well with corn? Garlic comes immediately to mind. Crush the cloves, briefly heat them in a nonstick pan or even in the microwave for a few seconds to release their flavor. Then add them to the salted soaking water. Don't hold back if you love garlic. Remember, you are soaking the husks to get this garlicky essence into those leaves. As you grill the husks the heat and steam will impart the garlic essence to the corn itself, but not overwhelmingly. This method gives the corn a background flavor of the herbs or spices you add at the soaking stage. I've used a garlic clove for each ear of corn I'm grilling and never thought it was too much. Your particular taste will dictate how much you use. Experiment.

Tasty Tips

I never throw away corn husks and used corn cobs—you know, after everyone has chewed away on the cobs to remove every last kernel. That's flavor in the garbage if you toss these leftovers. Instead, I put the husks and cobs in a pot of water and boil for about an hour. Strain the broth. Pour some into ice cube trays and freeze the rest in quart containers. This makes a wonderful taste base for rice, risotto, vegetable soup, or corn chowder.

Other soaking flavors I recommend include cilantro leaves, fresh ginger, Old Bay seasoning mix, Zatarain's seasoning mix (the sumac ingredient adds a zesty note), curry, and a ground chili powder like Anaheim or ancho. All these ingredients impart a subtle flavor as the smoke and steam from the charring husks transmits the herbs and spices to the corn. For a more pronounced flavor see recipes where these ingredients, or others, are added directly to the corn as it's grilling.

Selecting and Storing Corn

For the best-tasting grilled corn, you need to know how to select the highest-quality ears and how to properly store those ears to retain freshness. Here are some guidelines:

> ➤ Since heat hastens the conversion of sugar to starch, always shop for corn that is kept in a cool place—at supermarkets cooled in the produce section, at farmers markets kept under shade, never out in the sun.

> ➤ Husks should be dry, green, and fresh looking, tightly wrapping the cob, but don't worry if the top silk is brown—that's a good sign of ripe corn.

> ➤ Peel back a small area of husk, or ask the farm stand operator to do it, and inspect the kernels. They should appear plump and arranged in tight rows. If pierced with a fingernail, they exude a milky liquid. But be polite and don't rip open the husks. Just a peek inside will tell you if the corn is good enough to eat. Handle corn with the gentle respect it deserves.

> ➤ Try to consume the corn within a day of purchasing—corn loses sweetness and flavor quite rapidly compared to other fresh veggies. If you must, store corn without removing husks in a plastic bag in the refrigerator.

> ➤ You can freeze corn on the cob. Remove the husk, blanch in boiling water for about six to eight minutes depending on size, cool, pat dry, and freeze in bags. They will stay good up to a year. In my opinion, it's not worth the trouble to freeze corn kernels because there are many high-quality, economical bags of corn in your grocer's freezer.

Beyond Butter and Salt

Butter and salt are the traditional compliments to corn on the cob. But when corn is plentiful and we eat it several times a week, it's fun to vary the presentation. Here are some of our favorite corn on the cob grilling techniques.

Naked Corn on the Cob

Grilling naked corn on the cob, unlike my foolproof in-the-husk technique, requires constant vigilance. You can't grab a beer and go off chatting with your friends—especially if you're grilling over charcoal. The heat will vary each time you grill, so you'll want to master the art of compensating for heat differences such as moving corn to hotter or cooler grill locations.

Practice will make perfect. Allow yourself to get it wrong at first. It's worth the time and effort, and the slight expense of wasted corn. Don't do naked corn on the grill for a friends and family dinner party till you've gotten it right several times.

Basting With Spices

You can baste husked corn with spiced oil while grilling it. The best flavor in the spiced basting oil develops as you grill the spicy oil on the corn. Heating most spices enhances their flavor. But if you add oil too early in the grilling process, the corn may burn or the prolonged heat may ruin the spiced oil (especially true for extra-virgin olive oil due to its relatively low burning temperature). So begin painting the ears with the spiced oil partway through the cooking time, more toward the end than the middle. Because you're grilling oiled corn, you need to be more attentive to flare-ups and burning. The results, though, are worth the extra effort.

Corn With Lime Juice

There is something magical that happens to corn when lime juice touches it. Try rubbing a cut lime on hot buttered corn grilled in the husk. Be sure to salt the corn. I find that kosher or sea salt has just the right coarseness—you almost feel the salt crystals crunch as you chew the buttery lime-scented kernels. Or jazz up the lime and butter with some herbs. Try this lime butter sauce—or make your own variation.

Corn With Hot Sauce

Louisiana hot sauce—or its variations from nearly every part of the country—has so many fans it's no wonder supermarket shelves are crowded with brands from the famous to the obscure. Some people put hot sauce on nearly everything they eat. If you are one of them, add hot sauce to melted butter and drizzle it on corn grilled in the husk. The preferred proportions seem to be 1 tablespoon of hot sauce to one stick of melted butter.

Fresh Corn, Fresh Grilling Ideas

Grilled corn on the cob is so versatile you can prepare this vegetable frequently for your friends and family throughout the sweet corn harvest season, which lasts as long as three months in many parts of the country. They will never tire of it as long as you let your creative juices keep flowing.

Devise your own brine for grilling corn in the husk, create different brushed-on spice combos for naked corn on the grill, or slather different kinds of herbed dressings on grilled corn as you plate the ears. Think about the main flavor drivers in various ethnic cuisines and how you can use them in your corn presentations. Here are some ideas:

➤ Try brushing hoisin sauce, flavored butter, or peanut oil on naked corn near the end of the grilling time.

➤ Use chili rubs that coat your corn as you place the ears on the grill—dip the cobs in water, and then rub on the chili powder so it sticks to the kernels.

➤ Brine corn in the husks in beer or in sweeter wheat beers.

➤ Corn and pineapple go perfectly together in salsa, so why not figure out a way to introduce pineapple flavors when grilling corn? You can add pineapple to a buttery brushing sauce near the end of the grilling time, or to yogurt and slathered on grilled in the husk corn when served.

Maximize Flavor

The important principle here is to adapt the grilling method to enhance the flavors you're using. Most spices and some herbs get better with a bit of charring, but others are ruined. Using sugar (or sweet syrups and juices) in the grilling process hastens caramelization, a flavor booster, but also risks an unpleasant burned taste if not carefully monitored and controlled. The same goes for oils, especially extra-virgin olive oil that has a low smoke (burning) temperature compared to other oils like canola.

Always set up your heat source, whether gas or charcoal, so you have control over your grilling—so you can move corn between hotter and cooler areas on the grates as the need arises. Corn grilled in a soaked husk can withstand abuse or inattentive grilling; naked corn on the grill cannot. Choose to make corn in or out of husk based on how much attention you want to give it as you're grilling.

Corn Is All Good

There is no need to be concerned about the possibly carcinogenic chemicals HCA and PAB that can form when meat, poultry, and fish are grilled too hot and for too long or licked by open flames. Veggies, including corn, are not affected this way. No special treatment is required. Grill corn any way you like it.

Corn off the Cob

There are many delicious recipes from soups to salsas that are based on cooked corn kernels. If you begin by grilling the corn, instead of boiling it, you'll add a flavor dimension that enhances every one of these dishes. Grill the corn either with husks intact for a deep corn flavor and slight smokiness, or with the husk removed on well-oiled grates. This provides a more charred and smoky flavor to the caramelized kernels. In general, hot dishes use corn grilled in the husk and cold dishes use corn grilled with husk removed, but that's a generalization, not a rule.

Whether grilled in or out of the husk, removing the kernels from the corn is easy but takes a little practice. After the corn has cooled to a point where you can handle the cobs comfortably with bare hands, hold the corn vertically over a wide, shallow bowl or plate, your hand on top and the bottom of the ear resting on the plate. Use a chef's knife and run it down the cob just under the kernels—they will pop off into the plate. Don't worry if you go a little too deep and get some cob. You'll hardly notice it in the final product and it adds depth to the flavor. Sometimes, in fact, you will want to strip off the kernels still attached to the cob, by inserting your knife deeper as you run it down the corn. These intact strips are nice in a salad or floating as a soup garnish—but keep them small and easy to handle with a fork or soup spoon. Use your fingers to separate kernels that are still imbedded if you cut too deeply by mistake. Now you're ready to make dishes using corn off the cob.

Using Hot Corn off the Cob

Corn soups or chowders are a great way to enjoy the abundance of summer and autumn corn. Your imagination will keep you and your family from getting corn bored. Most traditional soup recipes call for the two classic ingredients: butter and cream. But we don't eat that way on a regular basis—too many calories and fat. Instead, we make our corn soup with a little butter and a lot of herbs and good corn flavor thanks to those grilled-in-the-husk cobs. This is a starting point for corn soups—there are dozens of cultural variations throughout the harvest months. In Part Three, you'll find our favorites among these recipes.

Master a basic corn soup, naturally sweet with rich corn and herb flavors. For these recipes, and most corn soups and chowders, grill the corn in the husks for a deep corn flavor and no charring, which really doesn't work well in a chowder-type soup.

My Basic Corn Soup with Herbs

I use basil and thyme in this soup, but these are just suggestions. Fresh herbs such as parsley, cilantro, tarragon, chives, and mint—or others you like—are perfect additions or substitutes. If using dry herbs, reduce amounts by half.

Ingredients
6 ears fresh corn, grilled in the husk (can be made ahead, or use up leftovers)
½ c chopped shallots
6 c chicken stock (vegetarians can substitute vegetable stock or water)
2 Tbs butter (or more if you've been real good lately)
2 Tbs fresh basil, roughly chopped
1 Tbs fresh thyme, roughly chopped
1 tsp each fresh basil and thyme finely chopped for garnish
Salt and pepper to taste

Directions

When corn has cooled enough to handle, strip off the kernels, reserving one cob's worth of kernels (about 1 cup) for garnish. Break three stripped cobs in half. Melt butter in a soup pot and sauté shallots until opaque, not browned. Add stock (or water), remaining corn kernels, and broken cobs. Bring to a boil, reduce heat, and simmer for ten to fifteen minutes. Remove pot from the stove, remove cobs from the soup, add roughly chopped herbs, and salt and pepper to taste.

Use an immersion blender to puree the soup (or puree carefully in small batches in a conventional blender). Soup should be on the thick side—if it's too thick, add liquid. Reheat soup. Add reserved corn kernels and salt and pepper to taste. Serve soup in bowls. Garnish with finely chopped herbs.

Tasty Tips

Don't throw away those stripped cobs. Use some of them immediately to boost the corn flavor in your soups. Freeze the rest to enhance other soups and stews—even when you're not using corn as one of the ingredients. No need to defrost, just add a couple of frozen cobs to chicken, veal, or turkey soup or stew, braised pot roast, and when making stock from assorted vegetables.

Grilling Tech Talk

A handheld immersion blender is a safe and convenient method for pureeing soup (no hot liquid blender explosion). And corn soup when blended takes on a velvety texture, more so than most other vegetables. For a change of pace, however, use the large hole side of a box grater to strip the kernels off the cob. The kernels pop and crush, releasing their milk as you grate them into a shallow bowl. Don't puree. Your soup ends up with a nice rustic consistency somewhere between whole kernels and pureed.

Using Cold Corn off the Cob

Charred corn kernels, stripped off the cob, are a wonderful addition to salads, salsas, and other cold or room temperature presentations. The slightly crunchy texture and the light smoky flavor enhance the taste of chicken salad, shrimp salad, and many other warm weather main courses. Keep charred corn kernels in the fridge for two or three days for a spur-of-the-moment addition to hot soup or cold salad.

Salsas and salads are best when the corn is grilled naked, the kernels a deep golden brown, the flavors concentrated by the caramelized natural sugars. A salad made with grilled corn kernels, fresh summer tomatoes, and sweet onion, dressed simply with a good extra-virgin olive oil and fresh squeezed lemon juice is a departure point for casual alfresco dining. Here are some ideas:

➤ Add shrimp or chicken for a satisfying meal.

➤ Add quinoa or barley toasted in a dry pan for a few minutes, then cooked in water or broth, cooled, and mixed in with the corn salad.

➤ Add cold whole wheat pasta like rigatoni, bow tie, or penne along with roughly chopped basil and parsley for a healthy and hearty corn pasta salad.

Grilling Tech Talk

When you grill husked naked corn, make sure your grates are clean. If the grates have any residue of previously cooked food, like fish, onions, fruit, or marinated meat and poultry, those unpleasant burned flavors will be imparted to the corn. Ugh! Use a wire brush, a folded damp paper towel, and then a clean oiled paper towel to prepare the grill for naked corn. Always use a neutral high-heat oil like canola or peanut to lubricate the grates, never olive oil, which has a lower burning temperature.

Fresh Corn—in Winter and Spring?

What about corn that's not fresh—days-old supermarket corn or off-season corn that's trucked in from Mexico or Florida, or flown in from an opposite season land? It's certainly edible and there is quite a lot you can do to improve flavor. Brining with a big dose of added sugar helps, as does a spicy sauce that is brushed on naked corn partway through the grilling process.

Of course, no treatment is as effective and wholesome as nature's sun, rain, and soil bringing corn to a perfect ripeness. The more days that pass between that ripe moment and your grill, the more you have to compensate for the loss of sweet freshness. So enjoy corn on and off the cob, in abundance, and in all its variations while it's locally harvested, inexpensive, and bursting with the ripe flavors of summer and early fall.

CHAPTER 13

Fruit on the Grill

It's been many years since grilled fruit seemed exotic. Way back in the last century, high-end restaurants, followed by food magazines and TV chefs, began featuring grilling as a preferred method of cooking fruit. This change in fruit preparation, a departure from baked or sautéed sugary, creamy recipes that were European based, has resulted in a wide range of healthier grilled fruit creations that are almost entirely New World inspired. Latino, Southwestern, and Caribbean flavors replaced heavier sauces and creams.

The Benefits of Grilled Fruit

Grilled fruit is an essential part of a healthy eating lifestyle, replacing the fattening desserts of yesteryear. Grilling fruit delivers fewer calories and little, if any, added sugar. It will satisfy your sweet tooth without spoiling your weight-conscious diet.

Grilled fruits are wonderful dessert treats on their own or with simple light enhancements. They are really a health food, a vital part of our daily nutritional needs. A common problem in many families is how to get the kids, and sometimes the parents, to love fruity desserts instead of our all-too-typical fat and sugar-laden baked goods.

One obvious solution is to stop serving raw fruit all the time. Let's face it, apple pie wins more fans than raw apples because the apples are cooked to a creamier consistency, they're loaded with butter, and they're nestled in a flaky crust. It's no contest—raw apples lose every time. So let's meet those sweet and fatty cravings partway. Grilled fruit almost gets you to fruit pie but stops short of too much butter, too much shortening, too much sugar, and too many calories.

Tasty Tips

Fruits are sweet because they contain fructose and other natural sugars that are metabolized more slowly and evenly than added cane sugar or high fructose corn syrup, major ingredients in soft drinks and sweet desserts. Grilling caramelizes these natural fruit sugars, intensifying their sweetness without adding any additional manufactured, refined, or artificial sweeteners. And high-heat browning of fruit (and veggies) does not result in the formation of potentially harmful HCAs and PAHs.

Grilled Fruit Variations

Here's my easy, foolproof method for grilling fruit. In almost all cases you want to produce attractive brown grill lines with a rich golden color in between, which is the evidence of caramelized sugar. You want to heat fruit through, but you don't want to completely cook them as you do meat or fish. The goal is a sweeter, juicier, warm fruit, the kind we all love in a pie but without the added fat and calories.

Make sure your grill is clean when grilling fruit. Charred leftover salmon bits or burned kielbasa scraps imbedded in pineapple or plums are a sure way to make grilled fruit a turnoff for family and friends.

As your grill heats up, scrape the grates free of residue, rub them with water-soaked paper towels, and dry with more paper towels to restore clean grates. Then lubricate the grates with canola or similar oil, and unless otherwise instructed, always keep the grill cover closed when cooking fruit. Medium heat is usually preferred. Keep a close watch, especially over coals, to prevent burning.

Pineapple Delight

Core and slice a pineapple into rings or half rings. Grill on well-oiled grates over medium heat, flip after two to three minutes, and continue grilling to achieve desired doneness, nice grill lines, and a deeper pineapple color between the lines. Remove to a warm platter and serve. You can garnish with a sprinkle of light coconut milk and chopped macadamia nuts, or shave a few chocolate strips onto the warm fruit using a vegetable peeler on a bar of rich dark chocolate. Just a little goes a long way and doesn't add significant calories for those of us who watch our weight.

Ed's Pineapple Delight

Marinate pineapple slices in coconut rum for a few minutes, then grill as above. Ed Hamlin of grillinnovations.com, a generous sharer of mouthwatering recipes and techniques, promises the alcohol is evaporated during the grilling, so you might want to sprinkle on some fresh rum just before serving.

Apple or Pear Un-pie

Slice apples and/or pears about ¼ inch thick, removing the core. In ¼ cup neutral oil, mix ½ teaspoon each of cinnamon, brown sugar, and freshly grated nutmeg—or slightly more to taste. Paint the fruit with these classic apple pie spices. Grill for two to three minutes per side over medium-high heat till fruit is seared and softened. Serve warm.

Nuts about Bananas

Slice bananas in half lengthwise and brush lightly with butter or neutral oil. Grill flat side down for two to three minutes over medium heat. Flip and carefully sprinkle crushed peanuts or pistachios onto the flat side and grill for another two to three minutes. You may want to remove the bananas to a plate to sprinkle and gently replace on the grill using tongs instead of a spatula.

Peachy Delight

Cut peaches or nectarines in half and remove the pit. Grill flat side down over medium heat for three to four minutes. Using tongs, turn fruit and fill the pit cavity with 1 teaspoon of the best blueberry or raspberry preserve and grill for about two minutes more. A rounded teaspoon of vanilla or chocolate ice cream into the pit cavity right after the fruit is plated adds a touch of sinful delight with very few actual calories. The ice cream and warm preserves ooze out over the fruit as you slice into it. Who says dessert has to be loaded with calories and fat to be luscious!

Tasty Tips

It may seem counterintuitive, but according to grilling guru Ed Hamlin, balsamic vinegar makes a luxurious grilled fruit sauce with no fat, added sugar, or significant calories. I tried it, and Ed has a winner. Buy relatively inexpensive balsamic vinegar, no need for the twenty-year-old product from Modena. You're grilling—stay casual. Reduce the vinegar by about half in a saucepan till it's velvety. Let cool and spoon over grilled mangoes, apples, pears, peaches, or nectarines. This couldn't be simpler, or more impressive, for that matter.

Rustic Bananas

Cut unpeeled bananas in half lengthwise. Prepare a mixture of ¼ cup neutral oil infused with ½ teaspoon each of cinnamon, brown sugar, and lemon juice. Place bananas on well-oiled grates fruit side down and grill for about three minutes. Flip the bananas and paint the cut side of the bananas with this infused oil. Grill skin side down for another two to three minutes. Serve warm in the skin—the bananas are now soft and scoopable. Or peel and serve with cool fresh blueberries or raspberries on the side.

Tasty Tips

Too often we buy pears that are hard and under-ripe. Instead of ripening at home, they get mushy. Skip this doomed ripening attempt and grill-roast them to extract maximum flavor.

Cut pears in half and core them. For four pear halves (two pears) combine 1 teaspoon of brown or white sugar, ½ teaspoon cinnamon and ½ teaspoon nutmeg in ½ cup white wine with a pinch of salt. Put the pears in a bowl, pour this marinade over them, and mix well. Let the pears sit a few minutes while you heat the grill.

Place the pears skin side down over indirect heat (turn off burners directly beneath the pears), close cover and roast for about fifteen minutes at around 350°F till pears are soft but still firmly holding their shape. (You may want to flip the pears partway through the grilling time, so check their progress after ten minutes.)

For charcoal grills, place pears on grates opposite the coals and close the cover. Sweet and a little smoky—delish. Serve immediately.

To Grill or Not to Grill

Like most food types, some kinds of fruit do better on the grates than others. In general, harder fruit like apples, pineapples, melons, and peaches grill better than softer fruit like plumbs, strawberries, and other berries. Bananas defy this generalization—if you like bananas foster or banana cream pie, you'll enjoy this lower fat and calorie alternative.

Grill with Flexibility

Don't take recipes for grilled fruit at face value and follow them to the letter. The recipe writers mean well (including yours truly), but the reality is all fruit, even in the same batch, are at different stages of ripeness, meaning they have an unknowable sugar and liquid content.

Grill flexibly. Test with a fork, flip more or less often. The key to good grilled fruit is to start with a clean grill and check on your progress by the appearance and feel of the fruit. The good news is even less than perfectly grilled fruit is delicious, provided it's not burned.

CHAPTER 14

 # Breads, Pizzas, and More

> ## In This Chapter
>
> ➤ How to make dough and grill bread to perfection
>
> ➤ Grilled bread techniques and the rustic loaf
>
> ➤ Pizza and flatbreads on the grill

This chapter is all about bread, with a dash of pizza, naan, and other flatbreads. Actually, there is nothing new about making bread on a grill, but it's become a lost art for most of us. That's a shame because mankind has been making various kinds of breads over wood and charcoal since we invented agriculture. This is how we ate grains when we first learned to cultivate them in the Tigris-Euphrates 8,000 years ago. All we've done since then is refine the technique. Notice I did not say improve the technique. If you want to conjure up those ancient Stone Age tastes, you can easily do it right on your deck. How many food experiences can we rightly say go back, virtually unchanged, to our prehistory? Bread on the grill—as old as the earliest wheat fields, and as comforting to us as it was to our cave-dwelling ancestors.

Bread on the Grill

There are three basic bread types that are ideally suited for your grill:

1. Flatbread, made from both yeasted and unleavened dough

2. Pizzas and the variations on this classic Italian style

3. Rustic homemade loaf breads

All three major bread types are very easy to prepare, no special equipment needed, and your grill gives them an extra dimension of taste and texture. Best of all, your active work time to make the dough, just using your hands, is a few minutes. Really. Read on.

Bread-Grilling Techniques

Similarly, there are three basic bread-grilling techniques, each a function of the type of bread you're making:

1. Naked bread grilling: Placing the dough directly on the hot grates over charcoal or gas. Use this technique for individual pizzas and flat breads.

2. Grilling on a very hot stone or grill topper: Use this technique for large pizzas or flat breads you are baking for a longer time.

3. Creating an oven: Grilling on a stone or grill topper in a cast iron or ceramic-covered pot over indirect heat, creating an oven effect. Use this technique for baking rustic loaves.

Grilling Tech Talk

No matter what grilling technique you're using for your bread, adding wood smoke creates a flavor dimension you can't get anywhere else without spending a fortune on a special wood-burning oven. Transform your grill into a wood-fired oven with a metal wood chip box placed directly on the burners or charcoal. Soak your favorite wood chips (I like mesquite, citrus, and grape wood) and smell the smoke working its magic on your pizza, flatbread, or rustic loaf. If you don't have a wood chip box, wrap soaked chips in heavy foil, poke holes, and rest the package on the coals or bars.

No-Knead Bread and Pizza Dough

My recipe is a variation on the famous no-knead bread developed by Jim Lahey, owner of the Sullivan Street Bakery in New York City. Mark Bittman of the *New York Times* further refined and varied the recipe for quicker no-knead breads, and dozens of other professional and amateur bakers have posted their versions on websites and in print. For the original recipe, go to the Sullivan Street Bakery website. For a video demonstration, go to YouTube and search "no-knead bread" to watch Bittman and Lacey make it together.

This dough is so easy even a six-year-old can make it. It requires no machinery and nothing to clean up but a bowl and a board. It's made in two or three stages, depending on your time frame. Active work time is about five minutes. That's not a typo. Really, just about five minutes.

Grilling Tech Talk

Just the thought of turning on the oven during the hot, muggy summer is enough to turn off the craving for wholesome and delicious homemade bread and pizza. My no-knead bread dough works just as well on your gas grill. You can enjoy this wonderful crusty bread with an added accent of rustic wood smoke, baked on your grill year-round. You'll need a good grill topper to protect your pot and provide more even heat. I use the Grill Innovations topper for bread baking because it provides a good convection oven effect. And I always use an accurate grill thermometer to maintain the correct baking temperatures.

My No-Knead Bread Dough (the basic recipe)

I've perfected this dough through hundreds of loaves over several years. I hardly ever buy bread these days because this technique is so simple—and so healthy. You control the ingredients, which is mainly flour, so you can use organic all-purpose flour or bread flour, partly whole wheat or 100 percent whole wheat, combo whole wheat and rye, and any other variations that strike your fancy. Active real work time is about five minutes. I promise.

This recipe should be practiced using your kitchen oven. Once you have the technique down pat—after about four or five loaves—you can do the grill variations for loaves or flat breads and pizzas with confidence. Get it right in the kitchen so you know exactly what to look for when baking on your less-precise grill.

Basic No-Knead Bread

Ingredients (for a rustic, crusty loaf)
3 c all-purpose flour or bread flour
¼ tsp active dry yeast
1 Tbs kosher salt (or less to taste)
1½–1¾ c warm water from the tap (more or less since all flour is different)
1–2 Tbs olive oil—only if making dough for pizza or many kinds of flat breads

Directions

Mix the dry ingredients by hand in a large bowl (I use a big glass or Pyrex one). Add about 1¾ cups of the water, nearly all to start and then more as needed—and you may need a few more teaspoons after the original measure of water is finished. Mix by hand till water is absorbed and dough comes together in a slightly wet mound. Add water as needed by wetting your dough-mixing hand after you use up the measured amount.

If you're making the dough for pizza or flat breads, you can add olive oil and/or herbs at this point. This entire hand-mixing, dough-making process takes just about two minutes. Have a warm, not hot, water source handy to add more water as needed. I just let the faucet run real slow and dip my hand under it. As you near the desired consistency, you'll be surprised by how suddenly the dough comes together. You want it wet and sticky—bakers call it shaggy—but with enough consistency to loosely hold shape. (This is where the YouTube videos really help.)

Cover the bowl with plastic wrap and let the dough rise for eight to twenty hours at room temperature. I often let it go for fourteen hours. It will double in size, so make sure there is room for this.

After it rises, lightly flour a work surface (I use a bamboo wood board about 18 × 24 inches) and tip the dough out of the bowl onto the board. Flour your hands. Using your floured hands, gently flatten the dough into a long oval about an inch or two thick. Fold it over onto itself from either end. Form the dough into a ball. For a tighter crumb (fewer large holes, more small ones in the bread), you can repeat this folding process a few times. Handle the dough gently, like it's a baby.

Dust the dough ball with corn meal and/or wheat bran. Let it rest for about two hours seam side down on the board, in a bowl, or in a proofing basket (experiment to decide on your preference). Lightly drape a cotton tea towel, paper towel, or plastic wrap over the dough. It will rise again, doubling in size.

About half an hour before you are ready to bake the bread, take your large covered enamel 6- to 8-quart Dutch oven, iron or enamel casserole pot, stoneware pot, or Pyrex pot, and put it in the oven. Heat the oven and covered pot to 450°F for about thirty minutes. Remove the lid. Turn the dough over in your hands or let it slide out of the bowl into your hands and gently place your dough in the middle of the pot seam side up. Don't worry if it's off center or looks sloppy—it will recover its rustic relax. Cover the pot and bake for thirty minutes at 450°F. Then remove the lid, lower the temperature to 425°F (you have to experiment because all ovens are different), and bake another fifteen to twenty minutes.

For the first few loaves, till you get the timing right, use an instant-read thermometer for an internal temperature of about 200°F-205°F.

Remove the pot from the oven, remove the bread with a spatula or tongs, and cool on a rack. Do not cut the bread for at least half an hour.

I know this long narrative set of directions looks daunting on the printed page. I know I said this no-knead bread is simple and easy to make. My guarantee—you can make this bread in just a little more active time than it took you to read the directions. Five minutes. Be sure to view a couple of YouTube videos to gain confidence and see the handling techniques that you'll acquire over time.

Tasty Tips

If you're using rapid-rise yeast instead of active yeast, your dough will be ready in two to four hours at room temperature. You can slow it down in the fridge if you want to let it go to the next day. If you make this in the morning before work, it will be ready when you get home if left at room temperature. If using active yeast, the dough will be ready in about eight to twelve hours at room temperature. If you like more fermentation taste, leave it for twenty to twenty-four hours at room temperature.

Tasty Tips

There are many variations on the no-knead dough, and your friends and family will enjoy the results of your experimentation. Use whole wheat flour instead of all-purpose, or mix them in different proportions till you find a formula that all agree is best. Whole wheat will not rise as much and has a tighter crumb, resulting in a denser bread. We like one-half whole wheat and one-half all-purpose flour, both stone-ground organic flours. Sometimes we add sunflower seeds and wheat bran. Hard red wheat flour is our preferred type for bread making. For rye bread, use two-thirds all-purpose and one-third rye flour. You can add some wheat gluten for a more resilient interior, a lighter bread with plenty of holes in the crumb. For gluten-sensitive people you can use gluten-free flour, available on most supermarket shelves.

How This Works

When dough is kneaded, the protein molecules in the wheat, the gluten, are stretched and become increasingly resilient. When the yeast begins devouring maltose—wheat sugar—the carbon dioxide that is produced gets trapped in the dough, thanks to your hard work when you kneaded it. That CO2 forms pockets in the dense dough. The dough rises, doubling in size. The yeast is literally blowing up the dough.

The no-knead method substitutes fermentation for kneading. After you've combined flour and water, the proteins gradually strengthen and become more resilient on their own, but it takes time, at least eight hours, better yet twelve to twenty hours or more if refrigerated. This long rising and resting makes the yeast work harder, which gives the bread flavor you can taste and texture you'll admire. Like many good things in life, time and patience are the essential ingredients.

Tasty Tips

Bread baking is so popular these days due to the no-knead method. As a result, the Internet abounds with recipes and variations on the method. Sourdough bread is everyone's favorite but keeping the starter alive is kind of like running a mini-greenhouse. Miss a feeding and your starter can die. Instead, there are a number of online recipes that instruct you to substitute beer for a quarter of the water and add 1 tablespoon of white vinegar. You'll get almost the real sourdough taste without the constant care and feeding the starter requires. There are many different beers to try, yielding a variety of intriguing flavors in your finished bread.

Grilling Tech Talk

No one I know keeps their grill as clean as their kitchen oven. The bread-baking pot you use on your grill will get some of the smoky residue from fat and grease that is impossible to completely remove. So use an old or second-hand casserole, Dutch oven, or cast iron pot that is dedicated to your grill. And make sure it fits with the grill cover closed.

No-Knead Bread on the Grill

Once you've perfected the recipe in the oven, you'll have the confidence to use your gas grill as an oven. Follow these steps to adapt the technique for your grill:

1. Use a grill topper or stone to distribute the heat more evenly.

2. After heating your Dutch oven or enameled iron pot on the grill as you would in a kitchen oven, follow the same directions for bread baking. A grill thermometer is essential to maintain the temperature at approximately 450°F for the half hour covered bake time and a little lower temperature for the uncovered baking.

3. Use indirect heat after you've preheated your grill topper or stone and pot. In my grill, it's the outside burners that I keep on during bread baking, and the pot sits on my grill topper in the middle between them.

4. Place a wood chip box on the burners filled with your favorite soaked wood chips—I like citrus or grape wood for bread—and get a good smoke going while baking with the pot lid on. This won't flavor your bread while the pot is covered, and in fact you don't want the smoke to dominate the taste. It's an accent.

Tasty Tips

On a balmy summer evening, begin your cookout by baking bread, using the dough you've prepared that morning or even the night before. Once the bread is baked you can then grill your dinner menu and you'll have tasty, crunchy, homemade bread to serve with the meal. For a real treat, slice some of the bread, brush with olive oil and crunchy sea salt, toast the slices on the grates and serve along with the rest of the fresh bread.

5. After the bread has baked for half an hour in the covered pot, carefully remove the lid. Allow the temperature to reduce to about 425°F and bake for fifteen to twenty minutes, depending on the size of your loaf and the temperature you have maintained during baking. At this point, the smoke from your chips will infuse the bread with a light accent of smokiness, reproducing the ancient flavors of wood-fired ovens that have been used for thousands of years.

6. Use your tongs to remove the bread to a rack and let it cool for at least half an hour before cutting.

Grilling Tech Talk

Bread baking is both science and art. Too much yeast in no-knead dough, for instance, will consume the simple sugars in your flour, and then the yeast begins to die, leaving an unpleasant taste. Don't be a yeast murderer; they are your friends. Follow recipes exactly till you begin to gain confidence. Most important, educate yourself. There are hundreds of websites and YouTube demonstrations. Check out stellaculinary.com for an authoritative series on bread making by a professional chef. Grillinnovations.com has recipes and demonstrations for grilled pizzas. Breadtopia.com has good videos and helpful products for serious bread bakers. Google *no-knead bread*.

Grill Speak

Active dry yeast was perfected about one hundred years ago by a scientist named Fleischman (whose son went on to found the *New Yorker* magazine, another gift from the world of bread baking). The name says it all. The yeast is dried to keep it in a state of suspended animation, becoming active when you add warm water. You used to have to proof yeast, add the yeast to a little water and sugar to prove that it's active. It bubbles after a few minutes (that's the yeast consuming sugar and giving off CO_2). But yeast is so dependable these days that I never proof and have only had one bad packet in years.

Rapid Rise yeast is treated to work much faster, in about a quarter of the time, and it can be used for no-knead bread. Since I leave my first rise for twelve to fourteen hours, I routinely use active dry yeast.

Bigger Bread

My bread is so popular these days I often make a bigger loaf to share with friends and family. Increase the amount of flour from 3 cups to 4. Increase the water to about 2 cups, add a little extra salt to taste. But keep the yeast measurement at about ¼ teaspoon. You'll have a big and beautiful crusty loaf—and a few more friends than you had before.

Frequent Bread Baking

Once you've perfected the no-knead method for baking bread, you'll feel liberated. No machine to clean, nothing but a bowl and a work board to rinse off. No unpronounceable chemicals in your kids' sandwiches. They will be spoiled for life, bread elites who sneer at supermarket baked "artisan bread," and, worse, store-bought packaged white bread. The more frequently you bake, the more yeast in the air in your kitchen, so you're creating a kind of sourdough without intending to. That means a richer fermentation over time. Dough for bread and pizza tastes better the more you make it.

Grill Speak

All-purpose flour is good for most kinds of baking but not all. I use it for bread baking instead of bread flour, which is fine but bromated to give a good rise. I rely on my yeast—and time—for that rise instead of artificially inducing it.

Organic flour is made from organically grown wheat and in general is a good indicator of flour quality. Unfortunately, stone-ground can be used on a label if part of the processing uses stone, so make sure the label says "100 percent stone-ground" if you are paying extra for that process. Stone-grinding wheat creates far less heat and therefore does a better job of preserving the nutrients we expect in high-quality organically grown flour. Whole wheat flour has the wheat germ and bran, a good thing, but it makes a denser dough so I prefer pairing it with white flour for the texture we like in our bread.

Grilling Tech Talk

Don't store bread in the fridge. That cold environment hastens spoilage. The bread tastes off sooner and the texture is ruined. Instead, keep bread in a loose, folded plastic bag at room temperature. Interestingly, my homemade preservative-free no-knead bread stays fresh longer than any store-bought bread I've had. Three, even four days after baking, my bread is still quite nice. We slice it as we use it. The toaster livens it up after a couple of days. I slice and freeze a loaf for emergencies, thawing in the toaster till a fresh loaf comes out of the oven.

Pizza on the Grill

There are two ways to make pizza on your grill. Most of the time we like to make small individual ones, grilled directly on the grates, where everyone gets a choice of toppings. If you are used to making family-size pizza in your kitchen oven on a pizza stone, you can replicate those large pies by using a grill topper or pizza stone on your grill. In either case, grill your pizza with the cover closed and the hottest heat you can muster. If you're using a stone, let it heat for at least twenty minutes. For pizza, you want your grill thermometer over 500°F.

Use the no-knead bread-making method but with these changes:

➤ For a New York-style pizza, the large resilient thin crust, use a higher gluten flour than all-purpose, such as bread flour, or add gluten, which is available in most well-stocked baking sections of your supermarket. Bob's Red Mill is the brand I like.

➤ For thin crust classic Neapolitan style pizza, I use Italian type 00 flour, which is available online or in grocery stores in Italian neighborhoods. It's more finely ground than American flour and is the choice of pizza makers in Naples—so how can I improve on that?

➤ For whole wheat pizza dough, I like to use half whole wheat flour and half all-purpose or bread flour. Friendly warning: when stretching your dough, don't do the knuckle air toss until you've had enough practice. I use a rolling pin for smaller pies and a rolling pin and gravity for larger ones by lifting and letting it stretch on its own. Be gentle with your pizza dough and let it rest.

➤ Add 1–2 tablespoons of olive oil to the recipe when you add the water to hand mix the dough.

➤ After the first rise, tear or cut off dough and form golf balls for individual pizzas or baseballs or softballs for larger pies. Let these rise again for about another hour. You can keep these for several days in the fridge, and they actually improve in flavor and texture. The dough freezes and thaws very well too.

Tasty Tips

You can make a variety of doughs, ranging from entirely whole wheat to lovely herbed organic white flour dough where you've added basil, rosemary, a little garlic powder, or herb mixtures like herbes de Provence. These dough varieties work best in small individual pizzas where everyone can choose their own flavors. It's fun to offer your guests a range of doughs with different flours and herbs. The more whole wheat you use, however, the less pizza-classic the dough, but you'll still have a very good pie if you give the dough resting time and grill on clean, hot grates.

Dough Shaping

Pizza dough varies from the Neapolitan style, almost cracker thin, to the relatively thick Chicago style. The thick dough can be shaped by hand by pressing and stretching on your floured work board. The thin crust pizzas should be prepared with a rolling pin. Professional pizza makers think this is a form of savagery but they're pros, we're not. A rolling pin is a good tool for making a thin crust, especially if you use this method:

➤ Dust the balls of dough with flour so they don't stick to your hands. If dough has be in the fridge, let it come to room temperature, which takes a half hour or so.

➤ Lightly cover your work board with olive oil and lightly oil the rolling pin.

➤ Press the dough on the board to flatten into a disk using your hands. Then use the rolling pin to flatten the dough to the thickness you desire, working from the center out in short rolls. Don't force this, easy does it.

If your dough was properly prepared according to these directions and rested before the final shaping, it should be very easy to work with. Forget about perfect circles—you want that homemade rustic look.

Grill Speak

Rises and rests, what are they and why? When making bread we use a little yeast, less than half a teaspoon, for 3 or 4 cups of flour. Yeast is alive, it feeds on sugar (in this case maltose, natural wheat sugar), and as it digests the sugar, it exhales carbon dioxide, which puffs up the dough, literally blowing it up like we do with bubble gum. We call this the rise. You'll see the bubbles.

When we push the dough down and either knead it or fold it, as in these recipes, the pockets of trapped CO_2 are forced out and, left to its own devices, the dough will rise again as the yeast eats more of the remaining sugar—the second rise. Dough needs to rest before shaping and baking to allow the yeast to do its work and enable the dough to form the consistency, the texture, we want. Every time I bake bread, which is about three times a week, I marvel at this yeast-driven alchemy.

Grilling Individual Pizzas

To grill individual pizzas, heat your grill and lightly oil the grates. Roll out your golf ball–size dough balls into thin rough circles, about 6-8 inches in diameter. Rest the dough for a few minutes.

Place individual pizza dough directly on the very hot grates, close the cover and grill for about three minutes till the dough bubbles and attractive grill marks appear. Remove the pizzas from the grill to a platter, placing them grilled side up.

Be sure to have your pizza toppings all ready to use on your kitchen counter or outside in your grilling area work station.

Grilling Tech Talk

Ignore those typical pizza-making instructions telling you to flour your work surface and flour your dough, then stretch by hand, using a closed fist and gravity. I've tried this and it's difficult, but some find it worth learning. It's much easier to use the technique I learned from Sara Moulton, that most accessible TV celebrity chef. She advises using olive oil on the work surface to avoid "chasing" the dough all over your board. A little oil on the board and the rolling pin makes this process so easy and comfortable you'll never use flour again when shaping pizzas with a rolling pin.

The classic margherita pizza is a good example of how to proceed. Use a spoon to spread tomato sauce over the grilled side of the pizza dough. Sprinkle shredded mozzarella cheese over the sauce. Arrange fresh chopped basil over the cheese. You can sprinkle on a little grated parmesan cheese. (Do not overload ingredients—let your dough be a star here.)

Ease the pizzas back onto the grates with a spatula. Close the cover and grill for about three minutes or more till the dough is cooked through, grill marks score the bottom, and the cheese has melted. Then remove pizzas to a cutting board, slice, and serve immediately.

Grilling Large Pizzas

For large, family-size pizzas, follow the same general rules. Bake one side on the grill as described above, remove, place your ingredients on the grilled side, and then finish back on the grates.

Or you can use a baking stone or grill topper and heat it as you prepare your pizza. Roll the dough to desired thickness. Coat a pizza peel with corn meal so the dough doesn't stick. If you don't have a peel, coat the bottom of a cookie sheet with corn meal—not the inside, the bottom inverted. This will enable you to slide the pizza onto your stone or grill topper. Apply your topping to the pizza as it rests on the peel. Don't try to apply toppings on a work surface and then move the pizza to the peel—you'll lose it.

Get the stone very hot, over 500°F if possible. Then gently slide your pizza off the peel or cookie sheet bottom onto the stone. Bake for eight to ten minutes, or more, depending on heat and thickness, till dough is cooked through, the edges are nicely charred, and cheese has melted.

Grilling Tech Talk

The grill topper from Grill Innovations is ideal for making pizza. It's easier than a stone to handle and if you drop it this grill plate won't chip or shatter as a stone could. It's made of much lighter cast aluminum. The design distributes heat in a convection flow, which bakes your pizza as evenly as a stone on a grill. When the grill plate is hot, slide the pizza onto the grill plate and close the cover. Bake for eight minutes or more if needed. You'll get perfect pizza every time.

Pizza Variations

There are dozens of cookbooks and hundreds of websites devoted solely to pizza. It would be redundant, and limiting to your creativity, to even attempt to discuss pizza iterations here. Pizza toppings are a joy to research and contemplate. It's even more fun to actually fire up the grill and let your imagination run wild. Anything goes. Most importantly, once you get the no-knead dough technique perfected, once you realize how simple it is to make and store the dough (it will keep for several days in the fridge and months in the freezer), you'll never again call that so-called pizza chain store for a delivery.

Pizza Is a Health Food

If you take control of your ingredients, you can make nutritious low-fat pizzas that form the core of a healthy family diet. Your homemade grilled pizza can truly be your own creation. Instead of a salty, high-fat fast-food pizza concoction dripping grease from the cheapest ingredients, your grilled pizza can actually be good for you and your family.

Use whole wheat flour and low-fat cheese and add your own fresh veggies to your topping. What a great way to use up leftover grilled vegetables. When you're feeding your family healthy pizza, it's never a guilty pleasure.

What's for dessert? No problem. Slice peaches or other fruit, lightly coat the grilled side of the dough with ricotta cheese, spread the fruit, a few teaspoons of fruit preserves here and there, grill several minutes more, and serve.

Grilling Tech Talk

After more than four days in the fridge, you're dough is beginning to need attention—it's time to use it or toss it. Now is the time to prepare individual pizza futures.

Flatten and roll as directed and grill one side till they bubble and have those lovely charred grill marks. Remove them from the grill and let cool. Stack these half-grilled flat breads with wax paper between each and store in the freezer in a ziplock plastic bag. When pizza cravings hit, simply remove the pizzas you need. Zap them in the microwave for ten seconds to thaw, top the grilled side with your favorite ingredients, and grill till hot and tasty. You'll never buy a frozen supermarket pizza again.

Tasty Tips

Now that you have those individual pizzas ready for the grill, paint a little olive oil on them along with crunchy sea salt (or one of the exotic salts from the spice aisle)—you can also sprinkle on your favorite herbs. Put the pizzas on the hot grates till bubbly and charred. Flip and grill another couple of minutes. Remove, drizzle on a little more of your best olive oil, freshly ground black pepper to taste, and enjoy this mouth-watering simple food. Wood smoke adds to the rustic sensibility. Kids love these naked pizzas. Use mostly whole wheat flour for whole grain goodness. Add slices of fresh mozzarella cheese if you like, or crumbled feta.

Indian Naan on the Grill

Can your gas or charcoal grill become a tandoori oven to bake naan? The short answer is no—there is really nothing like a tandoori where naan is baked at 900°F against the sides of the oven. But naan is such a luscious bread, it's a shame to enjoy it only at your neighborhood Indian restaurant. Using our grill, and adapting the grilling technique to bake the bread quickly on high heat, we can get close to the real thing.

Tasty Tips

Ghee is easy to make and it keeps for a month without refrigeration. It is the standard Indian fat for making naan, roti, or other breads.

Melt a pound of unsalted butter in a saucepan over medium heat. After it comes to a gentle boil stir a few times and remove the froth that forms on top. Continue to simmer the butter, stirring frequently for about ten minutes till it turns golden and the whitish solids settle to the bottom of the saucepan. Let the ghee cool. Pour it through cheese cloth into a glass jar. Don't use a wet or dirty spoon and the ghee will stay uncontaminated for weeks.

Almost Authentic Naan

Follow these steps to make naan that comes close to the real thing:

1. Use flour as in the pizza no-knead dough recipe, but instead of the olive oil use 3 tablespoons ghee. Add 3 tablespoons yogurt and a little less water when mixing the dough.

2. After the rise, cut and shape the dough into golf balls. Let these rest for at least an hour while they rise again.

3. Flour your hands and your work surface and press the dough into a disk. Use a rolling pin to flatten and shape the dough into rough ovals, no need to be exact.

4. Paint the dough lightly with ghee and fold it in half over itself. Roll the dough again till you have a round or oval less than a ¼ inch thick.

5. Heat the grill till very hot, lightly oil clean grates, and grill the naan in the closed grill till it bubbles and puffs, with attractive light brown grill marks. Flip the naan and grill another minute or two till the dough is cooked through. Serve warm with a little more ghee brushed on if desired.

Grilled Unleavened Bread

The biblical story of Exodus explains that the Israelites were in such a hurry to leave Egypt they had no time to wait for their bread to rise. Many of us lead such busy lives we can identify. Thankfully, our grill can come to the rescue, imparting a smoky char flavor to a simple dough made with flour, water, and a little salt—olive oil is optional. Follow these steps:

1. Mix the standard no-knead bread or pizza dough recipe but leave out the yeast.

2. Let the dough rest for at least an hour, then dust with corn meal, wheat bran, or more flour.

3. Form golf balls, then flatten and roll out thin ovals.

4. Let them rest for at least fifteen minutes, then brush them lightly with olive oil and grill over high heat.

Wood smoke adds a lovely flavor dimension. So do herbs and spices added to the dough at the mixing stage or seeds pressed into the dough just before grilling.

PART THREE

Healthy Grilling Recipes

CHAPTER 15

 **Burger Recipes**

When German immigrant butchers brought ground meat to the American table in the mid-1800s, the presentation was confined to meatloaf variations. The hamburger—named after Hamburg, the port city where many of these butchers emigrated—was a meatloaf mixture fried in a skillet with plenty of fat, or baked in the oven.

The true American burger emerged early in the 1900s, still a cheaper cut of ground meat but usually not mixed with bread and other fillers. This beef hamburger didn't exactly qualify as cuisine, unless we consider the 1950s greasy spoon diner experience, a part of our proud culinary heritage.

Only in the last couple of decades has the burger emerged from its humble origins, its iffy quality and battered reputation as a quick ketchup-laden lunch or late night hangover deterrent. We now inhabit burger nirvana, where chefs think nothing of charging $26 for Kobe beef burgers topped with foie gras on a homemade sourdough roll.

There is, however, a sensible, healthy, and delicious middle ground for ground beef and many other types of burgers. If you need proof, try these mouthwatering grilled burgers made with ingredients that top chefs never even dreamed about until quite recently. Your grill is the star here, giving your burgers extra flavor dimensions with fewer calories. You can keep these meals simple, or expand to an elaborate and impressive multicourse grilled dinner party. Here are inspirational grilling ideas, burger style.

Grilling Tech Talk

Always rest your burgers for at least half an hour up to eight hours in the fridge after you mix in the ingredients you'll find in the recipes. Flavors need time to infiltrate the meat or fish. The resting process also helps more delicate burgers, like chicken and salmon, hold their shape on the grill. It's a good idea to lightly coat these more fragile burgers with a neutral oil like canola, and, as always, start your grilling with very clean grates.

My Favorite Home-style Beef Burger Variations

I grill beef burgers frequently, especially for large groups of visitors. I choose very lean meat, which I always grill-roast, as outlined in Chapter 3. Most of the time I make my own mix of beef cuts, ground to my liking in the food processor. This technique is easy and quick, and enables me to control fat content and sanitary conditions. Follow the procedure outlined in Chapter 3.

Grilling Tech Talk

Making ground meat in your food processor is easy. A detailed how-to is outlined in Chapter 3. Here, in a nutshell, is the method. Put 1-inch cubes of beef or other meat or fish or poultry in the freezer till firm, not frozen, about twenty minutes. In batches, pulse the meat in the food processor to the desired consistency, usually about six to eight pulses for a course grind. Be sure to include all the different meats (or other ingredients) you may be grinding in equal proportions in each batch. Rest ground meat in the fridge after forming patties for grilling.

Sometimes my family is in the mood for a good old-fashioned cheeseburger (we use low-fat cheese) to remind us of the family cookouts that were a summer ritual when we were growing up. Today, though, we make smaller patties, 4 or 5 ounces each. We add lettuce, tomato, sweet onions, and other veggies. We've graduated from ketchup to other sauces, and serve our burgers on whole wheat buns. We use rubs with plenty of turmeric or rosemary, depending on the culinary traditions we're incorporating in the burger recipe.

These spices, along with a short searing time and grill-roasting over indirect heat, inhibit the formation of possibly harmful chemicals that occur in cooking meat over any high-heat source, such as frying and broiling. HCA, a possible carcinogen, is greatly reduced or eliminated if you follow the advice in Chapter 1 and grill-roast your burgers. Healthy grilling is our lifestyle, but don't confuse healthy with boring. Try these exciting recipes.

Bahn Mi Burgers (for six 4-ounce burgers)

Here's my version of the classic Vietnamese street food burger.

Ingredients
For the pickled carrots:
½ c shredded carrots
¼ c seasoned rice vinegar
1 tsp sugar
For the sauce:
½ c mayonnaise
2 Tbs tomato paste (or substitute ketchup if preferred)
2 Tbs Tabasco sauce
1 garlic clove, minced
Salt and pepper to taste

For the garnish:
¼ c thinly sliced jarred jalapeno peppers
¼ c roughly chopped fresh cilantro

For the burgers:
1½ lb lean ground beef
1 Tbs medium curry powder
Salt and pepper to taste

French or Italian baguette bread, split and cut for six sandwiches, and brushed lightly with softened butter (there's that French influence)

Directions
Mix carrots, vinegar, and sugar together, and let stand for fifteen minutes, drain and reserve. Mix sauce ingredients together; refrigerate or use within fifteen minutes. Mix garnish ingredients together and reserve. Incorporate curry powder into the meat and form six burger patties. Grill burgers according to my grill-roast method. When burgers are moved to the indirect heat, toast breads over the direct heat cut side down till golden brown. Slather bread with mayo sauce. When burgers are done, place them on the bread, top each with pickled carrots, and garnish.

Serve sandwiches immediately.

Argentine-Style Burgers (for eight 4-ounce burgers)

Argentina is famous for its grass-fed beef from the Pampas. It's no wonder this is a mouthwatering burger recipe. Use grass-fed beef, which is available in most supermarkets; it has less fat and better nutrition.

Ingredients
For the sauce:
2 c Italian flat parsley, loosely packed
3 cloves garlic
2 tsp fresh oregano or 1 Tbs dried
3 tsp red wine vinegar
3 tsp extra-virgin olive oil
1 tsp salt
1 tsp smoked paprika

For the burgers:
2 lb lean ground beef
Salt and pepper to taste
8 slices spicy Monterey jack or other sharp, spicy cheese (use low-calorie cheese if available)
8 thick slices of sweet onion

Directions
Put all the sauce ingredients in a food processor and pulse till completely chopped and mixed. Form burger meat into eight patties. Grill burgers according to my grill-roast method. When moved to indirect heat, top each burger with an onion slice and place cheese over the onion. Place eight rolls or other bread on direct heat and toast till golden brown. When burgers are done, place them on the rolls and top with a generous dollop of sauce. Serve immediately.

Mexican-Style Burgers (for eight 4-ounce burgers)

Mexican cheese, queso fresco, is available in most supermarkets and gives us this south of the border cheeseburger.

Ingredients
2 lb lean ground beef
2 garlic cloves, minced
½ c Spanish onion, finely chopped
1 tsp ground cumin
½ tsp smoked paprika
8 red onion slices

6 oz shredded queso fresco or 8 slices

Rolls or bread, enough for eight burgers

8 tomato slices

¼ c mayonnaise

Directions

Mix the first four ingredients into the meat. Form eight patties and grill according to my grill-roast method. When burgers are moved to indirect heat, top each with an onion slice and queso fresco. Toast rolls or bread over direct heat till golden brown.

When burgers are done, place them on the rolls. Place tomato slice on top of the cheeseburger, slather top roll with mayo, and serve immediately.

Fat Fighters

If you want to reduce the calories in burgers even more, or just want to reduce your meat consumption, you can still enjoy a nice juicy burger. Make semi-veggie burgers. Chop cremini (baby bellas) or other mushroom of choice and red onions. Sauté these ingredients till mushrooms and onions are nicely browned. Mix ground beef and this mushroom/onion sauté together in your preferred proportions—I like half and half, about 1 pound of meat and about 1 cup of the cooked mixture (so start off with about 2 cups of raw ingredients). Grill-roast the semi-veggie burgers and serve on grill-toasted whole wheat English muffins.

Fat Fighters

Another way to enjoy an almost veggie burger is to form the ground beef into a 2-ounce patty, about half the amount of meat (and calories) as our usual burger. Combine that grill-roasted burger with a whole grilled portabella mushroom of about the same size. You can even add a thin slice of low-fat cheese to the burger, top with the mushroom, grilled sweet onion, and crispy lettuce on a whole wheat English muffin. This kind of weight-loss diet food is so delicious and satisfying you will continue grilling these burgers even after you've lost that last 10 pounds.

Stuffed Beef Burgers (lower-fat version)

Serious grillers love experimenting with stuffed burgers, which are basically two thin patties with a layer of cheese, and often one or more other ingredient, between them—an inside-out cheeseburger. The patties are gently sandwiched and the edges sealed with your fingers so the stuffing between the patties doesn't leak out. A healthy stuffed beef burger is the guilt-free way to enjoy this family favorite.

Ingredients (for eight stuffed 4-ounce burgers)
4 slices bacon, fried crisp and crumbled, or 8 slices Canadian bacon
1 c red onions, chopped and fried
2 lb ground round, 90/10 mix lean to fat, or leaner
8 slices reduced-fat cheddar, Swiss, or other cheese, sliced very thin
1 c arugula, chopped
8 whole wheat English muffins (100 calorie option if available)

Directions
In a pan over medium heat, cook the bacon until it's rendered and crisp. Remove bacon to paper towels, pour out most of the fat, and fry the onions till slightly browned. Remove onions and chop. Crumble the bacon, or if using Canadian bacon, grill them briefly ahead of the burgers and remove to foil to keep warm.

Divide ground round into eight equal parts. Form into loose balls, cut each ball in half, and gently create two patties of equal size from each ball. Layer one piece of cheese onto the center of one patty. Top with crumbled bacon or Canadian bacon, and chopped arugula. Then add another patty on top and gently seal edges, forming a stuffed patty, about 3–4 inches wide and 1 inch thick. Repeat with the remaining patties to make a total of 8 stuffed patties.

Place all the patties on a medium-hot grill for three to four minutes, then gently flip and grill for another three to four minutes. Flip again and move the burgers to indirect heat and grill-roast for six to eight minutes till done. Grill-toast the cut side of the English muffins. Place the burgers on the muffins and spread the cooked onions on top. Serve with your favorite sauce. We like Russian dressing for these.

Tasty Tips

Beef and other burgers are the exception to the rule commanding us to rest the meat for a few minutes before serving. Burgers should be served hot off the grill, preserving their juicy succulence. Unlike steaks, in which the juices are redistributed during resting, juices leak out of the burgers as they cool. Besides, piping hot burgers taste better than cooler ones, and if you top with chilled lettuce and tomatoes, the hot/cold contrast results in burger perfection.

Beyond Hamburgers

The traditional beef hamburger and all its variations—cheeseburgers and other toppings, different herbs, spices, and sauces inspired by our more worldly cuisine—these are grilling staples. There's nothing wrong with that; we never tire of grilled beef burgers, and there are so many possibilities, you can grill burgers for a year without repeating a recipe. But you'll be missing even more burger surprises if you fail to venture out of the beef mode into other ingredients such as lamb, pork, poultry, fish, and vegetables. Here are some of my "beyond hamburger" recipes.

Lamb Burgers, Economical and Delicious

Ground lamb makes a terrific burger, especially if you use Mediterranean spices and aromatics like fennel and lemon zest. You can grind lamb at home in the food processor using the method for hamburgers, or buy ground lamb as long as you know it's fresh and locally ground. If you like a little pink when done, medium or even medium-rare, you need to be sure the lamb meat has been carefully handled—just one more reason to have a good relationship with your meat retailer.

Uncle Pete's Lamb Burgers

For over fifty years Uncle Pete ran his eponymous campground just outside Phoenicia, New York. The famous Catskill trout stream, Esopus Creek, runs through the campground, attracting fly fisherman (including yours truly) from New York City, one hundred miles to the south. But Uncle Pete's was, and still is, primarily a family campground in a bucolic valley, featuring meadows, woods, a pond, and wilderness trails. That's where my future son-in-law, Dan, and his family spent many summer vacations.

Uncle Pete was Greek-American, as were the majority of his campers back in those days. To celebrate their heritage, and to thank his customers, Uncle Pete hosted an annual summer barbecue featuring his famous and authentic Hellenic-style lamb burgers.

Many years later, Dan and his wife, my daughter Rebecca, bought Uncle Pete's Campground. They continue its family-friendly traditions. The woods are still unspoiled, campers still play ball in the meadow and tube or fish the Esopus. And at the end of every summer, they celebrate with their favorite customers, and serve Uncle Pete's lamb burgers hot off the grill accompanied by campers' donated side dishes. We never miss the feast. Now you can enjoy these Greek-inspired burgers too.

Ingredients (for eight 4-ounce burgers)
2 lb freshly ground lamb (or grind it yourself in the food processor)
2 cloves garlic, finely minced

1 c feta cheese, crumbled

2 Tbs fresh oregano, chopped fine, or 1 Tbs dried

¼ c fresh parsley leaves, coarsely chopped

Kosher or sea salt and black pepper to taste

Tzatziki (see recipe, or good store-bought brand)

Sliced crusty Italian bread, pita, or other rolls, grill-toasted

Directions

Gently combine the ground lamb and all other ingredients except the tzatziki. Make sure you don't overwork this mixture; it should be thoroughly mixed but not compressed. Form the lamb mixture into eight patties. Grill lamb burgers over medium-high heat for about three minutes till nice grill marks appear. Flip and sear for about three minutes more. Flip burgers again and move to indirect heat. Grill-roast for six to eight minutes till burgers are medium or at desired doneness. Grill-toast the bread or rolls.

Serve lamb burgers with a dollop of tzatziki on grill-toasted bread or roll of choice. Do not allow ketchup anywhere near these. They look like hamburgers but they are not.

Tzatziki Sauce

Ingredients

1 c Greek nonfat yogurt

1 cucumber, skinned, seeded, finely chopped, and drained

1 garlic clove, finely minced

1 Tbs fresh dill, chopped (or 1 tsp dried dill leaves)

2 Tbs freshly squeezed lemon juice

1 tsp lemon zest

Salt and black pepper to taste

Directions

Whisk together all ingredients at least one hour ahead and chill.

Pork and Shrimp Burgers (For eight 4-ounce burgers)

We learned to love the combo of pork and shrimp many years ago in Chinese restaurants, and now there seems to be about a hundred different grilled pork and shrimp preparations. Serious pork lovers are always tinkering with these two ingredients, combined with other aromatics and spices. Here's the recipe we serve to our pork- and shrimp-craving guests. Our kids love it too.

Ingredients

1½ lb ground pork, preferably pork shoulder

½ lb tiny shrimp, roughly chopped to desired consistency

½ c finely chopped scallions

1 garlic clove, finely chopped

2 Tbs low salt soy sauce

1 Tbs fresh ginger, finely chopped

Sesame oil for buns

Salt and pepper to taste, applied just before grilling

8 buns or rolls

Directions

If you're using a food processor, grind the pork following the procedure for beef burgers in Chapter 3. Use the food processor to coarsely grind the shrimp or chop by hand.

Mix the pork/shrimp with all the other ingredients and gently form eight balls, then press into burgers about ¾-inch thick. Let rest in the fridge for at least half an hour. Grill burgers over direct medium heat for about three minutes till grill marks appear, then flip and grill for another three minutes. Flip and move burgers to indirect heat and grill-roast for about six minutes till medium well done. While burgers are roasting, brush cut side of rolls lightly with sesame oil and grill-toast till light brown.

Serve burgers immediately when done.

Salmon Burgers

Salmon burgers are the more causal way to eat this delicious and healthy fish (see Chapter 19). Farmed salmon are abundant and the quality, while not equal to wild salmon, has improved significantly. For salmon burgers, the farmed fish are just fine, and so readily available in the supermarket you need not seek out a fish retailer. I also use the flash frozen wild salmon sold by the big-box stores—Costco has consistently high-quality wild salmon from the sustainable Alaskan fishery.

Once you get used to grilling fish burgers (for one thing, they are wetter so they need some oil to sear properly), this once-daunting preparation will be a regular part of your grilling routine.

To make salmon burgers in your food processor, use the method outlined in Chapter 3. A brief review here: Cut the salmon into about 1-inch chunks, spread them out on a large plate, and put in the freezer for about twenty minutes till very firm but not frozen. Add salmon in batches to the food processor till about 1 inch above the blade, and pulse to the desired grind. I like larger grind for some, resulting in ¼-inch pieces, and an almost sausage consistency for more of the salmon, which, when mixed together, helps bind the burgers.

Always let salmon burgers rest in the refrigerator for at least half an hour before grilling, and always serve them hot off the grill when done.

After lightly coating with oil, grill the burgers for about three minutes on each side over high direct heat, and then either serve immediately, very rare, or roast for another six to eight minutes over indirect heat till desired doneness. A sauce made of mayo, fresh chopped dill, and lemon juice is delicious on grill-toasted rolls.

Grilling Tech Talk

The moisture content in salmon differs depending especially whether they're wild or farmed salmon, as well as what species they are, the place where they were caught, and how the salmon were handled and packaged. If you find your salmon burgers are too wet, are not searing quickly, or not holding together as expected, don't give up. Mix in more panko or other bread crumbs and try adding a beaten egg to help the burgers bind as they cook. Spray burgers lightly with oil. Always rest burgers in the fridge for at least half an hour before grilling to help them bind.

My Favorite Salmon Burgers

These are the salmon burgers I make for family and friends when I have the creative urge to go beyond the basic salmon burger.

Ingredients (for six 4-ounce burgers)
1½ lb skinless salmon fillets
2 scallions, finely chopped
3 Tbs panko bread crumbs (or more if needed)
Salt and pepper to taste
Olive oil for lightly coating burgers and buns or rolls
Tartar sauce and chopped arugula for buns or rolls

Directions
Grind salmon in the food processor, in batches, to desired consistency. Put in a large bowl and add the scallions, panko, mustard, mayo, lemon juice and zest, a pinch of cayenne if desired, salt, and pepper. Gently mix until just combined. Form into six equal-size balls and gently press into 1-inch-thick salmon burgers. Refrigerate for at least half an hour to rest.

Lightly oil both sides of the burgers and place on a clean grill over medium-high direct heat. Grill for about three minutes till burgers release; flip and sear the other side for about three minutes. Flip and move burgers to indirect heat and grill-roast for about five to eight minutes, depending on how rare or well done you like salmon. While salmon is grill-roasting, you can grill-toast the buns or rolls after lightly coating with olive oil. Top salmon with tartar sauce and chopped arugula.

Chicken Burgers

Ground chicken used to be a rarity in the supermarket, but now the big chicken producers have packaged it so you'll always find it in the poultry section. You really need to pay attention to the label. The popularity of ground chicken has given poultry processors an incentive to grind anything from the bird, all the parts that don't lend themselves to the chicken display case. Nothing wrong with that, provided, of course, that chemical extraction is not used and you know the fat content. Just because it's chicken does not mean it's lean. Ground chicken can range from 25 calories per ounce to 60 calories, so there can be more than double the calories in the same product, a product with a reputation for low fat and calories.

Chicken burgers are easy to grind in the food processor using the same method used with turkey and beef. If you use all breast meat, as I often do to keep the fat low, you'll have 4- or 5-ounce patties that weigh in at about 150–180 calories. I like to add about 2 tablespoons each of chopped sweet red pepper, chopped celery, and chopped onion. These ingredients add moisture and flavor to the ground chicken without adding many calories. You can whip these up in a small food processor, add some dry thyme, sage, sweet Hungarian paprika, salt, and pepper as you process the vegetables, and then mix them into the chicken by hand.

Lightly coat a plate and the patties with oil, rest the patties on the plate in the fridge, and grill-roast. A mild Swiss or Muenster cheese topping is a kid favorite. Serve on whole wheat English muffins with lettuce, tomato, and Russian dressing. With a chunky vegetable soup, this is a very satisfying weeknight meal, nutritious, and well under the 800-calorie limit we try to maintain for our routine dinners.

Vegetable Burgers

Even we meat and fish lovers look forward to an all-vegetable dinner thanks to our grill. There is no tastier way to prepare veggies than on your gas or charcoal grill. So when it comes to vegetable burgers, even the store-bought frozen burgers, you can't beat them right off the grates.

Whole portabella mushrooms are the simplest and easiest type of vegetable burger, seemingly custom-made by nature to fit burger buns and grill to a consistency and taste that is almost like steak. When you think about what processed food manufacturers go through to create a fake meat burger, made from soy protein and other ingredients, it makes you wonder why anyone would buy an imitation when mushroom farmers deliver the product that tastes so good on its own. Vegetarians should search no further. Portabellas are the vegetarian grilled burger winner.

We start with clean portabellas, stem trimmed off (freeze and use for soup or gravy). Marinate the 'shrooms in olive oil, lots of finely chopped garlic, salt, and pepper. You can add fresh-squeezed lemon juice to the marinade if you like, or balsamic vinegar, red wine vinegar, or a teaspoon of instant coffee—trust me, you'll like this flavor with the mushrooms.

Marinate for a couple of hours and grill the mushrooms over medium heat till they are cooked through, yield softly to the touch but nowhere near mushy—those are overcooked and should be discarded. It usually takes about four minutes a side for perfectly done portabellas. Make sure you are not grilling over high heat and burning the marinade.

You'll notice I'm casual about the marinade ingredients and grilling times. Portabellas are very forgiving, have loads of flavor on their own, so it's quite safe to play around with marinade proportions and ingredients. Experiment, develop your favorite marinade from these basic three or four ingredients. Add low-fat cheddar or thinly sliced full-fat fontina or other cheese you like.

Sear roasted red peppers on the grates, slice into strips, and top the mushrooms with the peppers. Serve grilled portabellas on toasted whole wheat buns or English muffins with fresh tomato in season or grilled sweet onions, or both.

CHAPTER 16

 # Chicken Recipes

In This Chapter

➤ Healthy and tasty grilled chicken recipes

➤ Foolproof chicken kabobs and satays

➤ Roasting whole chickens on the grill

For health-conscious grillers, chicken is the go-to meat that seems to solve every dinnertime dilemma. It's inexpensive, nutritious, low in fat and calories, and flexible because it marinates into a world of different flavors. But one word of caution: boneless, skinless breasts, the most popular chicken part, can easily be ruined if not properly handled and grilled. It is vulnerable to drying out and being overcooked in just a few extra minutes on the heat.

High heat is the enemy of boneless, skinless breast meat, so grill gently. Use an instant-read thermometer until you have your timing down pat. A little care results in a highly satisfying dinner for the family or with a just a bit more creativity, a terrific impress-your-guests main course.

What You Can Do With Chicken

Those boneless, skinless breasts are just the beginning. Whole breasts, bone in and skin on, are juicier, and with brining, marinades, or rubs you can create a variety of main courses—even within the same grilled dinner party. (See Chapter 4 for great brines, rubs, and marinating concepts.) If you take the skin off when serving you get the low-fat and calorie benefits, plus you're removing any traces of HCAs and PABs, the chemicals that form with any high-heat cooking and are suspected carcinogens.

Thighs and drumsticks, while higher in calories and fat, are the choice of many grillers who prefer stronger chicken flavor and meatier meat. Try out kabobs and satays for family dinners. They offer loads of exotic flavor possibilities that will prevent chicken boredom. Once you've perfected kabob grilling techniques and timing, you'll see why people like to grill kabobs when entertaining a crowd. They cook quickly, you can do lots of them at one time, and kabobs and satays won't keep you chained to the grill for hours. The marinating and prep work can be done hours ahead, and you can keep them on the skewers in the fridge, ready to go when the patio festivities begin.

If whole roasted chicken is one of your favorite meals, wait till you taste grill-roasted chicken. Add some aromatic wood to the gas or charcoal grill and cook the bird slowly for maximum flavor. I offer three treatments here that produce a superb roast chicken—a starting point for your creativity.

Grilling Tech Talk

Before you begin using these recipes turn to Chapter 4. This will give you a good comprehensive overview of all things chicken, including how to buy, prep, and handle chicken for the grill, grilling methods for different chicken parts, some interesting labeling information, and a detailed look at brines, rubs, and marinades. This is important background before getting into specific recipes. It's designed to give you a firm foundation for your creativity.

Grilled Chicken Breasts

Grilled chicken breasts is the easiest dinner choice, ready for the grill in less than an hour, done to perfection in less than fifteen minutes of active prep and grilling time. Always marinate boneless breasts for at least half an hour to prevent the formation of HCAs. Marinades consisting of an acid, such as lemon, lime, vinegar, and even yogurt, plus olive or other oil, will suppress the formation of HCAs by up to 90 percent if you combine the marinating with lower heat grill-roasting. Turmeric and rosemary lower HCA formation, and they add good flavor, so add one of them to the marinade. The good news is that sensible practices such as marinades and lower heat grilling result in very tasty and safe family dinner fare.

Versatility is the major attraction of these chicken breast recipes. Use them as presented here, and then take off on creative grilling flights of your own. There are hundreds of culinary adventures ahead using your grill and your imagination.

Fat Fighters

Those of us who are busy and weight conscious find one of our biggest problems is the temptation to get fatty take-out food on the way home from work because we had no down time to think about dinner. Instead of stopping for fried chicken or getting a pizza delivered, it's so easy to thaw chicken breasts that are individually sealed in the freezer. I always keep a supply of frozen organic boneless, skinless breasts, as well as a bag of individually frozen tenders for kabobs and satays. They thaw in warm tap water in less than fifteen minutes, marinate in about half an hour, and grill-roast in twelve to fifteen minutes. Your dinner is ready to serve just over an hour after you get home. With a hearty made-ahead vegetable soup or tossed salad, you'll have an easy, nutritious guilt-free meal on the table.

Grilled Chicken Margarita

As the name implies, these marinated boneless, skinless breasts pick up summery tequila accents that continue the margarita cocktail's theme you started before grilling got underway. This is a festive chicken presentation at any time of year—perfect for a family of four to six, or double the recipe to make more for a crowd or for sandwiches and salads later.

Ingredients
4–6 boneless, skinless chicken breasts, organic preferred
½ c chopped fresh cilantro:
¼ c olive oil
2 Tbs tequila
2 Tbs fresh-squeezed lime juice
1 Tbs fresh garlic, minced
1 Tbs fresh ginger, minced
1 tsp ground chipotle chili
½ tsp salt

Directions
Mix all the ingredients and marinate the chicken breasts for at least half an hour up to eight hours. Place chicken breasts on grates over medium-high heat for about three minutes

till grill marks appear. Flip and grill for about three minutes more. Flip and move chicken breasts to indirect heat and grill-roast for about six to eight minutes more till breasts are cooked through.

When serving, add more chopped cilantro if desired and a splash of olive oil. Suggested side dishes include a homemade fruit salsa, grilled pineapple, grilled baby fennel bulbs, and grilled romaine lettuce with balsamic vinaigrette.

Tasty Tips

All these recipes are designed for convenient, easy family dinners, but that doesn't mean they won't be impressive for company. When planning an entire meal, go to Chapter 11 for delicious vegetable side dishes, Chapter 12 for creative corn ideas, and Chapter 13 for fruit grilling techniques.

Tarragon Grilled Chicken

I love the aromatic flavor of fresh tarragon, and when it's a main marinade ingredient grilled on a chicken breast, the heat infuses the meat with this delicious herbal taste. You can use dried tarragon at about half the amount here, but nothing beats the fresh herb.

Ingredients
4–6 boneless, skinless chicken breast, organic preferred
¼ c fresh tarragon
1 Tbs Dijon mustard
2 Tbs olive oil
2 Tbs fresh-squeezed lemon juice
1 garlic clove, minced
Salt and pepper to taste

Directions
Mix all the ingredients and marinate breasts at least half an hour up to four hours. Place chicken breasts on the grill over medium-high heat for about three minutes till grill marks appear, flip and sear for another three minutes. Flip and move chicken to indirect heat and grill-roast for about six to eight minutes more till breasts are cooked through.

Serve whole breasts immediately with a hearty soup or salad, or slice for sandwiches on crusty Italian bread that has been grill-toasted.

Greek Style Grilled Chicken

The Greek side of our family uses oregano and lemon juice in everything and believe me, it makes everything better. Here's my recipe when my Greek relatives join us for a weekend cookout on the deck.

Ingredients
6–10 boneless, skinless chicken breasts, organic preferred
½ c olive oil
½ c fresh-squeezed lemon juice
1 Tbs lemon zest
2 Tbs fresh oregano or 1 Tbs dried
1 Tbs fresh thyme or 1½ tsp dried
1 tsp dried sage
Lots of black pepper to taste

Directions
Mix all the ingredients and marinate the chicken for at least half an hour up to four hours. Place breasts on the grill over medium-high heat for about three minutes till grill marks appear. Flip and sear for about three minutes more. Flip and move breasts to indirect heat and grill-roast for about six to eight minutes more till breast are cooked through.

Serve immediately with a big Greek salad, couscous with oranges, and grilled fennel bulbs.

Grilled Chicken Florentine

No one I know claims to have eaten this in Florence, but anything with spinach on it—one of my favorite veggies—becomes Florentine by default. I experimented several times to get the timing right, and now this works perfectly every time. Remember, every grill is slightly different so make this at least once before serving it to company—especially if the company is your boss. It's a classy grilled dish, but not just for a special occasion.

Ingredients
6–8 boneless, skinless chicken breasts, organic preferred
For the marinade
¼ c fresh-squeezed lemon juice
¼ c olive oil
1 Tbs crushed dried rosemary

For the "Florentine"
3 garlic cloves, minced
1–2 roasted red peppers from the jar, chopped
1 Tbs olive oil
1 c steamed fresh-chopped spinach, or more for more breasts (can use frozen spinach)
3–4 oz shredded part skim mozzarella cheese

Directions
Mix the marinade and marinate the chicken for at least half an hour up to four hours. Sauté the garlic and peppers in olive oil. When beginning to brown, add the chopped steamed spinach and briefly heat the ingredients and combine. Remove to a bowl next to your grill.

Place chicken breasts on the grill over direct medium-high heat for about three minutes till grill marks appear, then flip and sear for about three minutes more. Flip and move chicken breasts to indirect heat and grill-roast for about six minutes till almost cooked through. Flip breasts and carefully spread the spinach mixture on top of each one. Add mozzarella cheese, close cover, and grill-roast for another two to four minutes till cheese melts and chicken breasts are fully cooked. Don't overload the cheese, just enough to melt through the spinach, which is the star here.

Remove the breasts, salt and pepper to taste and serve immediately. Suggested accompaniments include a fresh salad with Italian dressing, arborio rice risotto, or grilled roasted vegetables.'

Tasty Tips

Each of these boneless, skinless breast recipes can be made with bone-in skin-on breasts for those who prefer crisp skin and the extra flavor boost that bone-in brings to the bird. Increase the grill-roasting time by about four to five minutes due to the insulation provided by skin and bones. Thighs, boneless, skinless, or bone in and skin on are just as appropriate, again increasing the grill-roasting time by a few minutes for whole thighs with skin. Be sure to use a thermometer the first few times so your timing is perfected: about 165°F for white meat and about 170°F for dark.

My Favorite Stuffed Chicken Breast

Here's how to transform the humble skinless, boneless breast into an impressive, almost gourmet dinner centerpiece. Make a pesto—see recipe below for my everyday pesto, packed with flavor and nutritional goodness. Have on hand some solid hardwood toothpicks, or you can use thin bamboo skewers cut into a smaller piece. The trick here is not to stuff too much stuffing into the breast. Think of this as adding flavor, not bulk.

Ingredients
6–8 boneless, skinless chicken breasts, organic preferred
For the marinade
¼ c fresh-squeezed lemon juice
¼ c olive oil
1–2 Tbs crushed rosemary

For the Pesto
1 c packed fresh basil with added fresh parsley and/or arugula if desired
½ c or less very good olive oil
¼ c roasted unsalted walnuts, pistachios, or almonds
2–3 Tbs grated parmesan cheese
1 garlic clove

Directions
Mix marinade ingredients and marinate chicken for at least half an hour up to four hours.

Put all the pesto ingredients except olive oil in the food processor. Add about half the oil and pulse to puree, adding more oil a little at a time and scraping down the sides till you get the desired pesto (paste) consistency.

In the thickest part of the side of the breast, slit the chicken with a sharp paring knife to make a pouch that does not pierce the other three sides of the breast. Use a tablespoon to insert the pesto and gently press the breast to distribute the pesto in the pouch. Use a toothpick or two to close the open end of the pouch.

Place the chicken on the grill over medium-high heat and sear for about three minutes till grill marks appear. Flip and sear for about three minutes more. Flip the chicken and move to indirect heat and grill-roast for about five more minutes. Flip again and grill-roast for about three or four minutes more till chicken is well done, which will be when it reaches 165°F (because the breast has been slit and stuffed the heat transfer is not as efficient as a whole breast, so an added flip and more time is required). Insert an instant-read thermometer in the pouch of one breast to make sure it's at 165°F—that's the part that cooks last.

Serve immediately with grilled vegetables.

Tasty Tips

Once you've mastered this stuffed chicken breast technique—and it does take a little practice to make a nicely proportioned pouch—you can begin to stretch your chicken-stuffing repertoire. Add some part skim ricotta cheese, about one-third cheese and two-thirds pesto. Slice prosciutto into strips and add that to the pesto, or you can add a little crisply rendered sweet or hot Italian sausage (never uncooked or uncured meat). Have fun kicking up the flavors with imaginative stuffings.

Traditional Barbecued Chicken

This is as simple as it gets, proving once again that the grill is the most important ingredient. You can't beat barbecued chicken for the variety of flavors—delivered by different sauces— and that old-time taste that can't be produced anywhere but on your grill.

Be sure you have a variety of bottled sauces on hand, such as traditional Memphis style (Stubbs is my favorite), Carolina mustard-based sauce, vinegar sauces from South Carolina, white barbecue sauce from Alabama, a hotter Texas style, and your favorite homemade sauces (see Resources for some of the best mail order sauces we enjoy).

For a big crowd, a whole mess of chicken on the grill mopped with the sauce of your choice is always a hit. Nothing makes guests happier than an offer of several different barbecue sauces. This is the essence of hospitality, and it's actually very little extra work for you, the griller host.

Ingredients
8–10 boneless, skinless breasts (or bone-in skin on if preferred)
¼ c canola oil
¼ c apple cider vinegar
1 Tbs crushed rosemary or turmeric
BBQ sauces

Directions
Marinate the chicken in the canola, cider, herb mixture for at least half an hour up to four hours in the fridge. While the grill is heating up, prepare your sauces, pouring each sauce into small bowls with a separate tablespoon or brush for applying. Describe the sauces to your guest and take orders.

Place the chicken on the grill over medium-high heat and grill for about three minutes till grill marks appear. Flip and sear for another three minutes. Apply barbecue sauces to the tops of each chicken breast, flip and move breasts to indirect heat and apply sauce to their top side. Grill-roast for about six to eight minutes more till chicken breasts are cooked through. Just before removing from the grates, apply sauce to both sides of the chicken and place them on a warm platter to serve, grouping same sauced breasts together.

Serve with traditional cole slaw, potato or pasta salads, or mixed greens. Grilled veggies such as zucchini or summer squash go very well with this—see vegetable recipes. Or slice chickens and serve on burger buns with more sauce and coleslaw, and plenty of cold beer.

Grilling Tech Talk

Never apply barbecue sauces to meat when it's being seared. The intense heat will burn the sugars that are in all sauces, even homemade sauces with no sugar added because sugar is almost always in one of the ingredients you use. Apply the sauce when grill-roasting or after you've finished grilling.

Chicken Kabobs and Satays

When fuel is scarce or expensive it makes sense to develop cooking techniques that use very little fuel to cook the maximum amount of food. The Chinese wok, for example, is an engineering triumph for a fuel-poor cooking environment, transferring very high heat from a relatively small source. That combined with the bite-size pieces of the food being cooked maximizes cooking efficiency. A wok on a stove can't be beat for delivering food cooked in seconds.

Similarly, kabobs and satays employ the grill at its most efficient level. For us modern grillers, this means we can prepare a lot more food with less charcoal and propane when we make kabobs and satays. Tailgaters, picnickers, and boaters like me find that grilling this type of food is ideal for our portable lifestyle—less fuel to carry, quicker starts, and shorter grilling time, all add up to convenience without sacrificing taste or creativity.

Satays originated in what is now Indonesia, and kabobs hail from northern Africa and the Mideast. The satay, like the wok, was a response to a relatively high population in a confined area where fuel was, and is, in short supply and expensive. The kabob was a response to dry or desert regions where wood was rare and other fuels were relatively expensive. Without refrigeration in these warm climates, people used spices to suppress bacteria growth. When you combine spices with small pieces of chicken you get a mouth full of quick grilling flavor in every bite. That's why we love kabobs and satays.

Chicken Kabobs in Yogurt

Yogurt is an underused marinating ingredient in grilling, which is a shame because it gives chicken a richer, creamier taste. I love this recipe—it's simple, whips together in a moment, and results in perfect kabobs. We serve this every few weeks year-round with plenty of grilled vegetables, often shiitake mushrooms on skewers and other seasonal veggies. Chop the leftovers and combine with chopped red peppers, sweet onions, celery, and shredded carrots for a chicken salad dinner a couple of days later.

Ingredients
6–8 boneless, skinless breasts (depending on size) or 8 boneless, skinless thighs or both cut into 1-inch cubes
¼ c plain fat-free yogurt
¼ c fresh-squeezed lemon juice
3 garlic cloves, minced
1 tsp turmeric
1 tsp salt

Directions

Combine all ingredients and marinate chicken pieces for at least half an hour up to two hours. Thread chicken onto flat metal skewers (to keep them from rolling) or bamboo skewers. Sear for about two minutes over medium-high direct heat, flip and sear for another two minutes till light grill marks appear. Flip and move skewers to indirect heat and grill-roast for four minutes more till done. Serve immediately.

Grilling Tech Talk

Skewers can be dangerous. They are terrific to grill with but can be a hazard to adult diners who may have had a couple too many beers and to children. Hot off the grill, the flat metal skewers retain the heat and can give a nasty burn. Always use a potholder and remove meat from metal skewers before serving. Bamboo skewers don't retain heat but can break in the meat, and can cut the mouth or choke a child when eaten. Always remove meat from bamboo skewers before serving children.

Tropical Chicken Kabobs

Plenty of citrus flavor here. If you've never had grilled oranges, you're in for a treat. The grill evaporates the water, concentrating the orange flavor and caramelizing the sugar.

Ingredients

6–8 boneless, skinless chicken breasts, thighs, or both, cubed into about 1-inch pieces

1 large red onion cut into 1-inch irregular cubes—onion chunks

1 large navel orange, each section cut in half

For the marinade

2 Tbs fresh-squeezed lemon juice

3 Tbs olive oil

1 tsp ground cumin

¼ tsp cayenne or less to taste (it's hot)

Salt and pepper to taste

Directions

Mix all the ingredients for the marinade and marinate the chicken, onion cubes, and orange pieces for about half an hour to an hour. Thread the chicken cubes on bamboo skewers. Separately thread the onion cubes and orange pieces on skewers together, alternating onion and orange pieces on each skewer.

Place chicken skewers on grates over medium-high direct heat and grill for about two minutes till lightly seared with grill marks. Flip skewers and sear for another two minutes. Flip again and move chicken skewers to indirect heat. Place onion-orange skewers on grates over direct heat. Close cover and grill for about three minutes. Flip onion-orange skewers and continue grilling over direct heat for another three minutes till onions and oranges are nicely charred.

Remove chicken and onion-orange skewers and serve each person a skewer of each, and make sure there are extras on the platter. Accompany with rice and beans or whole wheat couscous.

Grilling Tech Talk

Kabobs provide an easy way to grill a combination of vegetables, fruit, and meat—in this case, chicken—but there are two good reasons not to grill them all together on the same skewers, despite the instructions in many recipes. Meat, chicken, and fish get done at different times and should be grill-roasted as explained throughout this book. Veggies and fruit are also grilled for different lengths of time, and many vegetables and some fruit love high direct heat. No HCA concerns at all with these ingredients, so grill them separately to maximize flavor and safe cooking methods.

Chicken Satay with Peanut Dipping Sauce

When I feel like grilling a special occasion chicken dinner but still want to keep it casual, nothing beats chicken satay. This is not a weeknight dinner. It takes a little more work than our kabob dinners, but it feels very festive and kids love the dipping sauce, even though it's a bit spicy. My tailgating friends think this is the perfect pregame celebration, especially when it's done on a patio instead of in a parking lot. Easily expand this recipe for a crowd by doubling or tripling all the ingredients.

Ingredients
6–8 boneless, skinless chicken breasts cut into ¼-inch strips lengthwise along the breast or chicken tenders, about 4 ounces for each serving

For the marinade
½ c reduced fat coconut milk
1 Tbs fresh-squeezed lime juice
1 tsp medium hot curry paste
1 tsp oil
½ tsp fish sauce

For the dipping sauce

¼ c reduced fat coconut milk
1 Tbs fresh squeezed lime juice
¼ c natural peanut butter—just
ground peanuts and a little salt
1 Tbs sweet chili sauce
1 tsp low sodium soy sauce

Directions

Mix the ingredients for the
marinade and marinate the
chicken strips for one to two
hours. Mix the dipping sauce
ingredients and let the flavors
combine for one hour. Serve at
room temperature.

Grilling Tech Talk

There is no need to soak bamboo skewers prior
to threading the meat on them. If you grill the
healthy way, briefly over high heat and longer on
indirect heat, the skewers will not burn. I promise.
This is another good reason to grill-roast. In fact,
I don't even soak skewers for vegetables and fruit,
which I'm often grilling on high heat. The food
insulates most of the skewer and the grilling time
is usually just a few minutes. So ignore the soaking
instructions you often see in recipes. Your skewers
will be just fine.

Thread chicken pieces onto
bamboo skewers, over and under so they stay secured, but as flat as you can so all the
chicken is in contact with the grates. Place chicken skewers on grill over direct medium-
high heat for about three minutes, flip and sear for three minutes more. Since chicken pieces
are only about a quarter-inch thick, they should be done at this point. Serve immediately
with the dipping sauce. Jasmine rice and cauliflower simmered in curry paste are ideal for
this meal.

Grill Speak

Fish sauce is a key ingredient in south Asian cuisine, and it's a staple in our spice and herb
pantry. A good fish sauce isn't fishy. The Greeks and Romans perfected fish sauces with
fermented anchovies and other fish such as squid. But before you say no way, consider
Worcestershire sauce. Its basis is fermented anchovies.

Fish sauces are rich in glutamates. Just a little enhances the taste of meat and poultry that are
marinated in it. In fact, these glutamates are known as the fifth taste after the four we refer
to as sweet, bitter, salty, and sour. The Japanese call glutamate-rich fish sauces *umami*, which
means yummy, and the great French chef Escoffier perfected it with sauces made from roasted
veal bones, which are also high in glutamates. Monosodium glutamate (MSG) is the artificial
version, so why not use the real thing to enhance and deepen flavors. Plato loved fermented
fish sauce, and you will too.

Roasting Chicken on the Grill

Everyone loves roast chicken, but there are so many months, especially in the southern parts of our country, when the thought of turning on the oven makes you sweat. Fortunately, your grill offers the perfect solution. Here are my two favorite roasting techniques, each resulting in a perfectly done bird with very little work.

Beer Can Chicken

This method has become a classic in just a few years. Variations on the theme abound. Here're mine. It's so easy and fun that I rarely consider roasting a 3½- to 4-pound chicken any other way.

➤ Prepare the chicken by massaging your rub under the skin and lightly coating the skin with a lemony olive oil mopping marinade, but don't truss it.

➤ Prepare your grill by turning on all the gas burners and heating to about 400°F, then turning off the middle burner(s). Leave the front and rear burners on medium-low and adjust to maintain a temperature of about 350°F–375°F. Or build your charcoal fire and bank the coals against both sides of your covered grill to achieve a temperature of 350°F–375°F. Place an aluminum drip pan between the banks of charcoal.

➤ Take a can of your favorite beer. Drink about a third of it. Or offer it to your spouse, lover, or friend, if you're feeling generous.

➤ Use an old-fashioned church key to make more holes in the top of the can and pour in some of the rub or other flavorings like citrus juice or garlic.

➤ Insert the can into the cavity of the chicken. The can and two legs of the chicken should form a triangular stand with the can at the apex, breast facing toward the side of the grill so there are burners on either side. You now have a beer can and chicken legs tripod. Carefully place the chicken on the grates in the middle over indirect heat, burners or coals on either side of the bird, on the leg or thigh sides.

➤ Close the cover and roast for about one hour for a 3½- to 4-pound chicken. Check for doneness with an instant-read thermometer showing 165°F for the breast and 170°F for the thigh.

➤ Using insulated rubberized gloves, carefully remove the chicken from the grill, making sure you don't spill any remaining very hot beer. Remove the can from the cavity, lay the chicken on its back, and let it rest for ten minutes before carving and serving.

Grilling Tech Talk

For an excellent video showing how to make beer can chicken, tune into www. celebritygrillshow.com. The host, JM, has so much enthusiasm and expertise you'll become a beer can chicken convert in a just few minutes of viewing pleasure. He makes it look as easy as it really is.

CHAPTER 17

 **Grilled Beef Recipes**

In This Chapter

➤ Healthy and tasty grilled steak recipes

➤ Beef kabobs and satays—and more

➤ Roasting beef on the grill

Steak is a grilling favorite for good reasons. Most cuts of beef are forgiving if your grill timing is off a little, unlike chicken and leaner pork cuts, because they have more intrinsic fat. Despite this, beef in moderation is a very healthy meat. With organic and grass-fed beef readily available, a grilled steak dinner remains a treat we meat eaters can enjoy without guilt or health concerns. Beef is rich in vitamin B12 in a readily absorbable form, which is essential for brain and nerve development, especially in children and older adults.

These recipes will give you a good foundation for many types of beef steak grilling, but be sure to check out Chapter 5 to learn the basics and get the essentials on marinades, various presentations, and healthy grilling tips.

Steak Recipes

All the steak recipes here are for boneless sirloin, rib eye, or London broil unless otherwise stated. Filet mignon, or flank steaks, and hanger steaks have different textures and other properties that require slightly different treatment, so I specify when those cuts are used in a recipe.

In all recipes, you should marinate for at least one hour up to four hours unless otherwise stated, and rest steaks at room temperature for fifteen to thirty minutes, depending on thickness, before grilling. Pat marinated steaks dry before grilling on clean, oiled grates because moisture retards the formation of attractive grill marks. When using a rub, you should apply it, or just salt and pepper, when you rest the steaks before grilling.

Grilling times will produce a medium-rare steak, assuming your grill is like mine in heat output, so practice to get the timing right on your grill to produce a steak done to your liking. Different gas grill brands and other factors affect heat output. For charcoal grilling, there are other variables that affect heat, such as type of charcoal and amount used. Even air temperature, wind direction, and speed affect grilling time, so get to know your particular grilling environment before showing off for company. Always rest grilled steaks for five to ten minutes before slicing and serving.

Grilling Tech Talk

Grill-roasting is the way to go with steaks. Briefly sear meat for two to three minutes on each side over direct medium-high heat, and then flip again and move meat to indirect heat. Grill 1-inch steaks for six to eight minutes more for medium-rare, about ten to fourteen minutes overall grilling time.

Marinating steaks for one or more hours in a solution of acid (vinegar, lemon juice, etc.) and olive oil along with grill-roasting can reduce HCA formation by 90 percent. Rosemary leaves and turmeric also seem to inhibit HCA. PAH won't form if you prevent flare-ups and charring over open flames. Moderation, in consumption and grilling technique, is the key to healthy grilling.

The Classic Grilled Sirloin Steak—My Way

When my favorite local New York area supermarket, Fairway, has a sale on USDA prime boneless sirloin, you'll often find me talking grilled steak with the experienced guys behind the meat counter. I let them pick my steak, and if it's too big for our usual steak dinner, we freeze the rest and grill it another time. Most of the time I prefer to buy grass-fed beef for both health and ethical reasons, but since only about 2 percent of beef gets the *prime* label, I take a happy fall off my beefy philosophical high horse and grill the best. Guilty as charged—but worth it. Nothing fancy here when the steak is prime, just my go-to everyday marinade, salt and pepper, maybe an extra splash of the best olive oil. The expressions of delight when I slice and serve this to family and friends epitomizes the grilled steak experience.

Ingredients (for six to eight servings)
About 2 lb boneless sirloin steak, cut 1 inch thick or a little thicker

For the marinade
Whisk together
¼ c olive oil
¼ c red wine vinegar
½ Tbs Dijon mustard
1 tsp Worcestershire sauce
1 tsp (or more) fresh garlic, minced—or rub a cut piece of garlic on the steak for a gentler garlicky background
Salt and pepper to taste

Directions
Marinate steak for at least one hour up to four hours. Remove from marinade and pat dry. Rub in salt and pepper or any other rub you prefer. Place steak on clean, lightly oiled grates and grill-roast. Let steak rest for five to ten minutes when done, then slice and serve. If you're feeling Italian, a sprinkle of your best olive oil is called for.

Grilling Tech Talk

For all steaks, remove any visible fat around the outside of the steak. This fat adds no flavor because it melts away into the coals or flavor bars as it cooks, but dripping fat can cause unhealthy flare-ups. There are people who love to eat beef fat, so if you want to indulge in that particular sin (and everyone is entitled to a few sinful moments in life), monitor closely to prevent flare-ups on steaks.

Beef Steak Florentine (for six to eight servings)

This is my other favorite way to grill steaks for the family, and when you have guests they will enjoy the added Italian accent that comes from rosemary and lemon juice. Always serve this with spinach, either steamed or sautéed in a little olive oil and garlic for a more authentic taste. And adding some grilled mushrooms is very Firenze style as well. Tuscany, here we come.

Ingredients

6–8 small 1-inch-thick T-bone steaks or 3–4 large porterhouse steaks or 2 lb boneless sirloin or London broil

1 Tbs olive oil and same amount of lemon juice for each steak, reserved

Salt and pepper to taste

For the marinade

¼ c olive oil

¼ c lemon juice

1 Tbs rosemary leaves, crumbled

1 tsp garlic powder

Directions

Marinate steaks for at least one hour up to four hours. Pat dry and grill-roast. Just before steaks are done, splash each steak with olive oil and then lemon juice, flip and repeat, and remove from the grill. Salt and pepper to taste, and let stand for a few minutes before serving. Use very good olive oil and freshly squeezed lemon juice—never bottled.

Grill Speak

When we grillers talk about searing meat, we are creating a misunderstanding. The common understanding of *searing* is to lightly char the meat surface and create attractive grill marks in order to seal in the juices. Sealing in juices is a myth. The charring and/or grill marks result from natural sugars on the meat surface caramelizing from the heat, literally turning into caramel. Instead of sealing in juices, searing actually eliminates juice, drying out the meat nearest the heat source. So in addition to the health benefits of searing briefly, you'll get a much juicier steak if the meat spends most of its time over lower indirect heat as in the grill-roasting method.

Flank Steak with Mustard (for six to eight servings)

This meat is so flavorful it almost needs nothing except salt and pepper. But I like to smear on mustard, which infuses the meat as it grills, enriching the taste and aroma. Another example of simplicity trumping complicated treatments when the basic ingredient is so good to begin with.

Ingredients
2 lb flank steak or hanger steak
Grainy Dijon-style mustard
Salt and pepper to taste

For the marinade
¼ c olive oil
¼ c red wine vinegar
1 Tbs fresh garlic, minced
1 tsp rosemary leaves, crumbled

Directions
Mix the marinade and marinate the steak for one to four hours.

Pat dry and apply a light coating of mustard to both sides of the steak, salt and pepper to taste. After steak has rested, place it over medium-hot direct heat on lightly oiled, clean grates and grill-roast.

When steak is done, in this case reducing grilling time by several minutes because usually these steaks are thinner, rest the steak before slicing against the grain and serving. See Chapter 11 for other grilled veggies or vegetable recipes or Chapter 12 for grilled corn ideas in this section.

Hanger Steak à la Française (for six to eight servings)

The French love this full-flavored beef cut that they call onglet. In keeping with that designation, we use a classic herbes de Provence–infused marinade. Ask your butcher to prepare this for the grill, getting rid of any silver skin that will tighten and toughen the meat as it cooks.

Ingredients
2 lb hanger steak
Fresh garlic clove, crushed
Salt and pepper to taste
For the marinade
¼ c oil
¼ c fresh-squeezed lemon juice
1 Tbs herbes de Provence
1 tsp Dijon mustard

Directions
Marinate the steak for one to four hours. Remove and pat dry.

Rub the steak with crushed garlic clove and salt and pepper to taste. Place steak on clean, lightly oiled grates and grill-roast. When done, let rest before slicing against the grain and serving.

If you're serving this to guests and you want to get a bit fancy, nothing accompanies this better than potatoes lyonnaise. But you must go to the gym the next day—and the day after.

Bloody Mary London Broil (for six to eight servings)

This cut of beef can be a little tougher than other steaks, so a longer time in an acidic marinade is a good idea. I suggest six to eight hours, and I find this tomato-based marinade is the perfect flavor enhancer. The tomato flavor will not be noticeable—it's a background that deepens the beef taste. Don't add salt when cooking because there is more than plenty even in low sodium juices and some of the other ingredients..

Ingredients
2 lb London broil or top round steak
Garlic clove, crushed
Grainy Dijon-style mustard, optional
For the marinade
¼ c canned tomato juice or V8
¼ c canola oil
1 Tbs prepared horse radish
1 Tbs Worcestershire sauce
1 tsp fresh-squeezed lemon juice
½ tsp celery seeds
Dash of Tabasco or other hot sauce, or to taste (or use spicy V8)

Directions
Mix the marinade and marinate steak for about four hours up to eight hours. Pat dry and rub with crushed garlic clove. Lightly coat both sides with mustard if desired. Grill-roast on clean, lightly oiled grates. Let rest for about five to eight minutes before slicing and serving.

Fajitas (for six to eight servings—increase proportionally for more)

When it comes to a casual and flavor-packed meal, you can't beat steak fajitas. And there is only one cut to use—skirt steak, although in a pinch you can get away with hanger steak. Skirt steak is a little fattier and tougher than many other beef cuts, so the way you marinate, grill, and serve it are the keys to terrific fajitas. This is the perfect tailgating, picnicking, beach party steak. It's easy to transport, most of the work can be done ahead, it grills relatively quickly, and you eat it with your hands. Every griller with an ounce of pride "owns" a fajita recipe, perfected over years of experimentation. Here's mine.

Ingredients

1½ lb skirt steak, after trimming fat

Chunky tomato salsa, favorite freshly made in store or make your own

¼ c fresh chopped cilantro leaves, or less to taste

2 onions, cut into six to eight slices across the rings, toothpick inserted to hold together

Salt and pepper to taste

6–8 large flour tortillas

For the marinade

¼ c freshly squeezed lime juice

3 Tbs canola oil

1 Tbs ground cumin

1 Tbs medium-hot chili powder such as ancho

1 tsp coriander seeds

1 tsp grated lime zest

Directions

Mix the marinade and marinate steak for two to four hours. Pat dry, salt and pepper to taste, and grill-roast, reducing roasting time by about two to three minutes till medium-rare (skirt steaks are usually ½- ¾-inches thick). After you move steaks to indirect heat, place onions, lightly oiled, on direct heat and grill for three to four minutes per side till charred and soft.

While steaks are searing, place tortillas over indirect heat and warm them till soft. Remove and wrap in foil till ready to serve. You can keep them on indirect heat, turning now and then so they stay warm.

Remove steak when done, rest a few minutes, then slice thin against the grain on the bias. Sprinkle fresh coriander leaves over the steak as it rests. Serve tortillas and onions. Serve the steak and pass around the salsa as everyone makes fajita wraps. No wine here, only cold beer.

Steak Kabobs

So many of the world's most intriguing and creative foods come from what we used to refer to as cultures of poverty, a phrase now deemed somewhat insulting so it's no longer used. But it never had a negative connotation—in fact, the opposite. It meant, with admiration, a cultural cuisine that maximized culinary possibilities despite a lack of disposable income and few imported or protein-rich ingredients.

These cuisines feature a variety of delightful flavors while overcoming the limitations imposed by fuel shortages and climatic challenges. Among these are the dry climate cuisines of North Africa and Asia, the wellsprings of kabobs. Kabobs are the tasty solution to leaner meat in limited supply, cooked with very little fuel. They're seasoned with flavorful, naturally antibacterial spices to retard spoilage, and marinated in tenderizing solutions such as yogurt, ginger, and citrus juices. Those frugal dry-land dwellers would never have sacrificed a cow for kabobs. They used much more plentiful—and tougher—goats, sheep, and chickens for their kabobs and satays. For us, kabobs are a good, healthy way to eat beef, using leaner and smaller servings with loads of spicy flavor.

Healthy Grilling, Taken to the Max

Kabobs are deliciously healthy. Very little fat and easy to configure for portion control, these meaty morsels can be a convenient family dinner or part of a showy, elaborate celebration for friends or business associates. Combined with an assortment of skewered vegetables and fruit, steak kabobs will delight your guests while keeping preparation manageable. You can marinate and skewer them hours or even a day ahead, store them in the fridge till just a few minutes before dinnertime, and grill them quickly with very little distraction—turn once or twice and they're done in less than ten minutes.

Grilling Kabobs

There are two basic steak kabob types:

1. Cubed beef about 1 inch square arrayed on the skewer with enough space between cubes for the sides to get grill heat. Crowding together inhibits even cooking and can leave those cubes nearly raw on two touching sides.

2. Thinly sliced beef strips about ¼ inch thick and several inches long, threaded onto the skewer in an over and under fashion, also called satays.

Grilling Tech Talk

For both types of kabobs, it's a good idea to use two bamboo sticks to keep meat from rotating as it's flipped, or, better yet, a single flat metal skewer that keeps the meat stable and actually helps cook it a little quicker due to heat transfer from the hot metal skewer. Use tongs or grill gloves to handle these kabobs, and never serve kabobs still on their hot metal skewers, especially not to kids. Bamboo skewers can be plated intact as these do not retain heat.

Grill Kabobs Quickly

Place kabobs on well-oiled, clean grates over medium heat and grill 1-inch (or smaller) cubes for about two to three minutes, flip and grill for about two to three minutes more for medium-rare. For strips, grill for about two minutes per side for medium-rare. Serve immediately.

Grilling Tech Talk

Many kabob recipes call for alternating meat with a vegetable on the skewer. The reasoning is that these other ingredients add a flavor component to the meat. The problem, however, is that the vegetables and fruits require different lengths of grilling time and insulate the sides of the cubes. Your choice of rare to medium doneness determines your beef grilling time, which will be quite different from vegetable or fruit grilling times. I recommend devoting each skewer to one type of ingredient so you can time each different veggie or fruit appropriately. You won't notice any flavor loss—the meat is marinated, remember—and the different ingredients will be perfectly done when combined on the serving platter.

The World of Beef Kabobs

From Asia, Africa, and our own home-grown adaptations, kabobs, satays, and pinwheels deliver varied, healthy meals right off the grill.

Tasty Tips

These kabob recipes work as well with satays. Instead of cutting the meat into rough cubes, you cut them into strips and thread them onto the skewers in an over and under weave. Satays are done in about half time because they are about half as thick so if you're limited on fuel, this is the best way to go. Round steak makes good satays. This is also an opportunity to trim the fat off chuck and grill this flavorful cut in a much lower-calorie presentation.

Classic North African or Moroccan Shish Kabobs (for six to eight servings)

Shish Kabob means skewered charred meat in the ancient Aramaic and Turkish languages. This classic beef dish was perfected in Morocco.

Ingredients

For the marinade
1 c plain yogurt—fat-free is fine
3 Tbs fresh-squeezed lemon juice
3 Tbs olive oil
1 Tbs ground cumin
1 Tbs ground coriander
I medium onion, minced
½ c chopped mint leaves, reserve half
2 garlic cloves, minced

For the skewers
2–3 lb lean beef, top round or sirloin strip, cut into 1-inch cubes
Assorted vegetables of choice cut into rough cubes, such as sweet red pepper, mushrooms, squash, cherry or grape tomatoes, onions, yams, or eggplant
Olive oil
Lemon juice
Salt and pepper to taste
Fresh mint leaves

Directions
Marinate beef cubes for at least eight hours—overnight is even better. Thread each type of ingredient on its own skewer, two bamboos or one flat metal skewer for stability. Using tongs, place skewers on well–oiled, clean grates over medium heat. Grill meat for about three to four minutes, flip and grill for about three to four minutes more till medium-rare or to taste.

Brush vegetables with olive oil and lemon juice, and salt and pepper to taste. Grill vegetables till nicely charred; tomatoes are done first, and other ingredients take longer (see Chapter 11).

Remove meat and vegetables from skewers and combine on serving platter. Sprinkle fresh mint leaves over platter, serve immediately.

Grilling Tech Talk

Kabobs and satays don't need grill-roasting because they get done so quickly. Grilling time for kabobs is about six to eight minutes total, and satays a couple of minutes less because they are quite thin. This also means that HCA formation is negligible due to the short exposure to heat, along with marinating. Eating beef in these two forms is not just delicious. It's a very healthy way to get your B12, protein, and other meat nutrients.

Malaysian Beef Kabobs (for about eight to sixteen servings)

This recipe is not for a simple and casual family dinner. It takes some planning, time, and effort. When you want to wow your guests, this is a memorable kabob feast. With a hint of India and the tropics, the sweetness of fruit, and a slight sour note, this marinade results in a taste sensation you'll serve again and again when a special occasion calls for some extra effort. It's an ideal entertainment choice because it must be made a day ahead for marinating. On the day of the party, all you have to do is a few minutes of grilling when your guests arrive. Serve with basmati rice or couscous.

Ingredients

For the marinade
1 Tbs garlic, minced
1 Tbs fresh ginger, minced
1 Tbs ground coriander
1 Tbs ground cumin
1 Tbs ground turmeric
1 Tbs sugar
2 Tbs apricot jam
3 Tbs medium curry powder
1 tsp allspice

The liquid
1 c tamarind juice (usually available in the Hispanic food section)
1 c white wine
½ c chicken stock
½ c cider vinegar or rice vinegar (not seasoned rice vinegar—you already have sugar in here)

The seasonings
1 whole cinnamon stick
2 whole cloves
2 bay leaves

Directions
Combine the ingredients for the marinade and sauté in neutral oil for about two minutes till the spice odors perfume the kitchen. Then combine the liquids and add to the marinade. Then add the seasonings to the liquid and bring to a boil. Simmer for about five minutes, remove from heat, and cool.

This can be made a couple of days ahead of the marinating day if refrigerated. This is plenty of marinade for 2–4 pounds of meat.

Ingredients

For the skewers
2–4 1b top round or sirloin steak, cut into 1-inch cubes (and you can include other meat like boneless chicken thighs, lamb, and pork shoulder)
1 c dried apricots, softened in water
1 c dried pitted prunes, softened in water
1 medium onion, quartered
1 sweet red pepper, cut into 1-inch pieces
(increase these last four ingredients proportionally if you are using more meat)
Fresh mint leaves, chopped

Directions
Thread the meat onto skewers, leaving a little space between each piece. Thread the apricots and prunes onto skewers, alternating and allowing them to touch. Thread the onion and pepper onto skewers, alternating and allowing them to touch. Place skewers into a large deep platter (a turkey roasting pan or similar is good too). Pour the marinade over the ingredients, cover with plastic wrap, and marinate for about twenty-four hours. Turn the skewers a few times so everything marinates well.

If this is impractical for you, then marinate the ingredients in bags and assemble the skewers shortly before grilling. If using bamboo or short, flat metal skewers, you can assemble meat and fruit-veggie skewers that are one serving for each guest, which makes portion control simple.

Grill ingredients on well-oiled, clean grates over medium heat. Meat takes about six to eight minutes, onions and peppers about six minutes, and fruit about five minutes. Turn each skewer once halfway through cooking time.

Meanwhile boil marinade and reduce. Apply sauce lightly to finished kabobs and sprinkle fresh chopped mint leaves over kabobs when you serve. Couscous and a North African parsley salad are the choice side dishes.

Grill Speak

Peri-peri sauce is sometimes spelled piri-piri sauce because it was originally made with the piri piri pepper, a Portuguese hot pepper similar to the bird's eye. Ever since Vasco de Gama explored the African coast in the fifteenth century, the Portuguese have established settlements, colonies, and their culinary culture around the southern third of Africa, from Angola on the west to Mozambique on the east, with South Africa in between. No matter how you spell it, you'll love this fusion of flavors when you use it to brighten poultry, beef, pork, and shrimp.

South African Beef Kabobs with Peri-Peri Sauce (for eight servings)

The cuisine of southern Africa is underappreciated. A combination of local African ingredients, Indian spices, and Portuguese tastes, the food of Cape Town is like no other in the world. Peri-peri sauce, a mixture of hot chilies, lemon, garlic, and spices, can be bought in well-stocked supermarkets, but it's much more fun to experiment and build your own peri-peri. It's easy, and you can control the spicy heat. Impala or springbok meat is in short supply in American supermarkets, so substitute beef for these delicious kabobs.

Ingredients

For the marinade
Whisk together:
1 c white wine
½ c red wine vinegar
½ c olive oil
2 garlic cloves, minced
2 shallots, minced
1 tsp dried oregano
1 tsp dried ground ginger
1 tsp cardamom

¼ tsp cayenne
¼ tsp black pepper

For the skewers
2 lbs top round or sirloin steak, cut into 1-inch cubes or strips (you can use about twice as much meat with this amount of marinade)
2 lbs yams or sweet potatoes, cut into 1-inch pieces and steamed or microwaved until tender but just short of done, cooled
2 large sweet red peppers, cut into 1-inch pieces
2 large sweet onions, cut into same-size pieces

Directions
Marinate meat for at least eight hours, up to twenty-four hours. Thread the meat onto skewers, leaving a little space between each cube. Brush the meat with peri-peri sauce (see recipe below). Thread the sweet potatoes and peppers on skewers, touching and alternating. Brush vegetables with olive oil and peri-peri sauce.

Place meat and vegetable skewers on well-oiled, clean grates over medium heat and grill for six to eight minutes till medium-rare or to taste. Brush with peri-peri sauce once or twice while grilling and turning. Combine all ingredients on a warm platter and serve with rice or couscous.

Peri-Peri Sauce

You can make ahead more peri-peri sauce than you need. It keeps for a month in the fridge and gets better, reaching its peak flavor in two weeks.

Ingredients
8–10 hot chili peppers, chopped, such as bird's eye, poblano, or Fresno, keeping some or all seeds for more heat
¼ c freshly squeezed lime juice
¼ c olive oil
2 garlic cloves, chopped
1 Tbs fresh ginger, grated
1 tsp salt

Directions
Heat the oil in a saucepan and add all the ingredients except the lime juice. Gently simmer for about ten minutes, and then let cool to room temperature. Add the lime juice. Use an immersion blender or food processor to puree the sauce. Store in a glass jar in the fridge for up to one month. If it's too spicy hot, you can add some sweet red pepper at the pureeing stage.

Making Pinwheels

Pinwheels are layers of beef and other complimentary ingredients that are rolled up, sliced through, and grilled on their sides. They look as appealing as they taste.

Start with a flank steak and carefully slice through the steak, with the grain from left to right as the steak lies on a cutting board with the front to you. Stop cutting just before you reach the end, open and flatten it so it's about the same thickness—half of what it was—all the way from one end to the other. You've butterflied the flank steak. Or ask your butcher to do it.

Grilling Tech Talk

If you started off with a flank steak more than a foot long, you'll probably have too much steak to roll up when you're done butterflying. You want about four to five steak layers in your pinwheels, each separated by the stuffing ingredients, with each steak layer about 1/3 to ½ inch thick. So longer flank steaks should be cut through at the end, then each half used separately for pinwheels.

Now decide on the stuffing. Here are some stuffings I like:

➤ Ricotta cheese and fresh basil leaves

➤ Grated parmesan, chopped spinach, and grated mozzarella in equal proportions

➤ Grated cheddar, mustard, and crumbled tortilla chips

➤ Chopped walnuts splashed with olive oil and balsamic vinegar, layered with thin slices of provolone cheese

➤ Soy sauce-marinated bok choy leaves sprinkled with sesame oil and crushed pistachio nuts

Let your imagination and good sense guide you to a combination none of us has thought of yet. Sausage bits, tomato sauce, fresh parsley, and oregano anyone? Chopped or tiny shrimp, chopped arugula, lime juice, and thinly sliced Muenster cheese—surf and turf.

Carefully slather the stuffing on the meat, end to end, but not so thick that it will bulge out—less is more in this case. Tightly roll the meat as you would a jelly roll, from one end to the other. Insert bamboo skewers through the rolled meat every inch or so to hold the roll intact. With your sharp knife, cut the meat roll between each skewer, leaving about ½ inch on either side of the skewer. You now have pinwheels, held together by skewers, each about an inch thick when laid on their side.

Lay them flat, brush with a little oil, salt and pepper to taste, and grill on clean, well-oiled grates for about four to five minutes per side till medium-rare, or more to taste. Use a spatula to turn them. You will have some stuffing loss as the ingredients melt, so don't make your stuffing layers thick—you want most of the stuffing to stay within the pinwheel rolls. Keep these layers thin and loss will be minimal.

Serve with grilled vegetables such as butternut squash, zucchini, or asparagus and rice or potatoes.

CHAPTER 18

Pork Recipes

> ## In This Chapter
>
> ➤ Healthy grilled pork chops
> ➤ Pork loins and tenderloins on the grill
> ➤ Pork kabobs for family or a crowd

Pork is a beautiful thing. Even raw it looks good. The meat is pink to red in color, and most cuts are quite lean. It's the perfect meat for brining, unlike beef or lamb, which means you can introduce flavors deep into the meat with just a little planning ahead.

Pork loves marinades and all sorts of rubs with spices and herbs. You can give pork a completely different taste any time you want a change of pace. In other words, pork is a creative griller's ultimate reward.

In Chapter 6, I discuss the different pork cuts and their applications. I cover the basic grilling techniques for each, along with brines, marinades, and rubs from around the world. In this chapter, I'll get into the pork details using recipes I've perfected or been given by generous family and friends.

Pork is the perfect main course for a crowd. It's economical—most cuts sell for $4–$8 a pound—and at Costco and similar retailers, you can buy big loins or whole tenderloins at considerable savings over prices at your local supermarket when you want a large quantity at one time. So whether feeding the family on a weeknight or entertaining all your neighbors with a summer cookout, pork is the way to go. Use these recipes as presented here, or, better yet, think of them as launching pads for your own creations.

Grilling Pork Chops

Whether bone or boneless, center cut pork chops are a tender, succulent grilling choice. A couple of minutes searing on each side to get those attractive grill marks, and then grill-roasting over indirect heat for a few minutes more results in perfectly done chops full of the marinating or rub flavors. Buy bone-in or boneless chops, about ¾ to 1 inch thick. Bone-in chops need to grill-roast a couple of minutes more than boneless due to the bone retaining and transferring the cooler refrigerated temperature.

For most grills, whether charcoal or gas, figure about two to three minutes per side for searing, and then flip and move over indirect heat and grill-roast for another six to eight minutes. Leave the meat alone as it roasts in a covered grill. Add two minutes for bone-in chops. Chops are done at 145°F on the instant-read thermometer.

The grill temperature for roasting under a closed lid should be about 400°F. Get to know your grill and adjust timing to account for different heat outputs. Each grill brand or model has different heating qualities, and other factors can affect grilling heat such as ambient temperature, wind speed, and direction. Over time you'll get increasingly comfortable adjusting the timing to suit the conditions, and that instant-read thermometer is a big help, too.

Grilling Tech Talk

As with all meat, fish and poultry you should grill-roast pork instead of grilling entirely over direct intense heat. Lower and slower grilling will inhibit the formation of HCAs, a possible carcinogen that forms when protein foods are exposed to high heat for longer time periods. Marinating with an acid oil solution and grill-roasting over indirect heat can reduce the HCA formation by up to 90 percent. And grill-roasted pork is juicer because this lean meat doesn't dry out from intense direct heat. Pork chops are not very forgiving because they are so lean, but you can boost the juiciness with brining and marinating, along with a gentler heat source.

My Favorite Grilled Pork Chops (for six servings)

This is the recipe my family counts on—nothing very creative, just the basics.

Ingredients
6 boneless center cut pork chops, about 4–6 ounces each
1 lemon, cut into six small wedges

For the marinade
¼ c freshly squeezed lemon juice
¼ c olive oil
1 Tbs Dijon mustard
1 Tbs crushed rosemary leaves
1 tsp ground thyme

Directions
Marinate the chops for one to four hours. Remove and pat dry. Grill-roast on clean, lightly oiled grates. Just before chops are done, squeeze lemon wedge over each and remove to serve immediately.

Easy Lime Marinated Pork Chops (for six servings)

This is another simple family dinner favorite with a lime-infused flavor. Pork and lime go perfectly together, as you'll see when you grill these chops.

Ingredients
6 boneless pork chops
1 lime cut into wedges
For the marinade
¼ c fresh lime juice
¼ c olive oil
2 Tbs fresh cilantro, minced
1 garlic clove, minced
½ tsp dried hot red pepper flakes (or less to taste)

Directions
Mix the marinade and marinate the pork chops for one to four hours. Remove from marinade and pat dry. Grill-roast on clean, lightly oiled grates till chops are done. Squeeze lime juice onto chops just before removing them from the grill. The chops should be about 145°F and have a light pink center.

Tasty Tips

The marinating possibilities for pork chops are endless. Use soy sauce and ginger along with rice vinegar for a Chinese accent, and include fish sauce (either Vietnamese or Thai) to deepen the flavor with the natural glutens. Chapter 6 gives give you plenty of marinades and rubs to try.

Korean Grilled Pork Steaks (for six to eight servings)

There are two areas in the world where pork on the grill has been perfected to a level of unrivaled taste.

1. The American south, where pork barbecue was developed and where it is practiced today with ethereal creations by countless pit masters and sauce makers.

2. Eastern Asia, especially the lands adjoining China, Vietnam, Malaysia, and Korea, where pork grilling is a high art practiced by street food vendors, market stall cooks, and homemakers.

Ingredients
6–8 pork shoulder steaks, trimmed, about 1 inch thick (or you can substitute pork chops)

For the marinade
¼ c gochujang sauce, store-bought (Korean chili paste available at Asian markets)
¼ c rice vinegar
¼ c light brown sugar
2 Tbs soy sauce
2 Tbs toasted sesame oil
2 Tbs canola oil plus more for the grill

Directions
Mix the marinade and marinate the pork for eight to twenty-four hours. Remove and pat dry. Place steaks on clean, lightly oiled grates over indirect heat and grill slowly for about one hour, flipping several times. On a charcoal grill, bank the coals against opposite sides with a drip pan in the middle. Grill steaks over the drip pan. In a gas grill after heating grates, turn the middle burner off, keep the front and back burner on low, and place steaks over middle burner. Maintain temperature in covered grill of around 250°F. If you are substituting pork chops, grill for less than thirty minutes over indirect low heat because this much leaner meat will toughen if cooked for too long.

Tasty Tips

Pork steaks are available in nearly all supermarkets, but they were a regional favorite in the Midwest until recently. They are cut from the same part of the pig as pulled pork barbecue, the shoulder, or butt. The steaks are cut about 1 inch thick and slow grilled over indirect heat for or up to an hour. This is tough but flavorful pork, so a long marinade is also required. I marinate for twenty-four hours in the fridge, and then one hour at about 225°F–250°F on the grill. They stay juicy and are perfect for entertaining large groups. Buy a pork shoulder and cut the steaks yourself, trim the fat, and marinate in your own concoction, or use this spicy Korean marinade.

Pork Kabobs and Satays

Because kabobs and satays grill so quickly, they are the ideal method for serving pork to a crowd—you won't be a slave at the grill. A few minutes on the grates, a couple of turns of the skewers, and you're done. Best of all, you can make a variety of kabobs for different tastes, all in the same grilling party. You can add skewers of vegetables and fruit to round out the party, with little extra effort. Here are a few suggestions that are among my favorites. Have fun experimenting and creating your own.

Sweet and Sour Grilled Pork Kabobs (for six to eight servings)

Ingredients
1½ to 2 lb pork loin, cut into 1-inch cubes (about six cubes for each serving)
Salt and pepper to taste

For the marinade
¼ c cider vinegar
¼ c canola or neutral oil
3 Tbs honey
1 Tbs Dijon mustard
1 Tbs dried tarragon
Canola oil for spraying
3–4 sweet potatoes, cut into 1-inch cubes, microwaved till almost soft (can be done day ahead)
4 medium ripe peaches or nectarines, cut into equal-size quarters
4 red peppers, each cut into pieces for the skewers
2 or 3 big sweet onions, cut into chunks and skewered to hold together

Directions
Mix the marinade and marinate the pork cubes for about one hour. Remove, pat dry, and thread onto bamboo skewers, about six cubes on each. Leave a bit of room for each cube to cook evenly. Skewer all the other ingredients (or some others you may want to include), each type on its own bamboo skewers. Lightly coat or spray with oil, salt and pepper to taste. Grill all the skewers over medium heat, turning several times. The pork will take about six to eight minutes total, and the fruit and veggies about the same. Other fruit and vegetables may take less or more time, so add them to the grates accordingly. When done, serve each guest a pork skewer and choices of the fruit and vegetables. (Grilled apples go well with this, and grilled pears too. For each, add a little cinnamon to a light coating of oil.)

Pork Kabob Variations

There are so many ways to vary kabob marinades. Use teriyaki sauce as your main marinade ingredient for an Asian accent, or for Indian flavors use lots of yogurt, curry powder, and ginger. Mix in garam masala, the spice mixture in every Indian kitchen. Precision is not called for.

For an old-fashioned barbecue flavor, mix bottled barbecue sauce, mustard, and white vinegar for the marinade. Because kabobs grill so quickly, you won't burn the sauce. Turn kabobs frequently if you see the sauce is getting charred. Marinate cubes of pork in beer and honey; marinate in red wine vinegar and olive oil, and then rub in rosemary, oregano and black pepper for a Mediterranean theme.

Grilling Tech Talk

Throughout this book I've used several opportunities to remind you of kabob skewer safety. Serving on skewers is attractive and reinforces the casual elegance of a grilled dinner. Kabobs and satays are exotic, bursting with flavor and easy to grill. But beware. Metal skewers retain heat and you should not serve food on metal skewers, especially if the beer and wine has been flowing. Remove the food and serve on platters. Bamboo skewers don't retain heat (and usually don't need soaking, by the way—they're only on the grill a few minutes). These skewers can break when meat is being carelessly removed, so don't serve skewers to children. A piece of bamboo inside a chunk of meat is dangerous to kids.

Pork Satay for a Crowd

Some folks swear that nothing beats barbecued pork butt, slow roasted all day, to feed a crowd. Once you have placed it on a low temperature grill, the meat basically takes care of itself. A little mopping now and then with the sauce, some attention to the coals or the smoking wood on a gas fire is all that's needed, leaving you free to enjoy your guests.

I prefer leaner, spicier, more exotic pork satay for a festive outdoor party on a warm summer evening. It takes just a few minutes to get the pork from the fridge to the dinner plates, so there's no worry that you'll be distracted with a heavy-duty cooking chore during the appetizers and drinks. Everything but the satay can be fully prepared ahead.

I grill my veggies earlier in the day and serve them at room temperature. Among my favorites are grilled asparagus, zucchini strips, and sweet red peppers, simply brushed with olive oil, salt, and balsamic vinegar. Or a more Asian emphasis for the satay theme could include grilled sweet onions. Slice them across the grain and skewer with hardwood toothpicks to hold the rings together. Brush with sesame oil and soy sauce. Or use this sauce on leeks and green onions, then place them across the grates for grilling. Slice small bok choy, skewer with toothpicks, and brush with sesame oil and soy sauce—a perfect partner for a pork satay dinner. Brown rice made in a rice cooker is a good accompaniment to these vegetables.

The stars of the show are many skewers of pork satay that have been marinating for several hours and are quickly grilled just before serving.

Pork Satay

For the marinade
Whisk together
¼ c canola, peanut, or corn oil
¼ c rice vinegar (not seasoned)
1 large or 2 small shallots, minced
2 cloves garlic, minced
2 Tbs toasted sesame seeds, crushed or ground
2 Tbs oyster sauce
1 Tbs fish sauce
1 tsp sugar (leave out the sugar if you only have seasoned rice vinegar to use in the marinade)

For the dipping sauce
1 c smooth natural peanut butter
½ c hot water
¼ c fresh-squeezed lime juice
2 Tbs dark brown sugar
1 Tbs red chili paste, or less to taste—it's hot (or 1 tsp Chinese hot oil, again to taste)

Directions
Put all the ingredients except the hot water in a blender or small food processor and emulsify, adding hot water to thin the sauce as needed. It should be smooth and silky when done—the consistency of ketchup. This can be made a couple of hours ahead. Don't refrigerate. Serve at room temperature and stir just before serving.

For the grilled pork satay dinner party, follow these steps:

1. Slice 1 inch thick boneless pork loin chops into ¼-inch strips so you have strips about 2–3 inches long and 1 inch wide.

Tasty Tips

When I think Vietnamese food, I think pork. No cuisine does pork better, in my opinion, so make classic Vietnamese dipping sauce, which you can use as a marinade for chops, kabobs, and satays, and also serve on the side for a stronger taste. In a food processor, add ¼ cup each Vietnamese or Thai fish sauce and freshly squeezed lime juice, 2 tablespoons seasoned rice vinegar, 1 tablespoon sugar, two garlic cloves, and 1 teaspoon hot chili oil. Puree in the processor and add a little water to lighten the flavors to your taste. It should be hot and sour with a sweet undertone from the lime and sugar.

2. Marinate pork loin strips for about one hour. Remove from marinade and thread onto bamboo skewers in an over-and-under weave, keeping them as flat as possible so they are in contact with the grates.

3. Wrap skewers in wax paper or pile on a covered plate and keep cool till ready to grill.

4. Before guests arrive, grill veggies and arrange on platters, ready to serve at room temperature

5. Cook rice in the rice cooker so it is done just before grilling the pork; keep warm.

6. Place pork skewers directly over medium heat and grill for two to three minutes per side. Remove from the grill with tongs to warm platter.

7. Use the tongs to immediately arrange the skewers on your guests' dinner plates—one or two skewers per guest. Serve the vegetables and rice family style. Place dipping sauce in individual small bowls so guests can double dip in their own sauce serving.

Tasty Tips

Satays are terrific with an Indian-style dipping sauce. Combine ¼ cup yogurt or ¼ cup coconut milk with 1 cup of nut butter such as pistachio or almond butter—again, like the peanut butter, make sure this is natural nut butter freshly made with no stabilizers or other ingredients. Add 3 tablespoons lime juice, 1 tablespoon garam masala, 1 tablespoon soy sauce, and one minced garlic clove. Use your food processor, and if needed thin out the sauce with warm water till it has the consistency of ketchup. Taste and adjust flavors to your liking. Everything gets better with more freshly squeezed lime or lemon juice, in my opinion.

Grill-Roasted Pork Tenderloin

Pork tenderloins are usually packed two to a cryovac package, ready to cook. Some are preseasoned or marinated. I never buy those, preferring to control the ingredients and marinating time rather than leaving that up to the producer.

These tenderloins, unseasoned and each usually around 1½–2 pounds, are excellent choices for a family grilled dinner. Just be sure to check the sell-by date because despite their relatively long shelf life, they can spoil if not stored perfectly in the supermarket. Given a choice, I buy tenderloins at the meat counter from the people who process them in the store.

Pork should always be fresh in appearance with no odor and no silverskin or fat on the tenderloins. Before grilling, you can brine them for an hour or two in a saltwater solution or other flavored brine. (See brining method in Chapter 6.)

Marinate the tenderloins in a simple lemon or lime juice—or both—and olive oil marinade with herbs and spices of your choice. Marinate for at least one hour up to four hours. Remove, pat dry, and decide on a rub, or not, or a glaze or sauce. We usually have pork tenderloins simply grilled after the marinating, with salt and pepper and add a light mustard and oil glaze as its cooking. The light smoke and caramelized natural sugars seem to us the perfect flavor ingredient. Served with grill-roasted sweet potatoes and grilled zucchini or summer squash, perhaps some grilled mushrooms on the side, this is pork grilling the way it should be. But even we welcome a change now and then.

Asian Accented Pork Tenderloin (for six to eight servings)

Marinate the pork in orange juice and teriyaki instead of my go-to lemon and olive oil for a very pleasing flavor of Japan.

Ingredients
2 pork tenderloins, each about 1½–2 lb

For the marinade
2 Tbs teriyaki sauce
2 Tbs orange juice
1 tsp orange zest
1 Tbs toasted sesame oil
3 Tbs canola or peanut oil

Directions
Mix the marinade and marinate pork for one to four hours. Remove and pat dry. Sear and grill-roast the pork. After brief searing, about two minutes per side, roast the meat over indirect heat for twelve to fifteen minutes till it reaches an internal temperature of 145°F. Rest the pork for five minutes, slice, and serve.

Fat Fighters

When you serve grilled pork chops, pork tenderloins, and loins, you are only getting about 200 calories per 4-ounce serving. Even a generous 6-ounce portion is around 300 calories on average. The oil that you add in marinades is usually wiped off or falls away in the grilling process, unlike when pan roasting or braising. When you add grilled vegetables and a fresh green salad or a small serving of rice or potatoes, your entire satisfying meal is well under 800 calories. But it is so delicious you might feel guilty. Don't.

Grill-Roasted Pork Loin

After brining or marinating—your choice—pat the loin dry. Rub with olive oil and crushed herbs and spices. I like fresh tarragon and thyme and coarsely ground black pepper. Lemon and lime zest is good, too, or coat the meat with a coarse French mustard and dry rosemary and garlic powder. There is no point in exact recipes here. It's your enthusiasm that counts, and any decent grill cook will dream up herb and spice combos that delight family and friends.

Directions

After rubbing the loin, or preparing the pork in other ways, let it rest for about fifteen minutes. Get the grill hot. If using charcoal, create a space in the middle with the coals banked against opposite sides. Put a drip pan in between. If you like, add aromatic wood like cherry or apple, soaked and wrapped in foil, to the coals. Keep the lid open till the coals cool a bit, add a few more coals so you have enough fuel for a low to moderate heat, about 300°F, for an hour or more.

Place the meat in the middle, between the coal banks, fat side up, close the cover, and slow-roast for an hour or more till done, which will be when the meat reaches 145°F and has a light pink center. You can rotate the meat a couple of times after half an hour, or not. Experience with your grill will teach you whether to leave meat alone or turn.

If using gas, once the grill is hot, open the top and turn off the middle burner. Turn the front and rear burner to low. Place the meat, fat side up, in the middle between the burners, close the cover, and maintain a grill temperature of about 300°F till meat is done, which will be when the meat reaches 145°F and has a light pink center. You may want to rotate the meat once or twice after half an hour, depending on your grill's heat characteristics. Experience will be your guide here.

After meat is done, let it rest for ten to fifteen minutes before slicing and serving. While it's resting, grill apples and pears over higher heat, and briefly sear peaches and nectarines. Serve with sides of fruit and assorted grilled vegetables. Grill romaine lettuce leaves, place them on a plate, and serve a tossed salad on top of the leaves for an unusual presentation.

CHAPTER 19

 **Fish Recipes**

> **In This Chapter**
>
> ➤ Grilled whole fish and steak recipes
> ➤ Grilled fish fillet recipes
> ➤ Tasty grilled fish kabobs

Grilled fish is the healthiest meat we can eat, full of omega-3 and many other vital nutrients that are too often missing or in short supply in our diets. Ask your doctor. She'll tell you to eat fish at least once a week, and twice is better. It's good for your heart, your arteries, and your brain. There is no tastier way to consume the nutrients that fish have in abundance. Even seafood avoiders can be converted with a few recipes that make fish taste like, well, meat. That slightly smoky undertone, an exciting marinade or rub, the concentrated flavors that grilling imparts. These three elements combine to make grilling the best way to prepare fish for family and friends.

Selecting Fish for the Grill

Selecting the right fish to grill is covered in detail in Chapter 7, so make sure you read that chapter before venturing out to sea or over to your neighborhood fish counter for today's catch.

In a nutshell, you should be grilling fish that will stand up to the rougher treatment the grates inflict on them. Delicate fish like trout or flounder can be grilled, of course, but with so many other more appropriate choices why grill fish that do better in a frying pan?

Another consideration when selecting fish is to avoid buying fish that are being overfished or are suffering from environmental degradation. Again, with so many choices why take the diminishing bluefin tuna or Chilean sea bass when you can eat equally delicious yellowfin tuna and black sea bass, two of many species that are abundant, or at least not threatened with extinction?

Delicious Grilled Fish

When grilling fish, keep it simple. Grill fish on very clean grates that are lightly oiled. Lightly oil the fish, too. Grill fillets briefly to sear, till just released from the grates, and then finish by grill-roasting to substantially reduce the formation of HCAs. When appropriate (see recipes), grill fish skin-on and then remove the skin which also removes any HCAs. This helps make a juicer fish as the meat cooks more evenly.

Grilling fish is much easier than inexperienced cooks think it will be, and much tastier than just about any other cooking method for the right fish. Enjoy these recipes, and use them to jump-start your own creative menu planning when the fisherman in the family brings home the catch from the boat or the seafood market.

Grilling Tech Talk

Even professional grillers seem to want to overcomplicate fish grilling. Many of these "experts" recommend a fish basket, where you place the fish between another set of grates and clamp them together, supposedly making it easier to handle the fish on the grill. I tried that once. Only once. The fish basket is just as likely to stick to the fish. It is just one more appliance to care for and keep as clean as your grill grates, so why double your cleanup?

Grill fish on the grill grates, keep the grates clean and oiled, learn your timing, and don't overdo the heat after that brief searing time. A few practice sessions following my recommendations in Chapter 7, and you'll be grilling fish as comfortably as you grill burgers. I promise.

Grilled Fish Fillets (for six servings)

This is the easiest and simplest way to serve grilled fish—easy on the grill chef and easy on the diners. But you're not sacrificing taste for convenience. The fish you select for grilling is quite important, so limit your choice of fillets to dolphin fish (mahimahi), snapper, black sea bass, striped bass, wahoo, or similar firm-fleshed white fish, and bluefish, mackerel, and salmon for darker fish fillets, as well as many other oilier fish-like sardines. Use lime or lemon, or both—your choice.

Ingredients

6 fish fillets, suitable for grilling, at least ¾ inch thick

For the marinade

¼ c canola or neutral oil

2 Tbs lime juice or lemon juice

1 Tbs lime zest or lemon zest

2–3 Tbs fresh basil, minced, or other favorite herbs

Salt and pepper to taste

Directions

Mix the marinade and marinate fillets for about half an hour (oily fish need more time). Remove and pat dry. Lightly oil fish and grates. Place fillets on very clean, oiled grates over high heat and sear for two to three minutes till fish releases easily. Flip and sear for another two to three minutes. Thinner fish may be done at this point. Flip and move fish to indirect heat and grill-roast for about four to six minutes more till center is opaque. Remove and serve immediately with grilled vegetables.

Grilling Tech Talk

The grill-roasting technique for fish fillets is a bit different from that used for other meat and poultry, primarily in the timing. Searing is done not just for grill marks, which we all find attractive, but also to form the slight crust that enables the fish to be moved without sticking to the grates. So you don't want to move them too soon. Gently slide a spatula beneath when you think the fish is scared to the release point. If it is not easily releasing, wait another minute or so. This takes some practice, but once you have the timing down, you'll feel very comfortable with grill-roasting fish. With thinner fillets, there may be no roasting time—the two to three minutes of high-heat searing is just enough.

Tasty Tips

My two favorite grilling fillets are mahimahi (dolphin fish) and striped bass. They both have the right texture for the grates and absorb marinades without losing their identities. You can taste the fish, and these two, as well as salmon, fresh bluefish, and mackerel, are indeed tasty. Vary the marinade to create all sorts of wonderful flavors. See Chapter 7 for marinating ideas from Asia to Latin America.

Grilling Tech Talk

Whole fish must be scaled to prepare for grilling (same for skin-on fillets). Don't try this at home. It's a mess. Have your fishmonger remove the scales, fins, head, and tail (or leave those on for presentation). If fish are fresh caught by you, your spouse, or friend, use a scaling tool, readily available at all tackle shops, at an outdoor fish table at the dock. Gut, descale, cut off fins, and thoroughly rinse the fish before taking it home. Remember, none of this messy work should be done in the kitchen—unless you plan on being the one doing all the cleanup.

My Foolproof Grilled Whole Fish (for six to eight servings)

Depending on the size of the fish and the appetites of the humans, you can use three larger red snappers, about 2–3 pounds each, or six small snappers about 1 pound each. Fresh porgies and farmed striped bass do really well with this recipe, too.

Grill the whole fish so the bone just peels out. If you want to serve these filleted, after they come off the grill, simply insert a knife into the back till you feel the spine, slide over it gently, and lift the upper side of the fish off its bones—a spatula helps with a big fish. Then lift the bones out of the other half by peeling the spine from the front end toward the tail. It and the ribs will easily lift out of the meat, leaving two fully cooked boneless fillets.

Ingredients
Three or more whole red snappers

For the marinade
¼ c olive oil
¼ c lime juice or lemon juice
2 garlic cloves, minced
1 big bunch of fresh thyme (a typical container full—2 or 3 ounces, sold in supermarkets)
1 big bunch of fresh tarragon, same container size
Salt and pepper

Directions
Using a paring knife, score the fish with several diagonal cuts through the skin about halfway into the meat from head to tail. Combine the oil, juice, and garlic for the marinade. Stuff the cavity of each fish with equal amounts of fresh thyme and tarragon. Marinate the fish for about half an hour, remove, and pat dry. Place oiled fish on lightly oiled grates and sear for two to three minutes on each side over direct high heat. Then move fish to indirect heat and grill-roast for another three to four minutes on each side till done—about two to three minutes longer on each side for larger, thicker fish.

Serve small whole fish to each diner or filet larger fish and serve half to each person. Grilled pineapple slices, grilled potatoes, and summer squash are perfect sides with this dish.

Fat Fighters

Most fish is low calorie and loaded with nutrition. Salmon, for instance, is less than 300 calories for a 6-ounce serving, with potassium (23 percent daily value), vitamin A (22 percent daily value), vitamin C (18 percent daily value), magnesium (15 percent daily value). Where can you get this much good stuff at such a low-calorie cost, not to mention all the heart-healthy omega-3 oil? And it tastes so delicious.

Grilled Seafood Steaks (for six servings)

This is my foolproof method for grilling tuna steaks, and it will work just as well for other seafood steaks such as swordfish, mako, halibut, or salmon, which are usually available at good seafood markets. The recipe calls for loads of fresh herbs, starting with rosemary (use sparingly, much less than the other herbs, due to its dominant flavor). Include any and all favorite herbs. The intense grill heat infuses the fish with the herbs—a powerhouse of great flavor. The grill at its best.

Ingredients
6 fresh tuna, or similar, steaks, 6 ounces each, about 1 inch thick

For the marinade
¼ c olive oil
¼ c fresh lemon juice
lemon zest from one lemon
1 or 2 tsp rosemary leaves, hand crushed
½ cup fresh parsley, tarragon, chives, sage and/or other herbs you enjoy
2 cloves garlic, crushed
Salt and pepper to taste

Directions
Mix the marinade and marinate steaks for about half an hour to an hour. Remove and pat dry, leaving a light oil coating and the herbs adhering to the steaks. Place steaks on lightly oiled grates over high heat to sear for two to three minutes on each side. (Rare tuna will be done at this point.) Flip and move steaks to

Tasty Tips

Whole fish are even easier to grill than fillets because the skin and bones provide a bit of insulation and help forgive your mistakes, like grilling a little too long or flipping too soon. Let fresh-caught fish rest several hours or overnight in the fridge before handling and grilling. See Chapter 7 for marinating ideas and vary the stuffing. I use herbs here, but try citrus instead. Fennel leaves, loads of dill, or garlic are all perfect ingredients to lie inside the fish while it marinates and grill-roasts.

indirect heat and grill-roast for about six more minutes, flipping after three minutes. Check one steak by inserting a knife sideways into the steak to see if it's done to your preference.

Serve with grilled fennel bulbs, grilled zucchini, and grilled polenta.

Tasty Tips

Check out your big-box store for frozen halibut steaks, tuna, and salmon. These are usually flash frozen on the boat, so they're really fresh. Thaw individually wrapped pieces in warm tap water, in which takes less than half an hour. See Chapter 7 for marinating ideas. You'll convert seafood avoiders with these ocean steaks, especially tuna and swordfish. If you're in a rush or short on ingredients, use bottled Italian salad dressing for swordfish and halibut, use bottled teriyaki and a little sesame oil for tuna and salmon. Yes, homemade marinades are better and it's always good to control the ingredients, but sometimes real life intrudes and we adjust.

Grilled Fish Tacos (for six servings)

All these ingredients are readily available and make a pleasing casual family dinner. Or increase this proportionately to feed a crowd. Buy your favorite salsa verde, and you can serve both kinds of tortillas if you like. Any meaty white fish does well here—even tilapia, which hasn't much taste on its own but will pick up the bold flavors of this traditional Mexican recipe.

Ingredients
1½ lb white fish fillets—sea bass, striped bass or other suitable for the grates
6 tortillas, corn or flour according to taste
1 large avocado, peeled, pitted, thinly sliced
1 c shredded cabbage
1 c mayonnaise, infused with juice of half a lime
½ c onion and cilantro (from marinade ingredients)
½ c salsa verde, store-bought

For the marinade
1 c chopped onion (reserve ½ c for serving when fish is done)
1 c chopped fresh cilantro (reserve ½ c for serving when fish is done)
¼ c olive oil

¼ c fresh lime juice
2 Tbs fresh orange juice
2 garlic cloves, minced
1 tsp dried oregano
1 tsp dried cumin
Salt to taste

Directions

Mix the marinade and marinate fish for up to one hour. Remove from marinade, leave light oil, herbs, and aromatics clinging to the fish.

Grill the fish over high heat for two to three minutes on each side, and move to grill-roast if it needs more time on the heat for four to six minutes till done. Remove fish to a board and roughly chop. Grill tortillas about half a minute, flipping once to heat through but still be very pliable.

Serve with lime-infused mayo on tortillas. Pass around ½ cup chopped onion, ½ cup cilantro, avocado slices, cabbage, and salsa verde.

My Perfect Grill-Roasted Salmon (serves six or more)

I love this recipe and make it all the time. It's so simple, yet the presentation and taste are sophisticated. Best of all, you can make the sauce ahead—it improves overnight—and the grilling process requires little time or attention. Get a real hot grill going and after searing, turn off the center burner(s) and roast the fish till done.

Ingredients

6 salmon fillets, skin on, each about the same thickness (I use flash-frozen Costco wild Alaskan, thawed in warm water for about half an hour—farm raised is OK, too)
½ c low-fat or fat-free plain yogurt
½ c fresh dill, finely chopped
1–2 tsp Dijon mustard (taste to decide)
1 tsp fresh lemon juice
1 tsp lemon zest

Directions

Mix all the ingredients for the sauce, yogurt, dill, mustard, lemon juice and zest, and chill for at least an hour. Lightly oil the grates and the fish, flesh side only. When the grill is very hot, sear the flesh side of the fish a couple of minutes till the fillets easily release. Flip and spoon sauce on the fish. Roast fish over indirect heat for six to eight minutes (closed cover, of course) till fish is done, shorter time for medium-rare, longer for well done. Gently slide a spatula between fish and skin, lifting fish easily off the skin, and serve immediately. You can

Tasty Tips

Searing salmon is a step you can skip if you prefer a roasted texture over a grilled crust. I often place the fillets skin side down on indirect heat from the beginning, apply the sauce, close the cover, and cook for ten minutes without going near the grill till done. Top-quality salmon roasts into an almost creamy texture, infused with the yogurt and dill flavors.

give the grates a quick scraping and brushing to remove the skin or just let it flake away, finishing the grate cleaning next time you turn on the grill. Be sure to remove every bit before grilling anything else. Clean grates are the rule.

Whole Roasted Coho Salmon (one per person)

Use the same salmon fillets sauce (above) for farm-raised whole cohos, about a pound each. Arctic char are also widely available and delicious with this sauce. Get your fish man to prepare the fish for grilling, removing the fins and tail, etc.

➤ Make a few diagonal slashes halfway into the meat on both sides.

➤ Rub with olive oil and lemon juice.

➤ Grill-roast from the beginning over indirect heat with the temperature inside the covered grill at about 400°F.

➤ Flip the fish at five minutes, and after another five minutes remove to a platter.

➤ Carefully insert a thin spatula or dinner knife from the dorsal side across the spine and lift the fish off the bones. Peel out the spine and ribs from the remaining side and serve the fish with the yogurt dill sauce on the side. Or serve the fish whole, one to each guest, and let them do this filleting with an ordinary dinner knife. It's real easy once you've either done it yourself or been shown how to do it.

Tasty Tips

This yogurt dill sauce, which I originally developed for salmon, is also a terrific chicken marinade, or salmon kabob marinade. I always make extra, doubling or tripling the recipe because it keeps in the fridge as long as yogurt does. Use it with a little more mustard, or add 1–2 tablespoons of honey mustard to marinate boneless chicken breasts for a few hours, or to marinate salmon chunks for kabobs. This is a tasty sauce for baked or mashed potatoes, or use the sauce in a veggie summer pasta salad, loaded with chopped red peppers, celery, fresh tomatoes, and sweet onions.

Whole Roasted Salmon

This is a festive grilled dinner centerpiece that you can show off on a platter.

Ingredients
4–6 pounds or more whole salmon
Lemon slices, enough to cover fish
Fresh dill, about a cup will fill the cavity
2-3 Tbs olive oil

Directions
Cover the whole fish with lemon slices over a light olive oil coating. Gently stuff the cavity of the fish with fresh dill. Slash the sides every couple of inches halfway into the meat.

I never rub salt on this fish as some recipes instruct, any more than I salt salmon when eating it.

A large salmon will take twenty to thirty minutes to cook on indirect heat with the grill covered at about 400°F. Remove the lemon slices and insert them into the cavity with the dill. Place the salmon on the grates, close the cover, and roast. Flip the fish after about ten minutes.

This is a rough guide based on the thickness of the fish. If each side is about 1 inch thick, you should roast for about ten minutes per side. Larger, thicker fish need a few more minutes. With these big fish you should flip by rolling the fish over, across its dorsal side, so the herbs in the cavity stay intact. You can ask for assistance—another spatula is very helpful. Easy does it. Use a spatula to gently lift the fish off the bones and peel the bones off the remaining side. Serve with the yogurt dill sauce.

Grilled fennel bulbs and sweet potatoes go very well with roasted salmon dishes.

Grilled Tuna Steaks

We often grill fresh tuna steaks using the foolproof method and marinade for grilled seafood steaks above. Like salmon, I tend to buy the frozen wild sashimi grade tuna from Costco or similar big-box store. But I can't resist fresh-caught tuna when traveling through an East Coast commercial fishing port like Port Judith, Portland, the Jersey shore towns, or the Outer Banks—or occasionally when I catch my own.

As with most really fresh fish, simpler is better. If we have a lot of tuna, we'll vary the taste to a Vietnamese or other Asian treatment, as you can see in the marinade varieties in Chapter 7. Tuna is what I call a convert fish because its meaty taste will convert almost all fish haters into, at the very least, tolerant seafood consumers.

Grilled Ligurian Tuna (for six to eight servings)

Sardinia is a magical place. Hills covered with wild rosemary and arugula, hidden beaches sheltered by towering cliffs over a turquoise sea. And at least two amazing fish dishes. Pasta with a sauce made with garlic, olive oil, white wine, fresh parsley, and fish eggs (bottarga), and grilled tuna served with a pesto sauce like this one.

Ingredients
6–8 tuna steaks, about 1 inch or more thick
Oil

For the pesto
2 c fresh basil
1 garlic clove
¼ c toasted pine nuts (or roasted walnuts, unsalted)
½ c extra-virgin olive oil (may need a little more)
½ c grated Parmesan cheese
2 Tbs fresh lemon juice
Black pepper to taste (optional)

Tasty Tips

Another traditional Ligurian tuna dish uses anchovy butter, as the Romans do with beef steak. This powers the great fresh tuna taste, and only a tiny bit of butter is needed. Combine 3–4 tablespoons room temperature butter with ½ teaspoon anchovy paste (or two very mashed anchovy fillets), 1 teaspoon of fresh lemon juice, and 2 tablespoons of minced fresh parsley. When each tuna steak is done to your liking, spread a bit of the anchovy butter on it. A teaspoon will be fine. This is terrific on swordfish, halibut, and mako steaks, too.

Directions
Lightly oil the tuna and the grates. Heat the grill to very hot. Sear tuna steaks for about two minutes on each side for very rare. Roast for an additional two to four minutes per side for rare to medium. Remove tuna and let rest.

Use a food processor to puree the basil, garlic, and nuts, first pulsing to chop, and then gradually adding the olive oil till the consistency is a classic pesto, a smooth consistency a little thicker than ketchup. Use a soft spatula to transfer to a bowl and add the cheese. (No salt needed because Parmesan is quite salty, but you may want black pepper to taste.)

Slice the warm or room temperature tuna across the grain, on a bias, into ½-inch-thick slices. Place the slices on a serving plate and splash with lemon juice. Serve the pesto on the side or put a dollop on each dinner plate. Arrange tuna slices attractively over the sauce. Drizzle a little more pesto on tuna and serve.

This lovely dish deserves a big salad with fresh greens, perhaps some grill-charred romaine leaves or grilled bunches of arugula and grilled polenta—see the chapter on grilled bread for more ideas.

Grilled Tuna Tuscan Style (for six to eight servings)

This couldn't be easier. You do all the prep work on a flat work surface, a big cutting board, or similar. Your grill does the rest.

Ingredients
6–8 tuna steaks, 4–6 oz each
3 Tbs rosemary leaves, finely chopped
Zest of 2 lemons
¼ c fresh parsley, chopped
2 Tbs crushed garlic
Sea salt and pepper
Olive oil

Directions
Spread some of the rosemary and zest on the work surface in one little pile, and some of the garlic, parsley, salt, and pepper in another. Lightly coat the steaks with oil. Press each tuna steak into each pile, one side and then the other, renewing the piles as needed till all the fish is coated with all the ingredients. Rest the fish at room temperature for a few minutes. Grill over high heat briefly to sear on each side. Very rare tuna is done. For rare to medium, move tuna to indirect heat and grill-roast for two to four minutes per side till done. I like to splash the steaks with a bit of olive oil as they are served, especially if it's the best unfiltered extra-virgin oil I can find.

Serve with grilled portabella mushrooms and a fresh tossed salad or platter of grilled veggies.

Grilled Swordfish My Way (for six servings)

When fresh swordfish from Montauk is in the Union Square farmers' market here in New York, I always strap a small cooler chest to the back of my bike, ensuring the fish I bring home stays as fresh as it is at the market. It's grilling time, with a Greek accent.

Ingredients
6 swordfish steaks
¼ c olive oil
3 Tbs fresh mint, chopped
3 Tbs fresh-squeezed lemon juice

2 Tbs fresh oregano, chopped (or less to taste—it's a strong herb flavor)
2 Tbs fresh basil, chopped
1 garlic clove, minced
Salt and pepper to taste

Directions

Marinate swordfish in olive oil and lemon juice for half an hour to one hour. Combine the rest of the ingredients in a bowl and coat both sides of the fish with the herbs and garlic mixture. Sear each steak briefly over high heat for two to three minutes per side. If steaks are ½ inch thick, they will be done. Grill-roast thicker steaks over indirect heat for three to four minutes per side till done. Center of steaks should be opaque and juicy.

Serve with couscous and grilled vegetables sprinkled with fresh herbs, more mint in the couscous, and shredded basil on the veggies.

Fish Kabobs (for six servings)

Grilling fish on skewers is a perfect party menu. You can serve a crowd without much distraction. The fish cooks relatively quickly and most of the work can be done ahead, so you're really busy for only a few minutes before this festive meal.

The key here is to select the right fish because you don't want the kabob cubes to come apart and fall off the skewers. I find halibut and salmon perfect fish for this. Swordfish works very well. So make sure your fish steak or fillet is about 1 inch thick and the texture is very firm, not easily flaked when grilled.

Thread the fish and vegetable on separate skewers to grill for different lengths of time. Some vegetables require longer or shorter grilling times than the fish. If you're grilling onions and sweet potato pieces, they will each require different treatment—the onions over moderate direct heat for about six minutes; the potatoes over indirect heat for about ten minutes. The fish over indirect heat will need about six to eight minutes or if seared over high direct heat, just a couple of minutes per side. Always leave a little space between kabob pieces so the heat gets the sides done, too.

Ingredients

1½ to 2 lbs halibut, salmon, or swordfish, cut into approximately 1-inch cubes
2 large sweet potatoes, skinned and cut into 1-inch cubes
12 small onions or onion chunks, about 1 inch diameter
12 pineapple pieces, about ½ inch thick
2 Tbs dark rum
Olive oil for brushing
Salt and pepper to taste

For the marinade
¼ c canola oil
3–4 Tbs freshly squeezed lime juice
1 Tbs cumin
1 tsp hot pepper flakes, or less or omit to taste

Directions
Mix the ingredients for the marinade and marinate the fish for about half an hour, and then thread onto flat metal skewers or shorter bamboo skewers (if bamboo,s you may want to use two skewers per kabob to prevent rotation—same for other ingredients). Thread sweet potatoes and onions on separate skewers and brush with olive oil, salt, and pepper. Pour rum onto a flat plate and dip pineapple slices to lightly coat.

Grill sweet potato kabobs for about ten minutes over indirect heat, turning as needed to prevent burning, till done. Grill onion kabobs over direct heat for about three minutes per side till soft and charred. Grill fish kabobs over indirect heat, turning two to three times till lightly browned and done to opaque in the center, about eight to ten minutes. Grill pineapple slices for about three minutes per side over medium-high direct heat till nicely caramelized.

Remove all ingredients from metal skewers, arrange on a platter, and serve. Bamboo skewers can be served intact to adults because they don't hold the heat.

Mock Tandoori Fish (for six to eight servings)

When we eat in Indian restaurants, I almost always order tandoori fish, halibut or salmon on a skewer roasted in a screaming hot clay oven. Here's my attempt at replicating this fish dish on my grill at home. It's almost as good as the best Indian restaurant fare.

Ingredients
1½ to 2 lbs salmon, halibut, or swordfish, cut into 1-inch chunks

For the marinade
½ c neutral oil
¼ c rice vinegar
2 Tbs grated fresh garlic
1 Tbs grated fresh ginger or twice as much dried
1 Tbs ground coriander seeds
1 Tbs ground cumin
1 tsp cinnamon
1 tsp cayenne
1 tsp salt

Directions

Mix the ingredients for the marinade and marinate the fish for about half an hour, and then thread the fish cubes onto flat steel skewers (leave a little gap between cubes) and let rest in the fridge for another half an hour before grilling. Oil the fish with a teaspoon, pouring a little oil and spreading it with the back of the spoon along the skewered fish cubes, rotating the skewers on the platter to completely coat the fish. Don't worry about using this much oil—it burns off during cooking and keeps the fish from sticking. Heat the grill to very hot, about 500°F covered.

Grill the fish over hot direct heat, cooking the fish briefly for about one minute on each of four sides, using tongs to rotate the skewers. This gets done quickly because the skewers are transferring heat inside while the outside of the fish cubes get a pleasing char. Do not serve fish on these dangerously hot skewers. Use grill-gloves or potholders and a grill fork to gently remove fish cubes to a warm platter to serve.

Separately grill red peppers and sweet onion chunks and serve with basmati rice and homemade yogurt/cucumber raita for dipping (many good recipes online).

CHAPTER 20

Shellfish Recipes

In This Chapter

➤ Grilling recipes for lobsters, crabs, and shrimp

➤ Grilling recipes for oysters and clams

➤ Recipes for the shell-less shellfish, squid

When you've develop a few shellfish recipes, especially for the "big three"—lobsters, shrimp, and squid—you have arrived in the pantheon of seriously accomplished grill chefs. This is a specialty that not all grill chefs want to tackle, but one that is well worth the time and effort.

Grilled Lobster and Crab Recipes

The ability to create a tasty lobster dinner or serve a platter of lightly charred stuffed squid will set you apart from the routine grillers who won't venture beyond steak and chicken. And for most of these delicious recipes, it's not your skill level that's critical, it's not the need for years of experience—it's just a sense of grilling adventure. So let's start with lobster, everyone's favorite but also the most daunting to newly minted grillers. Be sure to consult Chapter 9 to get a good feel for buying, handling, and prepping lobsters.

My Foolproof Grilled Lobster (for six or more servings)

If using 1¼-pound lobsters, figure on one per person; for 2-pounders, you can serve half lobsters to guests with smaller appetites. It's best to stick with lobsters that weigh in at 1¼– 1½ pounds for two good reasons:

1. It's more festive to present a whole grilled lobster to each person.

2. In general, lobsters are priced per pound and the smaller lobsters cost less per pound than the larger ones that weigh over 2 pounds.

So for both economics and enjoyment, I vote for buying smaller lobsters.

Ingredients
6 or more 1¼ lb lobsters split lengthwise, cleaned, claws and arms separated from the body
For the mop
¼ c olive oil
¼ c freshly squeezed lime juice
1 Tbs tequila
1 tsp Old Bay seasoning
1 tsp (or less to taste) hot red chili flakes
Salt to taste

Directions
Mix all the mop ingredients and coat the lobster tails, meat, and shell side. Use the back of a chef knife to crack the claws and arms, and dip those in the mop. Place tails meat side down on the grates over medium-high heat and grill for about two to three minutes till attractive grill lines appear. Flip the tails so their shell side is down and spoon a little more of the mop mixture on the meat. Grill tails over direct heat for six to eight minutes till cooked through with a white center, but carefully monitor so the meat is not overcooked and tough. Note: There is no agreement on which side of the lobster to start and end the grilling, so it's your choice. I do it either way, starting with the meat side down or starting with the shell side down. But grill the shell side about twice as long as the meat side. Total grilling time will vary due to heat differences and meat thickness, so practice your timing before serving company.

Meanwhile, grill the claws and arms, flipping once or twice till done, about eight minutes total. All the grilling should be done on a closed grill whether charcoal or gas. (Practice your grill cooking times before serving company—the worst that will happen is you'll eat a little more lobster that's a little too tough till you get it right.)

Serve lobster to each guest. No need for more sauce or even melted butter unless people insist. The lobster will be succulent and infused with olive oil and lime with a hint of heat and tequila perfume. In my opinion, butter smothers these nuanced flavors.

Accompany the lobsters with grilled corn and other grilled veggies. Grilled melon is a nice flavor contrast with this.

Grill Speak

Lobster terminology can be confusing—hard shell, soft shell, shedders, and culls. Hard shell is self-explanatory and sometimes priced a little more per pound because under that shell is a little more meat. Like all crustaceans, lobsters grow within their shells till there's no more room, and then they shed. So hard shell lobsters are nearly out of space beneath that shell. Soft shell lobsters are also called shedders because they've recently left their old shell behind and are gradually hardening this new one. That means there is some room within the shell, so a similarly sized shedder will have less meat than a hard shell. Some lobstermen keep the myth alive that shedders have sweeter meat. Nonsense. It's all the same meat, just less of it. I actually prefer soft shell lobsters because they're easier to break open. Culls are lobsters that have lost a claw and are priced accordingly. If you're a tail-only lover, buy culls.

Spiny Lobster Tails (for six or more servings)

Unless you live near a southern port or beach when lobsters are in season, you'll be buying frozen lobster tails from South Africa, the Caribbean, or Australia. That's a good thing because these sweet crustaceans are flash frozen immediately and thaw into a perfect grilling no fuss, no muss candidate. Just thaw them in the fridge and split them open, first cutting through the shell with kitchen shears, then with a chef knife through the shell side but not the opaque lining that is beneath that meat layer. You want to butterfly the tail. Spiny lobsters tend to be a bit dry, so use lots of mop and grill over lower heat than you would for North American lobsters.

Ingredients

6 or more spiny lobster tails, thawed and butterflied

For the mop

¼ c olive oil

¼ c freshly squeezed lime juice

¼ c fresh cilantro, finely chopped

1–2 garlic cloves, minced

1–2 Tbs dark rum

Directions

Mix the mop ingredients and liberally coat both sides of the tails with mop. Grill meat side down over medium-high heat for two to three minutes till attractive grill marks appear. Flip lobsters and apply more mop. Grill shell side down over medium heat for about eight minutes more till lobster is white in the center.

Serve with grilled pineapple, grilled corn, and/or other vegetables.

Grill Speak

Soft shell crabs and soft shell lobsters, how do they differ? Soft shell lobsters, also called shedders, have shells that are hard but pliable right after they've molted. Soft shell crabs, on the other hand, have paper-thin new shells that are as soft and as edible as apple skins. Only the carapace and organs are removed by your fish guy. All the rest of the crab is edible.

Grilled Soft Shell Crabs (for six to eight servings)

Once you grill instead of fry soft shell crabs, you'll never go back to the skillet. A light, smoky char adds flavors you can't replicate on the stove.

Ingredients

12–16 medium-size soft shell crabs (two per person), cleaned and ready for the grill
¼ c olive oil
4 pats melted butter, about a quarter stick
Zest from one lemon
Freshly squeezed juice from one lemon
¼ c fresh herbs, your choice (basil, mint, parsley, tarragon), finely chopped

Directions

Mix the ingredients and pour over crabs. Let the crabs sit for about fifteen to thirty minutes. Place crabs on the grates over medium-high direct heat and grill for about three to four minutes per side, flipping once, for a total of six to eight minutes. Crabs should be crispy on the outside with moist, succulent meat.

Serve with grilled corn, grilled zucchini, and grilled polenta.

Grilled Shrimp Recipes

Before you decide to try one or more of these recipes, go to Chapter 8 to learn more about buying, handling, and preparing shrimp. I always have several pounds of shrimp in the freezer for a spur of the moment family meal or a pop up grilling party for friends. Shrimp thaw in less than half an hour in warm tap water, ready for a brief marinade or mop before the shrimp hit the grill—freezer to dinner table in less than an hour.

The basic concepts remain no matter what marinade recipes you use. Marinate shrimp for a shorter duration than do larger fish, don't use too much acid or you'll begin making ceviche—a concept different from grilling—and skewer the shrimp to keep them from falling through the grates.

I use 2 pounds of large shrimp, about forty-five to fifty shrimp, enough for six guests, but feel free to be generous and add more. Recipes are easily tweaked for flexibility. The next day, the leftover cold shrimp are your treat for being a creative grill chef.

Grilled Shrimp Margarita (for six servings)

Ingredients
2 lb large shrimp

For marinade
¼ c tequila
¼ c fresh squeezed lime juice
¼ c canola oil
2 Tbs triple sec
¼ c chopped cilantro
Salt and pepper to taste

Directions
Mix the ingredients for marinade and marinate the shrimp for half an hour. Thread shrimp onto skewers and grill over medium-high heat on well-oiled grates for two to three minutes per side.

Tasty Tips

Are you in a hurry? Have unexpected friends dropped in and you need a quick, delicious dinner? Thaw your frozen shrimp in warm tap water for half an hour or less and pat dry. Lightly coat the shrimp with oil. Thread them onto skewers. Grill, turning after about two to three minutes a side. When just about done, brush both sides with your favorite bottled BBQ sauce, cook for another thirty seconds on each side to infuse the sauce and serve with grilled corn and rice or pasta with olive oil and freshly squeezed lemon juice, a sprinkle of herbs, and parmesan.

Grilled Shrimp Scampi (for six servings)

Garlicky shrimp in a buttery olive oil dressing is a classic, and it may seem almost sacrilegious to tamper with this Italian-American favorite. But for those of us who think grilling makes just about everything better (and healthier), here's a garlic lover's grilled shrimp scampi.

Ingredients
2 lbs large shrimp
¼ c olive oil
¼ c freshly squeezed lemon juice
2 Tbs melted butter
4 garlic cloves, minced
1 Tbs red pepper flakes
Freshly grated parmesan cheese
Bunch of chopped fresh Italian parsley

Directions
Mix the olive oil, lemon juice, and melted butter, then mix in the garlic and let that infuse for a few minutes. Reserve about 3 tablespoons for mopping. Add pepper flakes. Add shrimp and marinate for about half an hour. Thread shrimp onto skewers and brush with more garlic-infused oil, lemon, butter, mixture. Grill over medium-high heat on well-oiled grates for two to three minutes per side, brushing with reserved garlic-infused oil, lemon, butter mixture when you flip them.

If you're using metal skewers, carefully remove shrimp before serving. Shower hot shrimp with grated cheese and fresh parsley.

Tropical Shrimp (for six to eight servings)

You can make this with small chunks of tropical fruit, whatever you prefer, mango, papaya, kiwi, pineapple (my favorite), or even peaches and nectarines.

Ingredients
8–10 shrimp per person
8–10 fruit chunks per person, about ½ inch thick
¼ c or more fresh mint, finely chopped
For the marinade
¼ c freshly squeezed lime juice
¼ c canola oil
2 Tbs fresh ginger, grated
1 Tbs hot pepper flakes
2 shallots, finely chopped

Directions

Mix the marinade and marinate the shrimp for about half an hour.

Thread shrimp and fruit onto skewers, alternating shrimp and fruit. If they are the right size, you can curl the shrimp around the fruit chunk, cradling the fruit in the curve of the shrimp on the skewer for a more attractive appearance. To do that, pierce the skewer through the tail end, then the fruit chunk, then the head end of the shrimp so the fruit nestles between these ends.

Grill the skewers for two to three minutes per side for a total of about six minutes or less till shrimp is cooked through and fruit is heated and beginning to caramelize.

If you're using metal skewers, remove the shrimp and fruit before serving. Serve with grilled corn and grilled flat bread.

Grilling Clams and Oysters

In Chapter 9, you'll find a host of useful tips on buying, preparing, and grilling oysters and clams. If you savor fresh oysters and clams on the half shell, you'll enjoy them grilled, too. The light smokiness, along with the heat, creates a taste that's a variation on the theme rather than something entirely new. Grilling has the added benefit of virtually eliminating any risk of contamination because the meat reaches bacteria-killing temps in just a few minutes. When the shell fully opens, the oysters and clams are done. Be sure to place oysters cup side down on the grates so you don't lose juice, and practice getting your timing right. If you grill these too long the liquid steams away, leaving a rubbery, formerly succulent meat.

Tasty Tips

Not all shellfish are better on the grill than in the pot. Admittedly this is a personal preference, and there are, in fact, plenty of seemingly good mussel recipes in books and on the Internet. For me, though, half the joy of eating mussels is the steaming broth in all its tasty and exotic variations. Mussels are best cooked in a pot. Hard shell clams work well on the grill, and I prefer littlenecks or cherrystones for their size. I would not grill belon oysters from France, Maine, or Canada. They are too good raw on the half shell. Yes, there are a few foods that grilling does not improve.

Shell-Less Shellfish Recipes: Calamari on the Grill

Squid are everywhere, from tasteless fried rings in your neighborhood sports bar to exotic Chinese and Vietnamese sensations. They are an inexpensive weekday main course and can be turned into an impressive grilling event for friends. They grill quickly and require very little advance preparation. Your fish guy will gladly get them grill-ready, or if you buy the cleaned and frozen product, you can thaw it overnight. Chapter 10 gives you a good background on buying, handling, and grilling techniques for squid and octopus. Here are some of my favorite calamari grilled dinners.

Spanish Grilled Squid (for four servings)

Marinating squid for at least an hour in this sherry-based marinade transports you and your guests to the Costa del Sol.

Ingredients
2 lbs whole squid bodies

For marinade
¼ c olive oil
¼ c good sherry
4 cloves garlic, minced
1 Tbs oregano
1 tsp hot pepper flakes, or less cayenne, to taste
1 tsp paprika
Salt to taste
Chopped Italian parsley for garnish
Olive oil to finish

Directions
Whisk marinade ingredients together and marinate squid for up to three hours. Grill squid over high heat for two to three minutes per side, about five minutes total.

Serve on a warm platter, sprinkle with parsley and drizzles of your finest olive oil.

Squid Stuffed Squid (for four to six servings)

No, you're not OD'ing on squid when you serve this stuffed squid dish, one of my favorites because it's so versatile. Buy fresh or frozen cleaned whole squid with tentacles, plus some small shrimp or bay scallops. For four, five, or six people use about 2 pounds of squid and about ½ pound of the other shellfish. The size of the squid bodies and appetites of the diners will guide your squid buying.

Ingredients

2 lb squid

½ lb shrimp or scallops, or combine both, coarsely chopped

¼ c panko bread crumbs (or whole wheat)

1/4 c fresh herbs, basil, parsley or other

2 Tbs olive oil

1 Tbs fresh squeezed lemon juice

1 tsp lemon zest

1 tsp Old Bay seasoning

Directions

Chop the tentacles. Briefly sauté the squid tentacles and shellfish in 1 tablespoon of olive oil for about three minutes till cooked through. Add the remaining ingredients and sauté for another two minutes. Cool ingredients till warm and easily handled. Stuff squid bodies with the mixture and secure with toothpicks. Rub squid with remaining olive oil and grill over high heat for about two to three minutes per side till nicely charred.

Serve immediately on warm platters, garnish with more fresh herbs if desired.

Fat Fighters

Even foods like sausage and cheese can be included in your weight-loss diet when stuffed into squid. Don't use too much, stuff the squid loosely, and measure how much of these fattier ingredients you're using. Lots of flavor comes from just a little sausage, for instance, so use mostly fresh herbs and a few crumbles of delicious sausage. If you're adding bread crumbs to the stuffing mixture, use whole wheat instead of white bread.

Brick-Grilled Squid

Bobby Flay, in my opinion the most innovative celebrity grilling chef, introduced me and thousands of other viewers to the concept of using a brick when grilling calamari. Long used on chicken (see Tuscan Grilled Chicken in Chapter 4), the foil-covered brick set on top of the squid intensifies the heat and keeps the entire squid in contact with the grates. The results are very tasty.

I suggest the large Pacific squid, the bigger the better, cut through the tube on one side and laid out flat. Brush with olive oil and an acid like fresh-squeezed lemon, lime, orange, or pineapple juice, and salt and pepper to taste. Place the foil-wrapped brick on top, and grill two minutes per side over medium-high heat. Succulent, low calorie, and very satisfying alone or with various salsas for dipping.

A variation is to brush the squid with sesame oil, soy sauce, and rice vinegar. Infuse the oil with the Indian spice mixture garam masala and a medium-hot curry powder along with fresh ginger, then brush the squid steaks with the oil for an Indian theme. If you have the time, allow an hour or so for these various sauces to marinate the squid. If not, the brick grilling will hasten the flavoring process.

CHAPTER 21

 # Grilling Celebrations

---

In This Chapter

➤ Thanksgiving Turkey

➤ Cedar Planks and Salt Blocks

➤ Sibling Rivalry Clams

➤ Wings, Burgers, Vegetarian Dinners

We grill year round, even in the snow. Firing up the gas grill on a cold winter evening is not the most comfortable way to cook, but the results compensate for a few minutes of discomfort. The key element is to grill food that needs no attention because it's placed on the grill for a specified time period, no flipping, no moving around for different heat qualities. Two quick trips to the grill and you're done. Here are three of our favorite cold weather recipes that don't require grill monitoring and deliver wonderful flavors that justify a bit of inclement weather annoyance.

Thanksgiving—Tony's Turkey

I am always running out of oven or burner space at Thanksgiving. Everyone has a favorite side dish—or several—so I make two kinds of mashed potatoes, sweet potatoes, two kinds of stuffing, cranberry sauces, and the obligatory green veggies such as string beans that no one eats but everyone complains if they're not on the table. Meanwhile, my gas grill sits forlornly on the deck, our most useful and user-friendly cooking appliance in sleep mode when we need it the most. This is the one occasion when even a kitchen equipped with a double oven is a challenge for meal timing and cooking space. So many dishes, too many to get done or keep warm till that moment of serving. Ah, the grill, you think. But how?

My friend Tony Delio is not only a master outboard motor mechanic, an expert bow and arrow deer slayer, a horse racing enthusiast and an opera buff. He is a most creative grilling chef. He generously taught me how to roast turkey on the grill with no special equipment, and now it's my turn to pass his advice on to you. Here's what you'll need and how to do it:

Ingredients
10–12 lb turkey
2-3 slices bacon
Generous amounts of rosemary, thyme, and fresh-squeezed lemon juice
Pepper and paprika
Olive oil
About fifteen chunks of your favorite aromatic wood, soaked overnight
Aluminum disposable pan, about the length and width of the turkey
Aluminum foil to wrap the wood chunks

Directions
Dry the turkey inside and out and coat with olive oil and lemon juice. Put a couple of bacon slices and plenty of herbs inside the cavity. Sprinkle the outside of the bird with equal amounts of pepper and paprika, enough to see the turkey is covered with the spices. Fill the pan with water and place it under the grates beneath where the turkey will roast. Heat the grill to 200°F–220°F and maintain this temperature throughout the roasting. Wrap one or two pieces of wood in foil with holes in it. Place a couple of pieces of soaked wood next to or beneath the water bath.

When wood smoke appears, place the turkey on the grill above the water bath. Close the cover and roast for about five hours. Replace the wood as necessary and refill water bath as it evaporates. Use a thermometer. When the dark meat reaches 165°F, you can increase the heat to 230°F–250°F till the meat reaches about 175°F–185°F and the turkey is done. Allow the turkey to rest for half an hour before slicing.

This low and slow cooking, along with the fragrant wood smoke, produces a turkey both tasty and succulent. I highly recommend a gas grill for this because it's difficult to keep charcoal at a constant temperature for such a long period of time. But if you feel confident

Grilling Tech Talk

This turkey recipe almost cooks itself. You don't have to keep checking the turkey. If the smoke from the soaked charring wood diminishes, it means you should add more, and you'll be able to see that from inside your house. Once you've adjusted the burners to maintain the temperature—you may have to turn off one or two—there's no need to keep checking. Relax and let your grill do its thing—you've got enough to do in the crowded, stuffy kitchen.

about using charcoal, by all means do it. The key to success is the low temperature. You'll never roast turkey any other way again.

Cedar Planked Salmon (for six to eight servings)

Our favorite cold weather fish recipe is salmon filets roasted on the grill on cedar planks. The cedar chars as the salmon cooks, imparting its own deep flavors and delicate wood smoke to the fish. And once the grill and wood reach their grilling temperature, in this case a hot grill around 400-450F, you don't have to stand over the grates. The salmon roasts and you relax inside till the fish is done.

Ingredients
2½–3 lbs salmon filet, about 6 oz per person (approximately the same thickness, about 1 inch or slightly less), skin on
3 Tbs olive oil
Salt and pepper to taste

For the sauce
Mix together:
½ c fat-free plain yogurt
1 Tbs Dijon mustard
1 Tbs dill leaves, dried
1 tsp lemon zest
1 tsp lemon juice

2 cedar planks, large enough to hold three to four filets each placed diagonally across the planks for even cooking

Directions
Soak the cedar planks at least one hour or all day.
Place the salmon filets on a platter and lightly brush with oil on the meat side, leaving the skin side dry (you actually want the skin to stick to the plank). Salt and pepper the fish to taste.
Place the cedar planks on the grates and get the grill and planks hot till you see smoke and charring has begun.
Turn the planks over and place 3-4 fillets on each plank, skin side down. Careful, that side of the plank is very hot.
Use a spoon to generously coat each filet with the sauce.

Close the cover and roast about 8 to 10 minutes, depending on heat, for medium done. The salmon should be firm to touch, flake on the edges and the planks should be giving off good

Grilling Tech Talk

Like beer can chicken, no-knead pizza dough, and other exciting grilling techniques, cedar plank grilling is popular—and for good reason. I'm not exaggerating when I say this is a grilling revelation. The charring cedar releases oils and scents that you can get no other way, and the smoke infuses without dominating the salmon. With the popularity comes advice and instruction all over the web and on YouTube. In my opinion, the most reliable plank grilling recipes and advice is the Plank Grilling Cookbook (see resources). Be sure to view several cedar plank grilling videos on YouTube so you see a variety of techniques before you try any or all.

smoke but no flaming. (Keep a water bottle handy untill you get this right, a few practice meals before serving company)

When fish is done use tongs to remove planks to a large wooden board or convenient work surface. Slide a spatula just over the skin and gently lift the meat off the skin to a plate and serve.

Serve with oven roasted sweet potatoes, kept whole, with a little olive oil and lightly applied salt coating, done in about an hour at 350F. Oven roasted carrots and parsnips are good substitutes, and a hearty vegetable soup to start the meal. Slide a spatula just over the

Grill Speak

Cedar planks for grilling are labeled specifically for grilling food and are available in many supermarkets, in stores that sell grilling supplies, and online. Always buy planks that are specifically made for grilling and use words like *untreated wood*. DO NOT use cedar or any other wood that is not specifically labeled for grilling, such as cedar shakes or shingles, or even ordinary lumber. Many of these products are treated with chemicals that can make you very sick. Don't ask the guy who works in the lumber yard if the wood is OK for grilling food. He might say yes when it is not.

skin and gently lift the meat off the skin to a plate and serve.

Serve with oven-roasted sweet potatoes, kept whole, with a little olive oil and lightly applied salt coating, done in about an hour at 350°F. Oven-roasted carrots and parsnips are good substitutes, and serve a hearty vegetable soup to start the meal.

Reusing the Planks

I tend to use thinner cedar planks. When I'm done grilling on them, they don't look good enough to scrape off the remnants, scrub, and use again. And I don't use planks every week. They are more of a special dinner item when we're entertaining and want to delight our guests with flavors they've not had before. Thicker planks that seem in good shape can be used again, so you decide on a cost/elbow grease/benefit basis. Used planks make a good smoke source, soaked again, wrapped in foil and placed on the burner bars, or in cold weather they're perfect kindling for the fireplace.

Grilled artisanal bread rubbed with olive oil and roasted garlic, dipped in the leftover clam juice is the perfect accompaniment. Uh oh, there went the diet.

Tasty Tips

You can soak your planks in flavored liquid—add wine, lemonade or limeade, tea; add salt or sugar or both. Experiment with different flavoring concoctions that seem intriguing. Go beyond salmon to pork, chicken, and other fish. That's what grilling is all about—playing with fire, having fun with food.

Salt Block Cooking

Himalayan Salt Block cooking is the latest grilling innovation. Contrary to what you might expect, cooking on these blocks doesn't load your food with salt. In fact very little of the actual salt comes off on the food. Instead, the hot blocks sear your meat and vegetables with just a salty kiss.

We love to cook on salt blocks--also called bricks--on the classy granite *Firetainment* fire pit table (see Chapter 22 for more in Firetainment), but Himalayan salt blocks work just fine on a gas grill. You can order them online or buy them in well stocked grilling/BBQing stores. Here are two delicious recipes the friendly guys at Firetainment shared.

Parmesan Herb Steak

Firetainment suggests rib eye steaks for this flavor-packed recipe, but we like to use a leaner cut of beef such as tenderloin or London broil.

Ingredients
2 steaks, about 6-8 ounces each
1/4 cup shaved parmesan
2 sprigs of rosemary
2 sprigs of thyme
2 Tbs black pepper
2 cloves garlic
3/4 cup olive oil
Pinch red pepper flake

Grilling Tech Talk

To cook with your salt block, follow these simple instructions. Place your dry Himalayan salt blocks on the gas grill over low heat. Gradually increase flame to medium over about 15 minutes to heat to 475-500F. You may heat your salt block in the oven, but be sure to heat slowly. Do not place directly on oven rack or electric stove burner. Instead place them on an easy to handle shallow pan to deliver to your grill when hot. Use tongs; be careful, lightly toss your meat, fish or vegetables in oil, spices and herbs, or leave unseasoned to enjoy the simple but complex flavors imparted by the block. If you add extra oil to the salt block surface it will impart more salt to your food.

Directions

In a food processor add parmesan, rosemary, thyme, black pepper, red pepper, and garlic while slowly adding olive oil to form a paste.

Coat steaks with paste and let sit on the counter for about 30 minutes

 Heat salt block to high heat and place steaks on block

Cook for approximately 3 minutes on each side for medium rare and let rest for 6 minutes before cutting.

Salt Block Seared Tuna

If you like your tuna rare this is a terrific preparation. The slight saltiness imparted by the blocks enhances the fresh tuna flavor. Feel free to use other meaty fish such as salmon, halibut, striped bass and sword fish, to name just a few.

Ingredients
12-16 oz of fresh tuna
1/2 cup mayonnaise (low fat if desired)
2 Tbs lemon juice
1/4 cup capers
1/4 cup gin
2 Tbs black pepper or to taste

Instructions

For the aioli mix together mayo, lemon juice, and capers. Mix well and refrigerate for 30 minutes or a day ahead

Sprinkle tuna with gin and pepper, let stand at room temperature for 30 minutes

Slice tuna into ½ inch slices

Heat salt block to high and cook tuna slices for 1 minute on each side then set aside to rest for 3 minutes

Drizzle with caper sauce and serve

Sibling Rivalry Clams (serves six for appetizers, 2-4 as main course over pasta)

Whether it's Thanksgiving on the grill or cedar planked salmon, nothing beats steamed cherrystone or little neck clams as an appetizer with pre-dinner drinks or wine. Clams are so tasty but don't ruin your appetite—a light beginning to a festival of food.

My brother Norm works his clam bake for hours in the Great Salt Pond on Block Island, near his summer home, collecting the freshest clams, the perfect size for his mouth watering recipe. Then he buys the other 20 at the local seafood market for this dish. I call it Sibling Rivalry Clams because it pains me to admit his simple recipe is the best, better than I used to make them, better than any. If you like clams you will love these.

Ingredients
2 dozen clams
½ cup white wine
1 Tbs butter
1 Tbs olive oil
3 cloves garlic, sliced
¼ tsp red pepper flakes
Parsley

Directions
Take a 24 inch piece of heavy duty aluminum foil. Fold in half for double thickness. Turn up all sides of foil about one inch.
Place all ingredients except parsley in aluminum foil. Close and pinch (seal) top and ends of foil so it will not leak.
Place on covered grill for 15 minutes.
Don't lose the juice as you open the foil. Discard any closed clams. Sprinkle chopped parsley as you serve.

Serve alone as an appetizer or over pasta for a meal, using the liquid as the pasta sauce.

Grilled artisanal bread rubbed with olive oil and roasted garlic, dipped in the leftover clam juice, is the perfect accompaniment. Uh oh, there went the diet.

Ed's Air-Fried Chicken Wings

On the healthy grilling scale fried chicken wings would rate somewhere near the bottom. Whether you're deep frying or sautéing them in a heart healthy oil, you're still adding insult to injury. The wings themselves are quite fatty (that's what makes the little morsels so deliciously juicy) and the traditional cooking medium intensifies the fat content. Especially if you finish them off "buffalo" style.

Using his Grill Innovations grill plate and an inventive grilling method, my friendly outdoor cooking guru Ed Hamlin has transformed wings from a sinful indulgence to a lower calorie but just as tasty alternative. And his slower, indirect heat technique eliminates the formation of HCA, a possible carcinogen resulting from high heat cooking—whether grilling, frying or broiling.

You'll need Grill Innovations grill topper, a 1-2 inch deep disposable aluminum roasting pan with salt covering the bottom, and a stainless steel rack or extra grates set on top of this pan to hold the chicken wings. This arrangement should be large enough for a dozen or more wings. You can do the cooking in multiple batches to feed a crowd.

The concept is ingenious yet quite easy. The grill topper creates a convection effect thanks to the beveled design. With burners on high the topper causes the heated air to circulate within the covered grill, roasting the wings. Your thermometer should read in the 525-550 range, about as hot as you can get an average gas grill. The intrinsic fat drips through the skin as the wings cook, attractively browning them, and the salt beneath the grates keeps the fat from flaming. As the fat drips into the salt the combined effect of heat below and hot fat from above sets off tiny explosions of salt, misting the wings with even more flavor (so don't salt them as you would normally do prior to grilling). The grilling time varies of course, depending on all the usual factors like grill BTUs, ambient air temperature, height of the grate above the topper, but you should figure roughly 20 minutes to half an hour per batch.

Prior to cooking season the wings according to taste, omitting or reducing your usual salt amount, but pepper and other spices are good—as many and as much as you want. Serve naked the first time you make these so you know how good they taste "au naturale." Experiment with variations such as fresh squeezed citrus, a sprinkle of Thai fish sauce and sesame oil, a shake of garam masala or spiced up with hot chili flakes. My standby favorite, Old Bay, adds a bit of sweet salty flavor. Much less fat than the traditional wings…. and a lot more creative.

Healthy Burger Dinner

We love beef burgers so we often include them in our weekly dinner planning. I usually grind the meat at home using our food processor (review this method in Chapter 3, page 35). I can use the cuts of meat I prefer and create a meat mixture that's low in fat and high in flavor. I often use grass fed beef because it's more nutritious and we like the "grassy" taste. Grass fed organic beef is very expensive in most supermarkets, up to $25/pound… We take advantage of sales and stock the freezer with grass-fed steaks that we grind to order. And if you eat beef in moderation, making 4-5 ounce burgers, the cost per meal difference is less significant.

I've developed a burger dinner menu that satisfies our taste-buds while delivering plenty of nutrition. I vary parts of the menu according to the season, but I always feature my Home Style Burger as the ringmaster around which the other dishes perform.

The Menu

Beef burgers on whole wheat English muffins with pesto sauce and fresh tomato or balsamic grilled sweet onion (depending on seasonal availability)

Broccoli carrot soup

Bean salad with chickpeas

Grilled fresh fruit (see Chapter 13)

The Healthy Burger Dinner Recipes

Ingredients

For Home Style Burger

Lean beef cuts of your choice, ground in the food processor
Thomas' Lite Whole Wheat English Muffin, toasted (100 calories)
Pesto burger sauce (see page 41)
Fresh sliced tomatoes if in season or sweet onion sliced ½ inch thick

Grilling Tech Talk

We use toothpicks for a number of different grilling situations, from holding onion rings together (as here) to grilling radicchio and other leafy veggies that you want to keep secure. Make sure the toothpicks you use are the old fashioned hard wood type, not the more common plastic imitations. Plastic toothpicks will melt into your food and the cheaper wooden ones can shred into the veggie when extracted. I learned the hard way to use only hard wood toothpicks.

Directions
Follow recipe and grilling directions for Home Style Burgers (pages 38 and 180)
Slice tomatoes
If using onions instead (or in addition), slice about ½ inch thick and insert wooden toothpick sideways through the rings to hold onion together. Sprinkle with olive oil and balsamic vinegar.

When burgers are moved off direct heat begin grilling onions over direct heat, turning once untill golden brown. Remove toothpicks when done.

When burgers and onions are done, lightly apply olive oil and toast the muffins over direct heat, taking care not to burn them.

Brush muffins with pesto sauce, assemble burger sandwiches and serve

For Broccoli Carrot Soup

Fresh broccoli, cut up, trim stems and cut, about 4 cups

2 large carrots, split and cut or 2 cups bagged baby carrots

1 cup Spanish onion, coarsely chopped

1 garlic clove, coarsely chopped

1 celery stalk, chopped

1 small sweet potato, cut into cubes

1 Tbs medium hot curry powder

1 tsp cumin

1 tsp turmeric

½ tsp ground cinnamon or 1 tsp garam masala

½ tsp white pepper

2 quarts chicken or vegetable stock (more if needed), or water is OK too

½ cup barley

½ cup frozen peas

½ cup frozen corn

1-2 Tbs fresh lemon juice

Low fat/no fat plain yogurt

Shredded parmesan, Romano or locatelli cheese

Directions

(Can make ahead up to 3 days)

In a large soup pot sauté onions gently in oil untill opaque

Add curry and spices and sauté untill onions begin to brown and spice aromas fill the kitchen

Add all fresh vegetables, stir, cover pot and cook for a few minutes

Add stock, at least 2 quarts, more if needed to cover vegetables, bring to a boil, simmer about half an hour more untill vegetables are soft.

Remove pot from heat. Using an immersion blender puree the soup (if using a conventional blender be very careful and blend in small batches). Soup should be on the thick side.

Return pot to heat, add frozen peas, corn and barley, salt and pepper, cover pot and bring to a boil. Simmer 30 minutes or more untill barley is cooked.

Add lemon juice to taste. Adjust salt and pepper to taste.

Put a generous dollop of yogurt in each bowl. Serve soup and sprinkle with shredded cheese. Stir to incorporate yogurt.

For Bean Salad with Chickpeas

4 cups fresh string beans, trimmed, steamed and cooled

1 cup cooked cannellini or great northern beans

1 cup cooked red kidney beans

1 cup cooked chickpeas

(if using canned beans be sure to rinse)

1 red onion, finely sliced and slices separated (use a mandolin to slice)

2 Tbs seasoned rice vinegar

2 Tbs cider vinegar

3 Tbs canola oil

Salt and pepper to taste

Directions

(Can make ahead up to 3 days)

Add all beans and onions to large mixing bowl. If using canned beans thoroughly rinse them in a colander and remove as much water as possible

Whisk vinegars and oil and pour over salad

Toss salad, add salt and pepper to taste

For Grilled Fruit Dessert

As we say in Chapter 13, fruit on the grill brings out the natural sweetness and intensifies the flavor. But every now and then, especially when we have a festive occasion, it's fun to elaborate on the stripped down ingredients. Spices, low fat yogurt based sauces and even the indulgence of extra sweeteners are appropriate riffs on grilled fresh fruit. Here are five recipes to wow your guests and spark your creativity.

Pineapple Rum Kebabs: (serves 6-8)

Ingredients

1 large pineapple, cut into one inch chunks

½ cup dark rum

¼ cup brown sugar

¼ cup honey¼ cup orange juice

1 tsp orange zest

(Time saver—buy 1lb of chunked pineapple at your supermarket prepared fresh fruit section)

Directions

Mix all ingredients well and marinate pineapple chunks for a few minutes. Thread pineapple onto skewers leaving space between for heat penetration. Grill about 10 minutes, basting with the marinade, flipping once or twice till grill marks appear and pineapple has a deeper golden color. Remove from skewers and plate. Serve with chilled fresh berries and ice cream. The warm pineapple, cool berries and frozen ice cream work together for a beautifully textured dessert.

Grilling Tech Talk

Grilling Tech-Talk: Calculating the amount of fruit you'll need for the number of people you're serving is simple: About one large fruit or a cup of smaller fruit like figs per person.

Fruit Kebabs Indonesian Style:

Ingredients

Ripe peaches, plums, apricots, mangoes, pineapple chunks, pitted and cut into wedges for skewers, as many as needed (or other fruit you like at the market).

For the sauce:
¼ cup fresh lemon juice
Zest of one lime
1 star anise
1 cinnamon stick
6 cardamom pods, lightly crushed
1 tsp vanilla
1 cup sugar
1 cup water or a little more—enough to dissolve ingredients

Directions
For the sauce—can be made a few days ahead
Bring water and sugar to a boil in a sauce pan
Add remaining ingredients and simmer till reduced by 1/3 and slightly thickened, about 15

minutes

Strain sauce and let cool. Store in the fridge till ready to use

For the kebabs

Thread the fruit onto bamboo skewers, keeping the same fruit on each skewer with a little space between each slice or chunk. Brush with neutral oil.

Grill over medium heat for 8 to 10 minutes, flipping every 2-3 minutes, till fruit is done. Each type of fruit may need different grilling times to achieve nice lines and darker color. When fruit is done remove fruit from skewers and arrange in an attractive mixture on a warm platter.

Serve cool syrup on the side or drizzle over the platter of fruit

Grilled fruit with berry yogurt dip

Ingredients

Ripe peaches, nectarines, plums, mangos, papayas and/or pineapples, sliced into chunks for skewers, as many as needed

For the dip

8 oz container part skim ricotta or low-fat cottage cheese

4 oz plain low-fat yogurt

1 Tbs freshly grated ginger

8-10 large fresh or frozen strawberries or 18-20 raspberries

(reduce proportionally for fewer people—this feeds about 12)

For the marinade

½ cup balsamic vinegar

¼ cup sugar

Directions

For the dip (can be made ahead)

Place all ingredients in a blender or food processor and puree. Chill.

Whisk marinade ingredients

Thread fruit on to bamboo skewers, each type of fruit on its own skewer, with a little space between each chunk for heat absorption

Spoon marinade over fruit skewers and let rest a few minutes while heating the grill

Grill fruit skewers 8-10 minutes, depending on fruit types, turning every 2-3 minutes untill heated through and attractive grill lines appear

As fruit is done remove from skewers on to a warm platter. Serve family style with dipping sauce spooned on each guest's dessert plate

Grilled fruit burritos (this chocolaty splurge serves 4)

Ingredients
4 eight inch flour tortillas
1 cup semi-sweet chocolate bits
1 cup strawberries, raspberries or previously grilled peaches or nectarines, cut into small cubes
(or combination of these fruits and others you like—make sure they are in small pieces)
1-2 Tbs melted butter
1 tsp sugar and 1 tsp cinnamon, mixed

Directions
Warm tortillas 20 seconds in microwave or stacked in foil on the grill, turning untill soft and warmed
Place tortillas on plates and sprinkle the center with chocolate bits and fruit, about half a cup of these combined ingredients per tortilla
Fold the ends and roll burritos. Brush lightly with melted butter
Place burritos on grill over medium heat and cook about 3 minutes, flip and cook 3 minutes more untill attractive grill marks appear and chocolate is melted
Remove to a warm platter and sprinkle lightly with sugar/cinnamon mixture

Figs on the Grill (serves 4)

Figs and goat cheese go together like hope and marriage. Add some honey and divorce is out of the question.

Ingredients
8-10 figs, about 2 per person or more
1 Tbs olive oil
4-6 ounces fresh goat cheese thinly sliced
2 Tbs honey
Juice from ½ lemon

Directions
Thread figs on to bamboo skewers from the stem end, brush lightly with olive oil
Grill over medium heat about 2-3 minutes, flip and grill 2 minutes more till figs have softened and are heated through. Remove figs from skewers.
Place warm figs on dessert plates and arrange goat cheese slices over figs.
Drizzle lightly with honey and a splash of lemon juice
Serve immediately

Sausages on the Grill

Healthy grilled sausages may seem like an oxymoron. After all, there are two key ingredients that make sausages luscious and tasty. One is fat. About 30% in your average pork sausage or kielbasa. The other is salt. Too much salt. But you don't have to think of sausages as a delicious prelude to a forced visit with the cardiologist. There are many low fat, low salt sausages on supermarket shelves. Check the labels and find a brand you like. If you're as fortunate as we are to have a choice of old fashioned butcher shops nearby you can even order a batch of sausages made with less salt and fat. They freeze well and are perfect single serving grilled dinners where everyone has a choice—chicken, pork, beef, lamb and even seafood sausages from a good fish monger.

The key to grilling lower fat but juicy sausage is to partially grill them. I start by poaching sausages in a liquid I choose, depending on the main ingredient in the sausage. I use a toothpick or skewer to pierce a few tiny holes in the sausage casing. This allows fat to render out and some of the liquid to infuse the meat inside. For pork I use beer or cider. For chicken sausages I use beer or water/white wine, half and half. I poach lamb and beef sausages in water with shredded fresh mint or oregano for the lamb and a generous amount of rosemary and crushed garlic for the beef. Start them in cold liquid and, after they reach a boil, simmer them till cooked through, about 10-15 minutes.

Grilling Tech Talk

You can do the sausage poaching a day or two ahead and keep them in the fridge untill ready to grill. Be sure to grill over lower heat so the sausages have time to get up to temperature without burning or bursting. A couple of minutes more is all the time you'll need. Or poach your sausages right on the grill in a disposable aluminum pan filled with liquid, just as you would do over the stove.

Then place sausages on hot oiled grates and grill, turning frequently till they are "snappy". This two stage method enables lower fat sausages to retain moisture. Plus they pick up additional flavor from the liquid. The relatively quick finish on the hot grates gives them the texture we love without drying them out, as too often happens when we grill the entire cooking time. The formation of HCA, if any, is minimal thanks to the short time over the heat. You will enjoy thinking up new liquids or infusing the poaching liquid with flavors that enhance your sausages.

Vegetarians at the Grill

Vegetarians often feel shortchanged when friends gather around the grill. It seems like a mountain of beef and pork for everyone-- and maybe a fake hotdog as an afterthought for people who avoid meat. Veggie burgers can be delicious (see page 189), even for meat eaters, but the fake hotdogs leave me cold. Instead of disguising tofu with artificial colors and flavorings I believe in grilling the real thing. With real natural ingredients. Healthy eating, whether you're a vegan or a meataholic, means avoiding processed foods as much as practical.

Grilling Tech Talk

Is the soybean/tofu controversy serious science? There are two warnings about soy products that have gained some currency in the last few years. One is that tofu contains a substance that mimics estrogen and therefore may fuel breast cancer. There is little evidence that the amount present in soy products has any effect on breast cancer, or even that this substance acts in the body like estrogen. In fact there are studies showing that women who consume high levels of tofu have lower breast cancer rates. The other warning stems from the ubiquity of genetically modified soy grown in this country and in Asia. To date there is no evidence that GMO soybeans cause any health problems. If this issue is important to you, however, organic tofu is available everywhere.

Grilled Tofu Steaks (serves four)

Ingredients
1lb extra firm organic tofu, pressed dry and in cut ¾ to 1 inch thick pieces
For the marinade
¼ cup lemon juice
1 Tbs olive oil
3 cloves garlic, minced
2 teaspoons dried oregano

1/2 teaspoon salt, or to taste
Freshly ground pepper, to taste

Directions
Whisk the marinade ingredients in a bowl, marinate the tofu 1 to 8 hours in the fridge.
Reserve 2-3 Tbs for basting tofu on the grill.
 Drain marinated tofu and gently pat dry.
Lightly oil the hot grates and grill the tofu over medium-high heat, basting occasionally with
reserved lemon juice until lightly browned, 3 to 4 minutes per side.

Serve immediately along with assorted grilled veggies and/or corn (see Chapters 11 & 12).
With grilled fruit this is a delicious full course meal that vegetarians and meat eaters will
find equally satisfying.

Grilled Indonesian Tofu Steaks

As we all know, tofu is a terrific taste absorber. It's the chameleon of the food world,
becoming part of the flavor background. So this is your chance to take tofu on an exotic
trip.

Whisk together coconut milk, peanut butter, curry paste and hoisin sauce over low heat.
Cool, reserve 2-3 Tbs of the marinade.

Marinate tofu slices for 1 to 8 hours. Pat dry and grill 4-6 minutes per side on lightly oiled
grates.

Grilled Asian Tofu Steaks

Whisk together ½ cup hoisin sauce, 1 Tbs soy sauce, 3 Tbs rice wine vinegar, 1 Tbs lime
juice and ½ tsp garlic powder. Marinate the tofu slices for at least an hour, up to 8 hours,
then pat dry and grill on lightly oiled grates. Serve with grilled bok choy, cut in half
lengthwise and secured with toothpicks. Brush them with sesame oil and grill untill done to
your liking.

Tasty Tips

Why should pork eaters get all the good stuff. Whisk together ½ cup barbecue sauce, 1 tsp sugar (optional), 1 Tbs chili powder, 1 Tbs orange juice and lots of black pepper to taste. Reserve 2-3 Tbs marinade and marinate tofu slices for 2-4 hours. Pat dry and grill on lightly oiled grates 4-6 minutes per side. Brush lightly with reserved marinade. Serve with fresh corn (see Chapter 12)

CHAPTER 22

 Grilling Resources and Inspiration

In This Chapter

➤ Reliable resources online

➤ Grilling books

➤ Fire Pit cooking

There are literally thousands of websites for the grilling community and many offer valuable information. YouTube, ITunes and other sites abound with instructional videos. For those of us who are honing our grilling skills there is no better resource than the web. Be sure, however, that you are taking advice, instruction and inspiration from authoritative sources. Here are a few of my favorites.

Reliable Internet Resources

Let's start with people worth watching and listening to. Everyone knows the celebrity chef Bobby Flay. He really is as good as the hype. He knows his stuff and he shares it with enthusiasm and humor, exuding the grilling sensibilities we all value. Mark Bittman of the New York Times (The Minimalist) is a constant source of inspiration for me. A quick Google search will take you to numerous sites where he shows us "how to cook everything", consume more intelligently and humanely, a real champion of healthy cooking with an urban slant to grilling. His No-Knead bread video is excellent. Sara Moulton is another TV chef with great skills and the ability to convey recipes and techniques with ease and comfort. For all around culinary expertise in a most accessible style it's hard to think of a better source than America's Test Kitchen, Christopher Kimball's' creation that sets the standard for perfection with a practical down-home attitude. For overall cooking knowledge I greatly value Stellaculinary.com where Chef Jacob Burton teaches us everything from knife skills to bread baking. For a mini-culinary education this is the best place I've found online. For overall food knowledge and skills, each of these kitchen stars is worth tuning in, whether on the web, a podcast or their PBS shows.

Online Resources Essential for Grillers

> ➤ My website, *www.smartgrillingtoday.com*, is constantly adding recipes, techniques and links to the best grilling information and resources. Seasonal recipes include the best, freshest and most nutritious ingredients and focus on holidays and events. So visit often for the latest grilling inspirations

> ➤ Visit Ed Hamlin's *www.grillinovations.com* for the most versatile grill topper on the market. His revolutionary design creates a convection oven effect that turns your grill into a pizza oven, a roaster, even a pie and bread bakery. The website includes lots of recipes and techniques, a valuable resource with frequent updates. Videos too.

> ➤ For grilled fish, shrimp and shellfish lovers the Monterey Bay Aquarium is essential *www. montereybayaquarium.org* The aquarium's SeaWatch program is the most objective and authoritative source for those of us concerned about our effect on the world's fish stocks. The site features up to date information on threatened species, recommendations for seafood we can consume without guilt, and loads of recipes featuring fish and shellfish that are abundant.

> ➤ For roasting fish on the grill, especially the more delicate types, I like to use Frogmats, a non-stick screen that is FDA approved for food handling at temps of 400F. Use over indirect heat and you will never have those pesky stuck fish problems that plague even master grillers. Go to www.frogmats.com for all the details

> ➤ I really appreciate GrillGrates, a raised rail modular grill topper that can cover all or part of your existing grate surface. If you are cooking veggies like asparagus that can slide through your grates this topper eliminates that problem while still providing those attractive grill marks. When grilling fish, where you don't want any residue left to flavor other foods, the GrillGrate topper can be easily removed and washed without the ordeal of having to clean heavy greasy grates. And GrillGrates suppresses flare ups over charcoal, ensuring a healthier grilling environment. See details at *www.Grillgrates.com*.

> ➤ When it's time to replace those chipped porcelain grates, or you realize the thin stainless steel grates are not providing the kind of even heat distribution that's essential for great grilling, it's time to graduate to cast iron. The best I've found come from Craycort at *www. cast-iron-grate.com* and many BBQ retailers. They are pre-seasoned, providing a slick non- stick surface from day one, and evenly distribute the heat as only cast iron can. The charcoal models have hinges so adding more coal is a snap. This eliminates the problem with most other cast iron grate brands where you have to remove the entire hot, heavy

grate to put more coal on the fire. Designed to fit most charcoal and gas grills. A must for serious frequent grillers, virtually indestructible

➤ Amazingribs.com is misleading—ribs are there, but buried in encyclopedic grilling information. There are grill and ingredient ratings, instruction on all sorts of grilling techniques and preparations—a huge amount of knowledge all in one place. Be sure to visit this site where guru Meathead Goldwyn takes you on a tour of the grilling world. This guy knows it all and shares it generously. He's not a salesman and you can trust his judgment.

➤ Don't overlook the major grill manufacturers. Weber, Broil King, Fire Magic and Bull Grills are among at least a dozen grill makers who share tried and true recipes and techniques online.

➤ An innovative company, Firetainment, has reimagined patio fire pits. Grilling is the most social form of cooking because meal prep takes place in the midst of friends and family instead of the enforced isolation of your kitchen. Firetainment takes you and your guests to a more intimate level of this shared grilling experience. You are seated around a classy granite table with a lazy susan centerpiece. As the evening brings cooler air you remove the lazy susan to reveal a fire pit fueled by a hidden propane tank beneath the table. Flames spread warmth, delighting family and friends. You place the Firetainment universal cook mount over the flames and with the included cooking package for each table you can now cook on the cast iron griddle or Himalayan salt bricks (see recipes in Chapter 21). Or use a variety of other cookware you may have at home, such as a wok or Dutch oven. A leisurely feast around the fire is ahead. Salt grilled shrimp to begin, chicken, pork and vegetable kebabs to follow, and grilled fruit and 'smores for a festive dessert. Visit *www.firtainment. com* for inspiration and information. Happy healthy grilling—and you don't even leave the table.

Books and More

➤ For recipes, grilling books and more, check out the Barbecue Queens at Pig Out Publications. Not only do these two enterprising women dispel the myth that men are naturally better grillers, they prove it with their own books filled with recipes and techniques. They offer hundreds of other titles on grilling and barbecuing. Enjoy browsing through their virtual bookshelves at *www.pigoutpublications.com*.

➤ For plank grilling salmon, fish and other delicious meat and poultry get The Plank Grilling Cookbook at Amazon or BN.com

➤ The Smoke Ring is a community of grilling and barbecuing websites linked at *www. thesmokering.com*. Plenty of ads but a mountain of really good objective information, websites and specialized resources. For serious grillers this website offers layers of interesting and inspiring browsing.

INDEX

ABOUT THE AUTHOR

Ever since producing The Catfish Cookbook in the 1970s, Barry Fast has been a food-focused writer and editor. His articles have appeared in newspapers, magazines, and blogs. Most recently, he was a feature writer and restaurant reviewer for OffShore Magazine and Northeast Boating Magazine, publications dedicated to the recreational boating community.

His food interests led him to perfect healthy grilling techniques after many years as a local barbecue master chef. Combining the tastiest grilling techniques with the latest nutritional and heart health science, Barry has developed hundreds of recipes for everyday grilled meals, year round. Unlike most other grilling experts, he focuses on vegetables, fruit, lean meat, poultry, and seafood products, emphasizing low fat and calories in his flavor-packed recipes.

In addition to his passion for healthy grilling, Barry is an avid boater, kayaker, and bike rider. He lives with his wife Carol on City Island, the yachting capital of New York City, where he fires up his grill nearly every day to the delight of family and friends.